Managing Technology for Corporate Success

Managing Technology for Corporate Success

❖

Chris Floyd

Gower

Published by
Gower Publishing Limited
Gower House
Croft Road
Aldershot
Hampshire GU11 3HR
England

Gower
Old Post Road
Brookfield
Vermont 05036
USA

Reprinted 1998

Chris Floyd has asserted his right under the Copyright, Designs and Patents Act 1988 to be identified as the author of this work.

British Library Cataloguing in Publication Data
Floyd, Chris
    Managing Technology for corporate success
    1. Technological innovations – Economic aspects
    I. Title
    658.4'0632

    ISBN 0 566 07991 7

Library of Congress Cataloguing-in-Publication Data
Floyd, C. (Chris)
    Managing Technology for Corporate Success / Chris Floyd.
        p.   cm.
    Includes index.
    ISBN 0–566–07991–7 (hardback)
    1. Technological Innovations—Management.   2. Research,
Industrial—Management.   I. Title.
HD45.F615   1997
658.5'14—dc21   97–28405
                                                                          CIP

Typeset in 10/12 Garamond by Photoprint, Torquay, Devon
and printed in Great Britain by MPG Books Limited, Bodmin.

CONTENTS

LIST OF FIGURES

PREFACE

❖

OVER the past decade, executives have become increasingly aware of the importance of technology and innovation as a means for competitive advantage. However, knowing that technology is important and knowing what to do about it are two very different things. The modern corporation typically operates in many markets and product areas, using many technologies. Within the same corporation, some business units may well be technology leaders, investing heavily in advanced research, while others may be mature cost focused manufacturers, outsourcing all their technology needs. In such a scenario, it is not obvious which technologies the corporation should concentrate on and how technology and innovation should be managed to deliver the maximum added value.

Corporate executives therefore face a difficult task in setting technology priorities, allocating resources and engendering a supportive culture across business unit and divisional boundaries. The purpose of this book is to help them in these tasks. Corporate technology management is not just an issue for the chief technology officer or R&D director. Technology and innovation are so vital to corporate success that chief executives and other senior management should also be aware of the challenges and the possible solutions to them.

There is no single best way to manage technology and innovation in a company, and there is certainly no foolproof mechanistic route to success. There are, however, lessons that can be learnt from others, theoretical frameworks to guide thinking and decision making, and tools and techniques to assist in analysis. All of these are presented here to give readers a solid grounding in the art of technology and innovation management. As each organisation is unique, the way in which you choose to use this information, and the results you obtain, must be your responsibility.

This book is based on the author's twelve years' experience in consulting in technology management, nine of these with Arthur D. Little, the world's leading consultancy in this field. The book draws upon the author's experience, best practice in clients worldwide, and the collective wisdom of colleagues in the global Technology and Innovation Management practice at Arthur D. Little. The ideas expressed draw heavily on the approaches promoted by Arthur D. Little, but reflect the author's personal view of best practice.

Many colleagues and clients have made inputs to this book. In the Technology and Innovation Management practice at Arthur D. Little, particular acknowledgements are due to Jean-Philippe Deschamps, now at IMD, Richard Granger and Charles Boulton, for their thoughtful inputs. Many others in the practice have also made valuable contributions, including Christian Mouthuy, Frank Morris, John Brook, and Herman Vantrappen. Thanks are also due to Tim Simpson, Michael Younger, and Stephen Lawrence, all senior Directors of Arthur D. Little's UK management consulting operations, for their support and encouragement.

Theoretical ideas and concepts are of little value in isolation, and so thanks are due to the many clients of the author and his colleagues at Arthur D. Little. Their willingness to embrace the ideas expressed here and to implement them in their organisations has both helped develop ideas into practical concepts and helped their companies manage technology and innovation more effectively. In particular, thanks are due to the following, who have all been enthusiastic supporters of the need for effective technology and innovation management: Jan Oosterveld and Ad Huijser of Philips Consumer Electronics, Max Gowland and Vernon Sankey of Reckitt & Colman, Gareth Lloyd-Jones and Alan Suggett of Smith & Nephew, Arne Ingels of Norsk Hydro, Tony Kemmer of Boots, Mark Eames of BP, David Duncan of Unilever, and Martin Shelley and Alistair Keddie of the Innovation Unit of the UK Department of Trade and Industry.

I also owe thanks to my early mentors at Arthur D. Little, notably Bruce Thompson, Jim Staikos and Maurice Pearce, for showing me how to be an effective management consultant. Mentors earlier in my career also deserve mention: Norman Waterman, Mike Neale, Clive Wills, Don Rennie, and Richard Carmichael. They all provided me with the space and encouragement to develop my own thinking on business and technology management.

I am very grateful to Isobel Campbell, my editor at Arthur D. Little, who created clarity from my jumbled thoughts, and to Rebecca Mobbs, who not only typed endless drafts of the manuscript and created most of the figures but provided moral support and encouragement during the book's long gestation. I am also grateful to Joanne Rawlings for locating references and obscure facts with patience and forbearance, and to Tricia Osborne, Rosemary Triffitt and Mo Atkinson, who have provided excellent secretarial support.

Finally, I thank my wife Liz and my children Alex, Robert and Harriet for their tolerance and for reminding me that business is not the only thing that matters in the world.

Chris Floyd

INTRODUCTION

❖

I MAGINE you are the chief executive of a £2 billion turnover, £300 million profit, fast-moving consumer goods business. Your organisation, fairly typical for your industry sector, spends some £60 million a year on technology and new product development to deliver a steady stream of new products and the modern production processes needed for efficient low cost manufacture. However, all is not well. Much of your investment seems to be wasted, and you are usually second or third to market with new product innovations. Even your production processes lag behind the latest in process technologies used by your competitors.

Spurred into action, your colleagues apply a great deal of effort and succeed in streamlining the product development process and cutting out some of the development slack. You are told that this will deliver a net benefit of around £3 million to the bottom line. Net cash is always useful, but this is not enough to get excited about. You tell your technical director to try again. He comes back a few months later feeling well pleased that, by speeding up the process, he believes he can capture an additional £30 million of benefit. You tell him it's still not enough.

He then goes off and approaches the problem differently. Starting from the top, he looks at how technology adds value to the business, identifying what should be done in-house and what should be outsourced, how commercial and technical resources should be marshalled together, and what checks and balances should be put in place. Underlying this effort is the growing realisation that getting value from technology is more to do with improving the value of the output than controlling or limiting the costs of the input. In other words, value comes primarily from developing better products and processes rather than just increasing the effectiveness of the development process.

The results of this approach are staggering. An initial estimate shows that the net present value of this effort will be over £130 million, and that just comes from focusing on doing the right things. The consequential improvement in the management of technology activities will further help the organisation build on its strengths to deliver more profitable innovation-led growth in the future, leading to even greater returns.

This recent real example highlights how better management of technology can yield significant benefits. And this was not an organisation that managed technology badly. Far from it; the existing processes for setting priorities, managing projects and allocating resources were adequate and comparable to most European businesses. The real issue here was not bad technology management per se, but a failure to realise the impact that good technology-inspired innovation can have on sales, profits and long term business growth.

This book is about how to manage technology to deliver the sorts of benefits outlined above. The primary focus is on technologies used in products and processes, and the objective of this book is to outline how you can manage technology more effectively in terms of strategies, processes and organisation to deliver more and better products.

The idea that technology and innovation are critical to business success is not new, and over the past decade, managers have become increasingly aware of the importance of technology to companies as a means for competitive advantage. However, up to now, most managers and strategic advisers have adopted a relatively simplistic approach, assuming that companies function as a single entity, with a single set of objectives based on a single set of technologies. Decisions on whether to be a technology leader or follower, the consequent deliberations on technology strategy, and decisions on the most appropriate organisational framework have then been relatively straightforward.

Today's corporations are not like that. They are often decentralised conglomerates, focused on profit growth and covering a diverse range of products, technologies, geographies and markets. Within the same group, one business unit may be a low cost commodity producer, while another is at the leading edge of technology in its chosen market. At the same time, technology has never been more crucial for commercial success. Increasing competitive pressure is reducing the scope for differentiation, leaving technology as the only competitive weapon that many companies possess.

Corporate management therefore has the difficult task of trying to set technology priorities, anticipate longer term threats and opportunities, and allocate technology resources to the various businesses in the corporation, while ensuring that the value of the whole is greater than the sum of the parts. This book is intended to help corporate management in this task.

The target audience for this book is the corporate executive management team and their advisors. Not just the chief technology officer or the R&D director. The arguments presented in Chapters 1, 2 and 11 should be sufficient to show that corporate technology and innovation management is too important to the success of the corporation to be left solely to functional management.

The book is in three parts: Chapters 1 and 2 discuss the role of technology in the corporation and provide guidance on how critical effective technology management is to your business. In the second part of the book, Chapters 3 to 7 look at the mechanics of technology strategy. Finally, Chapters 8 to 11 cover the practical aspects of technology management: organisation, management processes, metrics and communication.

1

WHY TECHNOLOGY MATTERS

❖

T HIS chapter sets the scene; it explores what is meant by technology and looks at different ways in which technology can impact on a business. It then addresses the problems the larger corporation faces in managing technology across a diversified spread of business units, and looks at the merits of alternative corporate technology policies.

WHAT IS TECHNOLOGY?

First, what is technology? The word causes much confusion, particularly in the commercial and industrial world. Many take technology to mean information technology, and then stretch the definition further, using information technology as an all-embracing term covering all aspects of information systems, technological or not, within a business. Others use technology to imply something scientific. The technologist is the scientist: the man in a white coat in the laboratory doing long term speculative research. Neither definition is comprehensive or precise.

In the business context, you need to adopt a broader definition of technology:

> Technology is the practical application of scientific or engineering knowledge to the conception, development or application of products or offerings, processes or operations.

Each element of this rather long-winded definition is crucial. Firstly, technology is concerned with the practical application of knowledge not

1

with the knowledge itself. In this respect it is different from science. Metallurgy is a science: continuous strip casting is a technology. Technology builds on scientific knowledge, but the knowledge of itself is not enough. Technology is all about knowing how to apply knowledge.

Second, the only technologies which are of interest in business are those with a potential commercial benefit. Hence the phrase 'conception, development or application of products or offerings, processes or operations'. As will become clear, using a broad definition is critical if businesses are to succeed in making technology pay its way by delivering product and process innovation. Using conventional definitions, and particularly linking technology to science, can lock businesses into a mindset which misses many real opportunities for technology differentiation. Paper-making companies, obsessed with the science of paper-making, are likely to fail to exploit the benefit of new packaging technologies or logistics planning systems to the full. Consumer electronics companies, obsessed with electronics design and technical performance, will fail to give adequate weight to the touch and feel of their products which are key elements in the consumer buying decision.

In contrast, this broad definition of technology casts the net wide enough to pick up those aspects of business on which technology can have the biggest impact, even if they lie outside the core science base of the company. Knowing how to secure FDA (US Food and Drug Administration) approvals, operate automated canning lines or run a semiconductor fabrication facility at high yield rates may well be more commercially important than having a deep understanding of the sciences behind the products being produced. Spread the definition too wide, and there is danger that technology just becomes a synonym for business competitiveness, as every aspect of competitiveness will require the application of some scientific or engineering knowledge. Still, in deciding where your technology priorities should lie, it is better to start wide and narrow down, rather than limiting from the outset the options for using technology to develop the business.

With a working definition of technology clear in your mind, you need to reflect on why technology matters. Technology is critical for two reasons. First, technology is fundamental to the success of every product business (and of many service businesses). Without effective use of technology, you cannot sustain any competitive position. Second, technology-driven innovation is the only viable route to long term growth, and so you need to manage explicitly the application of technology for the longer term.

TECHNOLOGY IS FUNDAMENTAL TO EVERY PRODUCTS BUSINESS

Technology provides the principal, and often only, route to:

O   Differentiating products
O   Reducing costs
O   Providing new business opportunities (or meeting substitution threats)
O   Facilitating and supporting strategic change.

DIFFERENTIATING PRODUCTS

Differentiating products is the most obvious application of technology in business. Developing products that can do things that other products can't almost always requires the novel application of technology. Fast motor cars, small personal cassette players, draught beer in a can, microwaveable popcorn are typical consumer products benefiting from technological differentiation. Dry running gas compressor seals, pultruded reinforced plastic structures, and ink-jet printing machines are equivalent industrial examples.

Interestingly, technological differentiation often follows a maturity life-cycle pattern. When the product is first launched, its very existence is differentiation enough. Getting the product to work in the first place, and then increasing its performance until it is acceptable to the customer are the main foci of technology efforts. As the product matures, it moves into a growth phase. Customers are more willing to purchase competitors' rival products, and the emphasis of differentiation switches towards refining product features to best meet customer needs. Typically this will mean using technology to develop products which are more cost-effective, more reliable and easier to maintain. Finally, when all products meet these needs adequately and the market is more mature, there is another shift in emphasis towards differentiating features that extend the boundaries of the product's performance.

Taking industrial ink-jet printing machines as an example, the first stage was the development of a product to meet a regulatory need, namely the printing of sell-by dates on cans of soft drinks. EC regulations require that canned drinks indicate their sell-by date. Applying these dates by contact printing or the application of printed labels was impractical because of the very high speed of canning production lines. A modern canning line can run at well over one thousand cans per minute, whereas the fastest contact printing approach is limited to less than half that rate. In ink-jet printing, a line of ink droplets is sprayed at the product through a nozzle which directs the spray electrostatically to create printed characters. Very high speed printing is possible, and the initial poor quality and shape of the printed character were a small price to pay for keeping canning lines at full speed. Initially then, ink-jet printing was the only technology which could be used, and so the very existence of the product was differentiation enough. As competitors began developing rival products, the industry leaders attempted to continue to differentiate by adding better performance in terms of better printed character definition and faster printing speeds. Soon however, they had to shift their emphasis to meet the driving customer needs of better reliability and easier maintainability. Early products suffered from blocked nozzles and contaminated inks and were very unreliable, so much so that one canning business installed two printers per line, arguing that the cost of a back-up printer was a small price to pay for keeping the line running.

As the use of these products became more widespread, customer pressure grew for reliability and ease of use. More recently, over 20 years after the first products were launched, ink-jet printing has become a mature business, with all the main competitors offering comparable products. The focus of differentiation has now moved back towards product performance, and investment is directed towards edible ink technology for spraying on oranges and other fruit and vegetables, drop-on-demand technology giving lower ink consumption and more accurate character shapes, and water-based inks which are more environmentally acceptable. In parallel with these later stages of maturity, the number of product applications has expanded to include magazine address labelling and labelling of other packaging.

This ink-jet printing example highlights two general points. First, technology has been a vital differentiating factor for industrial ink-jet printers throughout their existence. Second, the focus of technology effort has been continually shifting as competitors strive for new opportunities for technical advantage. The control engineers designing better algorithms for character definition are replaced by electronics design engineers developing cheaper, more reliable products who in turn are replaced by food chemists developing edible inks. As it can take years to establish technical development teams, managing technology effectively was and is one of the top priorities of this business.

REDUCING COSTS

Not all businesses offer scope for differentiation as they mature. For products that become commodities, for example many primary materials businesses including steel and aluminium semifabricated products, base chemicals, and some polymers, the technology emphasis is on reducing costs. Aluminium smelting is an interesting example. This is a highly competitive capital intensive industry with limited scope for competitive action, because the unit costs of raw material and energy are largely given, as is the world market price of the metal produced. Companies have some scope for increasing profitability and/or market share by smelter location, material supply contracts and downstream alliances or integration, but the principal route to improved business performance is to reduce process costs by applying better technology.

The technology used is the Hall-Herault process, first developed in 1886. In essence, the process involves dissolving alumina in a current conducting molten salt bath operating at a temperature of around 950°C. A high amperage direct current, at a low voltage of around six volts, is then passed through the solution, causing liquid aluminium to collect on the carbon cathode. The process is simple in concept, but difficult in practice because of the high temperature and high amperage. Not surprisingly, since 1886, increases in plant size and productivity efficiencies have been enormous.

As Figure 1.1 shows, plant size has increased by a factor of 100 in 80 years, and smelting current by a factor of over 50. As a consequence of this move to larger higher power plants, the consumption of energy, the principal variable cost in aluminium production, has fallen from 40 kwh/kg of metal in 1890, to 24 kwh/kg in 1910 and below 14 kwh/kg in 1990. This trend will undoubtedly continue.

Year	Typical Plant Size (tonnes/year)	Smelting Current (amps)
1910	3,000	5,000
1950	100,000	36,000
1990	300,000	280,000

FIGURE 1.1   Aluminium Smelter Developments
Source: Arthur D. Little

Countless incremental technology developments over many years have produced ever larger, better designed smelters operating under more accurate control systems. Technology is changing more slowly than in ink-jet printing, and the direction of technology development is more predictable. However, the cost of new plant and the disproportionate impact of small technical improvements on the variable cost element of the business, mean that every technical decision is critical to overall profitability.

Effective technology management is therefore again a top priority for management.

PROVIDING NEW BUSINESS OPPORTUNITIES

This third role for technology is one that everyone likes to talk about, as it is inherently glamorous and exciting. Sadly, it is rarely as important as more prosaic efforts to cut costs and enhance existing products. Despite the hype about technology push, most commercial innovation is still a consequence of market pull not technology push. Very few companies use technology as a driver for new business, and those that do find it a difficult strategy to follow. One company that has chosen to follow this route and build on its technology is Raychem. Founded by some scientists, expert in radiation chemistry (hence the name), the company has built a large business making specialist components based on changing the physical properties of plastics, metals and ceramics. Shape memory metals, heat shrink plastics and specialist circuit protection devices are typical products.

Since its creation in 1957, Raychem has expanded to have current sales of around $1.6 billion, with around 10,000 employees in over 40 countries. Much like 3M, Raychem's strategy is to serve numerous market niches with specialist applications of its materials. Fire resistant cable sheathing and heat shrunk cable connector sleeves both use the heat shrink polymer technology, but are targeted at very different market niches. One of the advantages to this approach to business is that it can yield very high margins, as the products are often uniquely suited to their applications and usually well covered by patents. However, by definition a niche offers little scope for growth, so that growing the business overall requires a steady stream of new niches. What is worse, if the business is to grow at a steady percentage rate, the pressure to find more and bigger niches grows as the number of untapped opportunities diminishes. As a consequence, companies following this strategy can find it increasingly difficult to sustain growth as the search for new sales often leads them into niches where the margins fall well short of those on existing sales. This problem is often compounded by the need to add new marketing and distribution channels each time a new product niche is found. Building a complete business strategy around a core technology is therefore a high risk approach appropriate only for those with vision, technology good enough to sustain many business areas, and the commercial scope to justify it.

That is not to say the technology push approach should be ignored completely. All businesses should use technology to open up new business areas, if the opportunities present themselves and if the new business areas are consistent with the overall objectives and strategy of the business. If the opportunities are *not* consistent with the existing business direction, you should beware. Technology alone is rarely justification for entering a new sphere of business activity.

One company's new technology-driven business opportunity is another company's technology substitution threat. When Raychem developed heat shrink plastics for cable connecting sleeves, the companies which produced resin filled diecast metal connecting boxes found themselves out of business. Similarly calculators replaced slide rules, CDs and tapes have replaced records, and transistors replaced diodes only to be replaced in turn by integrated circuits. Technology threats often come from outside the industry, frequently causing such a radical change in business operations that adaptation is difficult, even if the threat is anticipated. The only way out is to be sufficiently aware of possible threats early enough to allow time to develop an appropriate strategy in response. Once again, this is further evidence that technology is so fundamental to business success that all top managers need to understand how to manage it effectively.

FACILITATING AND SUPPORTING STRATEGIC CHANGE

Technology can have a major role as a lever for strategic change. To illustrate this point, consider the experience of a light bulb manufacturer based in Europe. Lacking the scale economies of the market leader, and facing low cost competition, the company decided to switch from high volume domestic light bulb manufacture to lower volume niche domestic products such as spotlights and candle bulbs. Recognising that this strategy would result in a wider variety of products and higher stock levels, managers changed their production management systems. However, because they did not understand the basic process technology, the managers failed to anticipate the very high scrap levels that resulted. Every time the production line was switched on, the first 5,000 bulbs were scrap, as they were used to fine tune the process parameters. On a high volume production run this was not a problem; 5,000 scrap out of 2 million was considered acceptable. On a low volume batch of 25,000 or so, 5,000 scrap was disastrous. On investigation, it became clear that to compete economically in low volume batch production, the whole manufacturing process would have to be modified, with considerable capital investment in sensors, instrumentation and automated process control systems. The cost threw into question the economic viability of the new strategy. By now, however, top management was so wedded to the idea that it carried on anyway. As a result, the company's financial performance suffered, and this was one of the factors contributing to its subsequent acquisition. The message is clear: think through the possible impact of technology on your proposed business strategy, and factor in the costs of the modifications required to realise your chosen strategy.

As these four examples have shown, an understanding of technology is fundamental to business success, because it provides the main competitive weapons that a business needs to call upon. Technology matters, and it matters to the extent that all top management should understand it and participate in making technology decisions.

THE ROUTE TO LONG TERM GROWTH

Technological innovation is the only viable route to long term growth. Innovation, and particularly technology innovation, is the prime driver in today's industrial environment. Companies that fail to innovate enter a downward spiral of uncompetitive products, declining sales volume and declining margins.

Moreover, the trend is accelerating. First, product lifecycles are getting shorter, so that products are quickly made obsolete and need to be

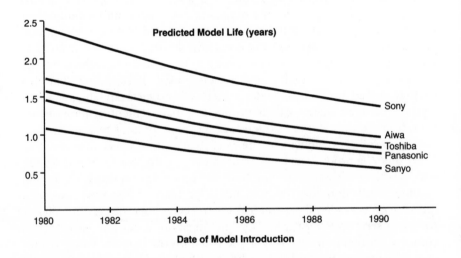

FIGURE 1.2   Decline in Model Life in the Consumer Electronics
             Industry
             Source: Sanderson and Uzumeri (Ref. 1.1)

replaced by new, more advanced products. The electronics industry (Figure 1.2) is a good example.

Even outside the electronics industry, you cannot afford to be complacent. A study conducted by the Fraunhofer Institute in Germany found a similar reduction in the length of product life cycles across a wide range of industries. In the automotive parts industry, products that lasted ten years in 1980, now last only seven, and even in a mature industry like machine tools, product life cycles have shortened significantly, from twelve years to eight years.

Second, technologies are always evolving and advancing. Again, the electronics industry is a well-documented example, with the capacity of solid state memory chips, know as DRAMs, increasing logarithmically, doubling roughly every eighteen months (Figure 1.3). The development of impact-resistant polymers shows the same pattern, although over a longer timeframe (Figure 1.4). The same overall trend is visible in most industries; when one technology reaches its natural limits, the next generation is developed to replace it. New materials to increase aero-engine operating temperatures are another clear example (Figure 1.5). All of these examples are ones where the advances are in a single group of technologies.

Similar trends occur in complex systems dependent on several technologies. Power to weight ratios in railway locomotives, for example,

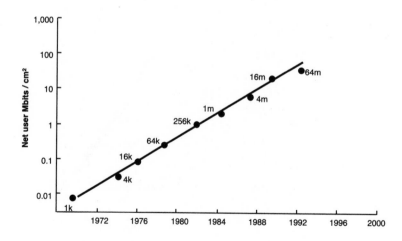

FIGURE 1.3   Evolution of DRAM Information Density
Source: Arthur D. Little

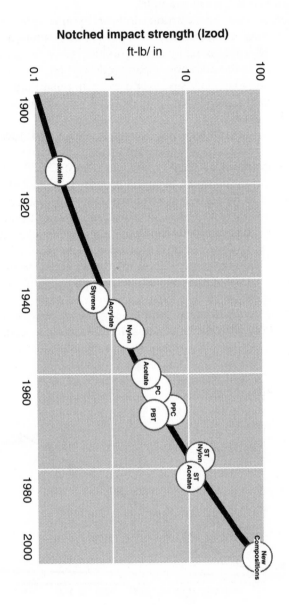

FIGURE 1.4 The Development of Impact-Resistant Polymers
Source: R. Porter (Ref. 1.3)

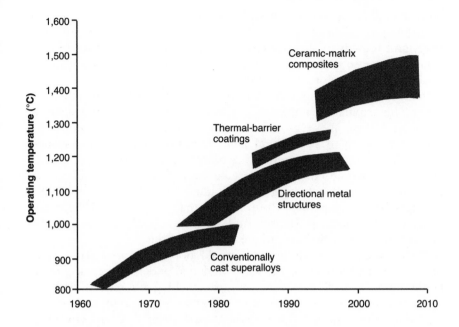

FIGURE 1.5   Evolution of High Temperature Materials for Aero
             Engines
             Source: J. P. Clarke & M. C. Flemings (Ref. 1.4)

improved 70-fold from 1810 to 1980, reflecting the sum of numerous incremental developments in the technologies of materials, components, sub-assemblies and overall system design (Ref. 1.2).

Why, though, are innovation and technology the only possible route for expansion and growth? Surely, growing geographically, or taking market share by lower cost production or acquisition are viable alternatives? And, in any event, why grow at all? If shareholders are happy, why not just keep chugging on?

Taking the second objection first, there are numerous economic arguments why growth is a necessary condition for prosperity. From the management viewpoint, there are two compelling drivers for growth. Firstly, standing still is not an option. The alternative to growth is decline. Competitive advantage accrues to those who grow, enabling them to grow even more. Secondly, shareholders expect growth in dividends and share price, and if growth is not forthcoming, they will not stay happy for long. In the short term, better management practices and increased utilisation of assets can provide such growth. In the longer term, however, growth in profitability and hence dividends can only come from growth in sales, and growth in share price can only come from increase in asset value or increase in the present value of future growth opportunities.

Companies, therefore, have to grow.

In the short to medium term, it is true that such growth can come from geographic expansion, improved cost competitiveness, or acquisition. In the longer term, these growth options hit natural limits. Geographic expansion clearly has a natural limit. Increasing cost competitiveness tends towards diminishing returns. Acquisition, similarly, runs into problems as the acquiror both has to take over ever larger companies to maintain a constant percentage growth rate and has to demonstrate it is adding value by acquiring. The problems that some of the UK's largest conglomerates, such as Hanson and BTR, have had to face up to in maintaining their growth record are evidence of this.

These other routes for growth should not be ignored. They often provide a route for building the scale needed to underpin organic growth. Furthermore, if well managed, they can yield good returns. Hanson, whose shares rose from some 12p in 1980 to around 200p in 1996, has over that period provided a consistent performance record envied by many. In the end, however, it is inevitable that such expansion will peter out unless there is strong underlying organic growth, fuelled primarily by improved products and processes and driven by technology development. To reinforce the point, a wide-ranging survey by *Electronic Business* in the US showed that technological innovation was the single most important chief executive concern (Figure 1.6). If American electronics CEOs are concerned, so should you be.

There is a final practical reason why technology management needs to be given more attention, and that is the paradox of technology and business planning. It is rare for companies to drive their business with technology, and it is much more common to use technology to support a business strategic thrust. This is as it should be, but in practice is very difficult to do well. Most businesses plan accurately for the next quarter, have outline budgets and plans for the next year, and have vague ideas and objectives for the two years beyond that. In contrast, for a technology plan to be workable, it must have a time horizon of at least five years, and probably longer, to be consistent with the time span of projects and the time taken to establish a team of specialists. Technology plans need therefore to anticipate business plans in most companies, while still nominally reflecting the requirements of such business plans. For this to work, both technical and non-technical top management need a good understanding of the issues so they can hold a constructive dialogue about what might be possible and what might be needed. This is

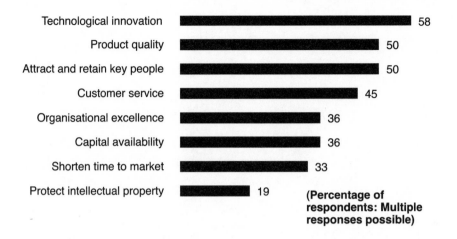

Technological innovation	58
Product quality	50
Attract and retain key people	50
Customer service	45
Organisational excellence	36
Capital availability	36
Shorten time to market	33
Protect intellectual property	19

(Percentage of respondents: Multiple responses possible)

FIGURE 1.6   The Critical Concerns of US CEOs
Source: Reprinted from *Electronics Business*, March 1991,
© Cahners Publishing Company (1997). A division of
Reed Elsevier, Inc.

increasingly important. As examples later in this book will show, most businesses today face an unprecedented challenge in adapting to the opportunities and threats posed by new technology.

It is not surprising that many current management thinkers are arguing that corporations need to become much more proactive in deciding their strategy than they have been in the past. Hamel and Prahalad's ideas on core competence and corporate intent (Ref. 1.5), Campbell's work on mission and vision (Ref. 1.6), and work at Arthur D. Little on ambition-driven strategy (Ref. 1.7) all point to the need for businesses to look ten, or even twenty years into the future, defining the type of business they wish to be and identifying the key strategic steps they need to take.

Long-range technology planning provides one of the most important elements in this strategic visioning process, giving solid information to allow corporate management to have a rational debate about what the future might hold. Long-range technology planning techniques also provide a template to assist in long-range business strategy development.

For the strategic reasons outlined earlier and the practical reasons presented here, it is clear that technology matters to top management and should matter more.

2

TECHNOLOGY AND CORPORATE INVOLVEMENT

❖

THE DRIVERS FOR CORPORATE INVOLVEMENT

IF you accept the premise that technology matters because it underpins current competitiveness and provides opportunity for future growth, you should be concerned about how well your business is managing technology. You may still feel, however, that active corporate involvement in technology management will interfere with local company management without adding value. However, it is not enough for corporate management to exhort their subsidiary companies to be more innovative and use technology more effectively. The problems are so far-reaching, and the impact of decisions on the business is so great, that active corporate involvement is inevitable if you are to succeed in making technology add value to the business.

There are three drivers for corporate involvement:

O   Corporate growth and corporate strategy are dependent on technology choices.

O   From a defensive viewpoint, the scale of investment required for technology development is so great that corporate involvement is necessary as a safeguard.

O   Within the corporation, the divisions and the strategic business units (SBUs) are unlikely to make the technology choices that best meet the needs of the corporation as a whole.

CORPORATE GROWTH AND TECHNOLOGY CHOICES

Two examples illustrate the linkages between corporate growth and technology choices: Glaxo and Zantac, and the TI Group and mechanical seals.

15

Glaxo was a middle sized UK-based pharmaceuticals company before it launched Zantac in 1982. The success of Zantac since then has allowed Glaxo to expand internationally, establish a global manufacturing and marketing presence, and acquire competitors. Glaxo became Number Two in the world ethical pharmaceuticals industry and has a sufficient cash stream from Zantac to fuel extensive R&D on new drugs to find the next big products.

The success of Zantac was no accident. Glaxo pushed the development of the drug very hard, taking only seven years from patent to launch compared to the industry average of 12. Five extra years of patented sales of Zantac are equivalent to about £2 billion of pre-tax profit at today's prices. Realising early on that it had a winner, Glaxo marketed the drug as vigorously as possible, stressing the benefits compared to Tagamet, the anti-ulcer drug produced by SmithKline French (now SmithKline Beecham). Glaxo then used Zantac to help it become a global business giving it the production capabilities, regulatory knowledge and distribution channels required to underpin the launch of the next generation of new products.

Zantac is now off-patent, but Glaxo is continuing to build on its success.

Throughout the 1960s and 1970s, the **TI Group** maintained an extensive research programme at its corporate research laboratories to ensure that Crane Packing Ltd., its 51 per cent owned subsidiary in the mechanical seals business, maintained a strong market position. John Crane, a subsidiary of the US group Houdaille Industries, with a 49 per cent stake, was the other major shareholder in Crane Packing. It also invested heavily in technology development, and there was considerable interchange of ideas. However, despite this technology effort, the two companies achieved only average commercial success. In 1987, the situation changed. The TI Group began a radical restructuring programme, divesting its bicycles and domestic appliances businesses, and focusing on high technology industrial components. In the same year, the group acquired Houdaille Industries in order to gain complete control of John Crane. John Crane / Crane Packing became the world leader in mechanical seals, and achieved the commercial success that its technology strength had always promised.

At the time of its development, the seal business of the TI Group was a small part of one of the group's four main divisions. A decade later, this small part had become one-third of the total business, growth fuelled by acquisition and geographic expansion, but underpinned by corporate faith in the company's technology capabilities in this specialist niche.

The two cases have similar features:

O   The technology breakthrough took many years to bring to commercial reality.

O   Commercial success was not just a function of good technology, but also depended on many other factors.

O   Management used the technology capability to underpin a new strategic direction and so support the reshaping of the corporation for the future.

The message is clear. Without corporate involvement, it is unlikely that these products would have received enough support for long enough to make it out of the research laboratory. Furthermore, even if they had made it to the market, corporate involvement was fundamental to their growth, success and impact on the company.

Racal's cellular telephone business provides an interesting contrast. Racal started life in defence electronics, concentrating on portable radios for battlefield use. In 1984, Racal decided to enter the embryonic cellular telephone business and set up Racal Vodafone. In 1991, Vodafone was floated off as a separate public company, with market capitalisation in excess of £3.5 billion. The commercial success of Vodafone has been undeniable, but it could be argued that, for a period of some years, the rest of Racal suffered from neglect in its shadow. After the demerger of Vodafone, the residue of Racal was criticised as financially weak, over extended in too many markets, and vulnerable to takeover. It would seem that Racal did not take the strategic opportunity to use the stability and rewards provided by the Vodafone technology to buy time and space to reshape the company as a whole. Instead, Racal managed Vodafone as a bolt-on stand-alone unit and, as a consequence, lost the opportunity to realise synergistic benefits.

Regardless of the outcome, all three of the examples quoted above show that technology is one of the basic building blocks of corporate growth, opening up strategic options and providing scope for competitive advantage. However, technology development is risky and expensive; indeed ultimately it provides scope for bankruptcy. Corporate involvement is therefore also needed for defensive reasons.

SCALE OF INVESTMENT

The collapse of Rolls Royce in 1971 was at least in part due to excessive development cost and time overruns on the RB211 engine programme. Other less publicised examples of over-investment in technology include Chloride's costly, time-consuming and unsuccessful attempt to develop commercial sodium-sulphur batteries and GKN's expensive and at the time of writing still commercially unsuccessful foray into the development of composite components for the automotive industry. Don't be deceived by the relatively low budget typically assigned to a research project. For most technology developments, the Pi rule applies: £100,000 spent on research typically requires over £300,000 on development and over £900,000 on starting production. Moreover, once a research project has started, management is often reluctant to stop it. The more the project develops, and the more it costs, the greater the reluctance to pull the plug. Instead, management often commits more and more of its own time to trying to make the project successful, further increasing the opportunity cost of the project. That is why corporate involvement is vital at the *early* decision stage.

Given the scale of investment from research to market introduction, no company can afford to develop all the products it would like to. Choices have to be made. Make the right choice and you provide the corporation with the tools it needs to grow. Make the wrong choice and you could bankrupt the company. Can you run the risk of delegating such decisions?

TECHNOLOGY SYNERGIES

Finally, corporate involvement is necessary to ensure that the benefits of technology to the corporation as a whole are greater than the benefits to the separate divisions or businesses. Many companies delegate decisions on technology development and funding to the divisions. The consequences are not surprising; divisions spend money on technologies relevant to them, and the big divisions spend more than the little divisions. While this approach satisfies the divisional management, it makes no strategic sense at corporate level.

Corporate management should be more far sighted in its approach to allocating resources: from each business according to its ability – to each according to its strategic need. Consider, for example, a primary materials company with two divisions, one making aluminium and one producing structural polymers. Today, the aluminium division accounts for 80 per cent of group sales, but the polymers division is growing faster, and should account for half of group sales within five years. How should the company's R&D effort be allocated – 80 to 20? Obviously not. The polymers division is in greater need of R&D effort, both because technology is moving faster there and because, as a business, it is the division with the greater growth prospects. However, in this simplified version of a real company, the aluminium division did indeed spend 80 per cent of the total technology development budget, maintaining three separate research centres and conducting a wide ranging research programme into new aluminium products and production processes. Some of these projects, such as a study into harder wearing extrusion dies, made good commercial sense. Others, such as a project on fibre reinforced high strength aluminium matrix composites, did not, even though technically such projects were both interesting and challenging. The polymers division, meanwhile, struggled on, lacking the development resources required to exploit all the commercial opportunities available. The company's policy of allowing divisions autonomous control meant that the situation continued and, as a consequence, both divisions of the company fell behind its principal competitors. The aluminium division squandered its resources and was not managed tightly enough to remain profitable when the aluminium industry went into recession. The polymers division grew too slowly and failed to achieve competitive economies of scale.

Divisions can also suffer from being inward looking, as all the pressure from corporate level is to focus on their own area and deliver the prescribed returns. The consequences can be serious. One paper company, with an office plain paper division and a coated paper division, mainly producing fax paper, was caught out as plain paper fax machines gained in popularity. The technology expertise and production capability existed in the plain paper division, but the business requirement, applications knowledge and customer base were in the other division. The performance pressures exerted on each division gave little incentive for the divisions to work together, even though to do so would have been in the interest of the company as a whole. As in the previous example, too much power was devolved to the divisions. In this case, the only solution was to merge the divisions.

Even when the corporation is able to take a more active role in managing technology, there is a danger of misallocation of resources. In Philips Consumer Electronics, the success of the CD player meant that resources were thrown at developing optical recording technology further, long after the returns had started diminishing. Since many of the senior managers in the company had risen to their positions because of their involvement with the CD player, they were inherently biased towards that area of development. As a consequence, they viewed magnetic recording as something of a poor relation. It took the personal intervention of Jan Timmer, the Head of Philips Consumer Electronics at that time, to redress the balance and put more resources into the magnetic side, leading to the development of the Digital Compact Cassette (DCC). Even then, the lack of resources devoted to the DCC has meant that its technology is not far enough advanced to allow it to be manufactured at a competitive cost. Consequently, its performance in the market has to date been disappointing.

For this variety of reasons, the individual businesses and divisions of a group cannot be relied upon to use technology resources to the optimum benefit of the corporation as a whole. What is needed is a greater degree of corporate involvement, providing guidance and focus for technology development without meddling in the day-to-day activities of the operating units.

Most corporations, however, are moving in the opposite direction towards ever more decentralisation, pushing strategic decision making down to the lowest possible level. ABB, for example, now operates with over 100 autonomous business units, all at arm's length from the corporate centre. The benefits of decentralisation are not in doubt: improved efficiency in the daily operations of the business, increased management responsibility, faster management response time and reduced central overhead costs. However, unless carefully managed, decentralisation can also result in lack of technology synergy, duplication of effort and waste of resources, and inappropriate technology priority setting. How to manage technology at a corporate level, to exploit synergies, transfer technologies between divisions and set priorities are underlying themes of this book.

These are critical issues. A recent comprehensive research project, documented by Goold, Campbell and Alexander (Ref. 2.1), has looked more generally at the role of corporations. The project concluded that corporations must deliver some sort of 'parenting advantage' to justify their existence. Otherwise they should relinquish control and allow business units to be managed separately or as part of other corporations which can deliver parenting advantage. Obviously, technology management is not the only possible form of parenting advantage a corporation can offer its subsidiaries. However, it is one of the most significant advantages for many product businesses, and so is an area deserving of active corporate management.

The starting point has to be both a recognition of the need for a corporate policy on technology, and a realisation that such a policy should complement other aspects of the corporate style.

CORPORATE STYLE

Companies come in all shapes and sizes and the nature of corporate technology policy will vary enormously in scope and scale. Nonetheless, there are some fundamental guidelines which apply, depending on the generic style of the company. The three styles derived by Goold and Campbell in 1987 (Ref. 2.2) provide a useful starting point. They conducted a wide ranging study into how diversified corporations are managed, and identified three distinct styles:

O   Strategic planning
O   Strategic control

O   Financial control.

Strategic planning companies do what the label suggests. The corporate centre is closely involved in planning the future of the business, coordinating the strategies of the individual businesses to give maximum overall benefit. This management approach leads to strong organic growth and good financial performance in the longer term. However, there is a danger that this type of company can be slow moving and inflexible in times of crisis. BP and Cadbury Schweppes in the UK, Siemens in Germany and Xerox in the US are examples of businesses whose style approaches this model.

Strategic control companies use the corporate centre to monitor the performance of the individual businesses, to focus resources on building up growth areas and to invest in poorly performing businesses. Individual businesses are given the scope to develop long term strategies, but little attempt is made to realise possible synergies between the businesses. This management style gives some organic growth, coupled with stability and reasonable profit levels. Safe and steady, this style can, however, be risk averse, bureaucratic and inefficient. ICI and Vickers in the UK, and Philips in the Netherlands, could be viewed as representative of this style.

Interestingly, many Japanese companies following the Jigyobu organisational structure are also essentially strategic control companies. Jigyobu was introduced by Matsushita in the 1950s and is now the dominant organisational structure for large Japanese and other Pacific Rim companies. Sanyo, the consumer electronics giant is a typical example. At the time of writing, the group was divided into nine product divisions ranging from Audio-Video products to Housing Systems. Each product division is then further divided into business units. The Audio-Video division, for example, includes separate TV, video cassette recorder, Hi-Fi and Components businesses. Product planning and design, and all manufacturing and assembly, are carried out at business unit level. R&D is carried out at product division level, together with a limited amount of product design coordination. Separate geographically grouped sales organisations handle sales and marketing. Under this system, individual business units have the freedom to move quickly within their chosen product segments, while retaining group economies of scale in the marketplace. The corporate centre has the power to divert resources into new areas of strategic importance using well-established strategic planning approaches to differentiate between cash absorbing rising stars and cash generating mature businesses.

As in Europe, this management style has historically delivered consistently good growth performance. However, it is now generally accepted as sub-optimal, with problems such as multiple procurement from suppliers, duplicated R&D, and an inability to handle cross-business products, such as a combined TV and video cassette recorder. Attempts are now being made to solve these problems by increasing the level of central involvement in business unit operational decisions.

Financial control is the third distinct style identified by Goold and Campbell. Financial control companies focus on financial performance. Very decentralised, these companies allow their subsidiaries almost complete autonomy of management, provided that they meet a comprehensive set of financial targets. Financially successful, usually with very high share price growth, such companies can suffer by concentrating too closely on short term results. GEC, as a typical example, has, for 20 years, managed to grow by acquisition and merger and so deliver ever greater returns to shareholders. However, underlying organic growth has been disappointing. This style of management tends to be unsustainable over the very long term, requiring ever-greater acquisitions to deliver constant growth rates. As outlined earlier, organic growth driven by innovation is the only secure route to long term success. However, there is no doubt that the financial control management style can be very effective in the short to medium term. Many a strategic control company has improved immeasurably in efficiency and use of overheads after acquisition by a financial control oriented predator.

This framework of three distinct management styles, strategic planning, strategic control and financial control, provides a template for assessing what type of corporate technology policy is appropriate and deciding at what level policy issues should be determined (Figure 2.1). For strategic planning companies, technology policy is set at corporate level and the centre plays a strong role in managing technology across the company. For strategic control companies, technology policy is set at both corporate and divisional level and the degree of corporate technology management

Company Management Style	Decison on Technology Policy	Time Horizon
Strategic planning	Corporate centre	Long term
Strategic control	Division	Medium term
Financial control	Business unit	Short term

FIGURE 2.1   Corporate Technology Policy and Management Styles
Source: Arthur D. Little

is more limited. For financial control companies, there is no explicit technology policy, and management of technology is concentrated at business unit level.

The model is, of course, simplistic. Even financial control companies need some corporate monitoring and coordination to ensure that not all long term technology competences are sacrificed for the sake of short term financial gain. The content of this book is therefore still relevant to financial control companies, although the depth of central involvement will obviously be less than in strategic planning or strategic control companies.

CORPORATE TECHNOLOGY POLICY

All companies need some form of corporate technology policy. This policy should set clear guidelines on the degree to which the company plans to compete as a technology leader. With this clear, the company can decide on the level of active involvement of corporate management in the company's various technology activities, and the degree to which corporate management should monitor the technology activities in the business units.

First, companies need to decide whether they want to be technology leaders or followers. Companies such as IBM, Xerox, and Hewlett-Packard have all made this corporate technology decision. Xerox has positioned itself as a technology leader. Investing heavily in long term research, Xerox competes across the board in all its chosen markets on the basis of technology and product performance. Not only that, but Xerox's ways of doing business are also innovative, reinforcing its image as a company at the leading edge. Hewlett Packard is also positioning itself as a technology leader, moving rapidly to stay ahead of the competition by offering high performance, high technology products at competitive prices. Leading products in workstations, printers, and test equipment are all evidence of the success of this policy.

In contrast, IBM regards itself as a fast follower. The company does not like pioneering a product and carrying the risk of market failure. Instead, it aims to be ready to launch a follower product quickly, building on its market muscle and the IBM name, and fine-tuning its response to satisfy market queries about the leader product. IBM still has to maintain a high level of technology competence, investing enough in R&D to be able to move fast when a new market develops. In fact, at the time of writing, IBM invests almost as much in R&D as Hewlett Packard (5.2 per cent of sales compared to 7.1 per cent of sales in 1996) to try to ensure that it is not wrong-footed when a new market takes off. This strategy works well when markets are relatively stable, but carries the risk that the company can fail to spot new trends fast enough. If IBM had followed a leader strategy, it might have been less vulnerable to the shifts in the PC industry than it proved to be.

The fast second-to-market strategy adopted by IBM is not the only possible following strategy. One alternative is to focus on applications engineering, liaising closely with customers to develop reliable products of adequate, but not leading edge, performance. Applications-based companies spend heavily on product development, but rely on others to do the fundamental research and longer term advanced development. Most applications engineering companies are OEM (original equipment manufacturer) suppliers, working in markets where reliability, cost and consistency of quality are more important that out-and-out technological performance.

Amstrad adopted another different following strategy. It focused management effort on identifying attractive market niches and on sourcing manufacturing from low cost external supplier. The corporate technology policy was to spend as little as possible. This strategy is workable, if the company can stay ahead of the game in spotting new opportunities and production sources. However, it can be high risk and few companies adopt it, preferring to keep some product and technology competence in-house, rather than become just a trading business.

Whether a company can adopt a clearly defined corporate technology policy, and stick to it, depends on the type of company. Companies which follow the strategic planning model, such as Xerox and IBM, have little difficulty in defining a company-wide policy on technology. Their management style is one of long term corporate thinking, which is in line with the concept of corporate technology policy.

For many strategic control companies, though, the picture may be less clear cut. Companies such as Vickers, with interests ranging from medical equipment to tanks, may lead in some divisions and follow in others. Indeed, trying to be a technology leader on all fronts is a daunting task for all but the largest of global corporations. The corporate technology policy adopted by strategic control companies should therefore allow for the different needs of the divisions while maintaining some degree of corporate coherence. A full spectrum of policies in one group is unlikely as it would suggest the group is not contributing to the success of the individual businesses. Even worse, conflicting policies across the group could damage the group's image. Companies which are technology leaders in one area tend also to be at least technically capable in all other areas. The need for some consistency in corporate culture in strategic control companies places some limits on the range of technology policies followed.

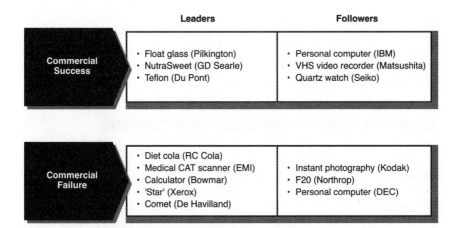

FIGURE 2.2   Technology Leadership and
              Commercial Success
              Source: Adapted from Teece (Ref 2.4)

This has been one of the problems suffered by Philips over the past decade. With businesses ranging from light bulbs to telecommunications, and a variety of technology policies, it has been difficult for the group to retain a coherent image. The group's technology leadership image in key areas, including interactive media and optical data systems, is diluted by its less differentiated 'me too' image in mass market audio systems and light bulbs.

Taken to the extreme, if technology policies across a group cannot be reconciled, then the rationale for the group's existence must be questioned. With little opportunity for synergy, the individual businesses may well be better placed outside the group, rather than within, unless in reality the group is justified by its financial control mechanisms and not by its strategy. Financial control groups do not need corporate technology policies, as the synergies between the business units come from how the units are managed, not from what they are doing.

In considering technology policy, do not confuse leadership with success. Leaders are not always successful, as Figure 2.2 shows. EMI, with the medical CAT scanner, is an example of a company that developed technology leadership, but failed to manage its exploitation successfully and ultimately succumbed to takeover by Thorn. Conversely, followers are not always failures. IBM in personal computers and Seiko in quartz watches are good examples of successful followers.

Commercial success is not dependent on whether you are a leader or a follower. It is a function of your company's ability to link technology and business strategy closely, so that technology activities are focused on strategic needs, and business growth builds on technology strengths. Both technology leaders and technology followers can be successful, provided that this link is managed effectively, and as a consequence, they continue to develop and launch new innovations (Ref. 2.3).

AREAS OF ACTIVE CORPORATE INVOLVEMENT

Once the appropriate technology policy for the corporation has been identified, you need to decide which technology activities can be left to the business units and which require the active involvement of corporate management.

In essence, whatever the overall policy, corporate management needs to take an active role in:

O   Positioning the corporation in the longer term:
        – Managing corporate thrusts into new technology areas
        – Identifying technology threats and opportunities
O   Ensuring that the portfolio of technology activities spread across the business is in balance
O   Realising synergies across the corporation
O   Creating and overseeing joint ventures and alliances
O   Monitoring business unit activity.

These five areas are all corporate rather than business or divisional issues.

LONGER TERM POSITIONING

Only corporate management can position the corporation in the longer term. The business managers, and even the divisional management, are quite rightly more focused on short term issues. Most businesses plan accurately for the next quarter, have outline plans for the next year, and have vague ideas and objectives for the two years beyond that. However, for a technology plan to be workable, it must have a time horizon of at least five years, and probably longer, in line with the time span of projects and the time taken to establish a team of specialists and build a solid competence. Technology plans need therefore to anticipate business plans in most companies, implying the need for constructive corporate dialogue about what is possible and what might be needed for this mismatch in time horizons to be dealt with. For example, a business unit manufacturing sintered metal components and serving the automotive industry components market, may recognise the threat posed by high strength plastics, but will still focus on sintered metal, driven by the pressure to maximise returns on the next assets, most of which are elements of the sintering plant. The decision on whether to build up a plastics business to maintain a presence in the market or to gradually withdraw and focus on alternative sintered metal markets can only be made at corporate level.

The need for corporate involvement in longer term planning is particularly acute when, as in this example, a new technology is involved. At business unit level, it can often be difficult to justify investment in new technology and associated capital plant solely on the basis of the next product programme. New technology projects often have negative net present value when dealt with in isolation, and their true value only becomes apparent as subsequent generations of products follow through. Even worse, investing in new technology may imply equally large write-offs of assets associated with the current technology. Switching costs are therefore often prohibitive when viewed at business unit level, and so decisions on investment in new technology often have to be made on the strength of corporate strategic intent, rather than simple financial hurdles.

BALANCING TECHNOLOGY PORTFOLIOS

Ensuring that the portfolio of activities is in balance is also a corporate responsibility. Within each business unit, management is able to assess the risk-reward trade-off of specific projects, and to ensure that the business unit is not over-dependent on one high risk project. However, this should also be done within an overall company-wide picture. At the corporate level, it is important to maintain the balance between high risk, high reward projects and low risk, low reward projects across the businesses. For every breakthrough project costing millions, there needs to be a collection of smaller, but safer projects that will generate those millions. Timescale is also important. Each division in isolation might plan a major project with maximum cash outflow in five years' time, but good returns thereafter. Taken together, the effect on the company could be catastrophic, if the weakened financial base of the company made it vulnerable to take over. Someone somewhere at corporate level needs to keep an eye on this, taking action where necessary to ensure that the portfolio does not become too imbalanced.

In a similar vein, the centre should take the responsibility for ensuring that those parts of the company that need technology invest the right amount in it and that those parts that do not, don't, even if they have the spare resources to do so. How you make this happen depends on the type of company. In strategic planning or control companies, the centre can take a direct role and manage the focus of resources. In financial control companies, more indirect measures are needed. Setting different financial

Magnetic tape drive mechanisms are used in cassette tape recorders, video tape recorders and video cameras. In many respects, the technologies used in mechanisms for these three products are similar. Each product requires a mechanism which will move the tape from one reel onto another, past a read / record pick-up head. Each product also requires a tape tensioning mechanism, and motor control circuitry. However, there are many significant differences. Cassette tape mechanisms are, in the main, cheap and cheerful commodity products, built to well-established specifications at very low cost. The technology push in this area has been for cheaper manufacturing and more compact components. Video tape mechanisms are more complex, with the tape wrapped around a rotating angled cylinder. Close tolerances are necessary to give adequate picture quality, and the technology push in this area has been for better resolution pick-ups to give finer pictures. Video camera mechanisms are also different, with a focus on miniaturisation and shock sensitivity.

So, although a technology development project on tape tensioning could benefit all three products, there is a risk that, even if the project led to a high resolution shock insensitive component, it would be too expensive for use in cassette players, too big for use in video cameras, and probably too late for all three products.

targets for different businesses, depending on how mature they are, is one option.

REALISING SYNERGIES

Realising technology synergies across the corporation is difficult, mainly because it is not in the immediate interests of each of the businesses. A technology developed to meet the needs of two businesses is unlikely to meet the needs of either. So compromise and negotiation are required. This is the responsibility of the centre: acting as arbitrator to make sure the businesses suppress their own specific ambitions for the greater benefit of the company as a whole. There can be a risk attached to this. Attempting to realise synergies can have big negative effects and may not benefit the corporation as a whole. At worst, compromising on technology develop-ment can result in a technology which is so much of a compromise that it is unusable by any of the individual businesses for which it was intended. Even if that doesn't happen, the costs and delays arising from trying to develop a single technology that satisfies everyone can result in uncom-petitiveness and lost market share (see panel). Technology synergy is therefore a double-edged sword. Often valuable at the fundamental research level, where several businesses can spread the cost of research into, say, high temperature materials or precision assembly techniques, the benefits of synergy usually decrease dramatically the closer you get to real products. The role of the corporate centre is therefore to decide when synergy is worth the management effort and, as importantly, when technology development is best left to the businesses.

CREATING JOINT VENTURES AND ALLIANCES

The fourth corporate responsibility is creating and managing joint ventures and alliances. Joint ventures and alliances are often cited as good approaches to rapid technology development and business growth. However, like synergies between business units, synergies between corporations are difficult to achieve and may not give the benefits desired. Inevitably, the partners in a joint venture or collaborative technology development project have different objectives and different ways of working. There is little double that, if all goes well, the benefits can be great, particularly in relationships down the value chain, such as between a materials supplier and a parts fabricator. The way in which many of the plastics companies, notably Dow and BASF, have collaborated with automotive companies to explore greater use of plastics in cars is a good example of this. However, the negative effects can also be great: sub-optimal technologies, delays, management distraction and leakage of company confidential knowledge are all possible. Joint ventures and alliances on technology issues can also have wider effects, influencing market perceptions, customer and supplier relationships, and share price. Corporate involvement is therefore vital.

MONITORING BUSINESS UNIT ACTIVITY

Finally, no matter what the style of the company, the centre needs to get involved at business level at least to the extent of confirming that the technology plans developed by the businesses are sensible. Corporate managers need to be confident that the businesses have thought through their plans, and need to know that such plans are specific, practical and consistent with other investment and business plans.

The checklist given in Figure 2.3, adapted from material in the Innovation Advisory Board's *Innovation Plans Handbook* (Ref. 2.5) provides a useful summary of the questions that corporate management needs to ask in assessing business unit technology policy.

Developing a clear idea of *what* to do in technology is only half the battle. You also need to decide *how* you are going to make it happen. How much are you going to do within the company and how much will you buy in from outside? How useful are universities and other sources of

Are the technology development plans consistent with business strategy?
- How important is technology to the business strategy?
- Are the plans focused on meeting market needs?
- Are we investing enough compared to national and international competitors?
- Have we got the right balance between investment in technology and investment in other aspects of the business?

Are we confident that the business unit has the skills needed to achieve the desired results?
- Have previous efforts resulted in business growth?
- Are appropriate systems and procedures for the management of technology development activities in place?
- Are any plans to use external sources of technology well thought through?

Do we have an appropriate balance of technology development activities?
- Have we got the right mix of incremental and more radical innovation?
- How much longer term research effort is needed?
- Have we allocated the investment appropriately between the different parts of the business?

Have we got the best balance between low and high risk and short and long term projects?
- Have we identified the expected risks and timings?
- Have we acknowledged that only some of the projects will succeed?
- Are we over-dependent on the outcome of one project?

Have we calculated the net financial impact?
- What returns do we expect, and when?
- Do we have sufficient cash flow to finance the innovation effort?

FIGURE 2.3   Technology Policy Checklist
Source: *The Innovation Plans Handbook* This, and other figures from *The Innovation Plans Handbook* elsewhere in this book are Crown Copyright, reproduced with the permission of Her Majesty's Stationery Office. (Ref. 2.5)

intellectual property? In what areas do joint ventures or collaborative R&D projects make sense? How should you organise the R&D within the company to ensure that the results feed through to the business? These questions are dealt with in subsequent chapters. They need to be answered as a corporate management cannot afford not to get involved.

3

ASSESSING TECHNOLOGY POSITION

A S the first two chapters have emphasised, technology is important to every business, and senior managers need both to be aware of the role of technology in their spheres of activity and to develop policies that ensure that technology can be applied to give maximum impact on business performance. As a general principle, this is indisputable. However, recognising that technology matters to corporate management and taking specific steps to increase its impact are two different things. The difficulty is that there is no simple recipe for deciding how much to spend on technology or what to spend it on.

The most obvious starting point is to look at the R&D spend of all your competitors to try to get at least some indication of how much you should be spending, if not of what you would be spending it on. Unfortunately, this line of attack doesn't really help. *The 1997 UK R&D Scoreboard*, published by Company Reporting Ltd. in conjunction with the UK Department of Industry (Ref. 3.1), shows wide variations between the R&D expenditure of similar companies. For example, the R&D spend in 1996 as a percentage of sales in similar types of companies in the chemicals industry ranges from 0.1 per cent to 3.9 per cent. In the electronics industry it is from 0.2 per cent to over 20 per cent and in food from 0.3 per cent to 2.7 per cent. Even in a stable mature industry such as construction materials, there is a wide range from 0.1 per cent to 3.7 per cent. One of the causes of this wide variation is the difficulty of ensuring that we are comparing like with like. There is no precise definition of what should and what should not be included in the accounting definition of R&D. *SSAP 13* (Ref. 3.2) gives one, but it is not wholly satisfactory. The Institutional Shareholders' Committee gives the following explanation of *SSAP 13* (Ref. 3.3).

SSAP 13 splits R&D into the following broad categories:

- *Pure (or basic) research*: experimental or theoretical work undertaken primarily to acquire new scientific or technical knowledge for its own sake rather than directed towards any specific aim or application.

- *Applied research*: original or critical investigation undertaken in order to gain new scientific or technical knowledge and directed towards a specific practical aim or objectives.

- *Development*: use of scientific or technical knowledge in order to produce new or substantially improved materials, devices, products or services, or install new processes or systems prior to the commencement of commercial production or commercial applications, or to improving substantially those already produced or installed.

Attempts have been made to improve the definition (Ref. 3.4) but interpretations still differ, in particular with regard to how to account for the grey areas of product design and manufacturing process development. For *new* products, the development costs are clearly included, but what about tooling, prototype testing, and regulatory compliance testing? For *existing* products, costs should only be included if they relate to *substantial* improvements. This begs the question of what constitutes substantial.

Even if these definition and interpretation problems were resolved, wide variations in spending would still occur, for two reasons. First, *R&D* spend is not a reliable measure of *technology* spend. Companies can apply resources to R&D, but just as legitimately could apply such resources to acquiring new process machinery that incorporates advanced technology, or to sourcing more technologically advanced components and sub-assemblies. In all three cases, the company has invested in developing its competitive position through technology, but only the first will show as an R&D spend.

Second, companies in the same industry, which on the surface appear similar, often compete in different ways. Some companies are technology leaders, others are followers. Some compete solely on product technology, others more on sales, delivery and service. In the UK construction materials industry, for example, Hepworth, manufacturing drainpipes and other products reported a percentage spend in 1996 of twice as much as Blue Circle, manufacturing cement and concrete, which in turn reported a spend higher than those of Marley and Redland, two comparable competitors. Hepworth's higher percentage spend does not necessarily imply that Hepworth is more technically advanced. It is rather a reflection of the different balance between commodity materials, such as bricks, and differentiated materials, such as gas pipes, in the different businesses. Blue Circle, Marley and Redland have a higher proportion of bulk sales to the industry, where price and delivery response are more important than product technology. Therefore, looking at competitors, though interesting, does not necessarily give a good guide on how much to spend and of course gives no clues at all on which technologies to spend the money on.

How then can you decide what to invest in and how much to spend? There are no mechanistic approaches which work adequately. The decisions have to be based on judgement and on fit with business objectives. However, techniques and tools are available to help you and your managers analyse the technology needs of a business and guide decision making. In particular, there are approaches for:

O   Deciding which technologies you need to support the strategic objectives of your business
O   Determining competitive strengths and weaknesses in the technologies that matter
O   Setting corporate technology priorities
O   Deciding on strategic actions to strengthen your position.

Taken together, these approaches give a framework linking business objectives with technology competences to integrate business and technology strategies (Figure 3.1). Remember though, that they are a framework for guiding thinking, not a mechanical strategy development tool. As

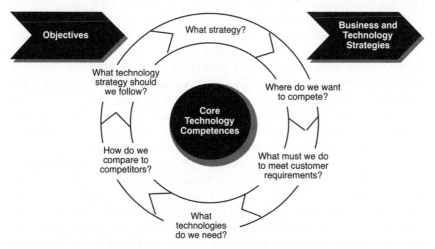

FIGURE 3.1   Structured Approach to Business and Technology Strategy
Source: Arthur D. Little

always, there are no substitutes for intuition and management judgement.

This chapter and the next discuss each of these approaches in turn, providing the basics for the formulation of a technology strategy. The first two, covering technology needs and competitive position, are covered by this chapter. These issues should be dealt with initially at business unit level. They can then be brought together and combined with corporate strategic initiatives to give the corporate priorities. Therefore, responsibility for strategic decision making will shift towards the corporate centre between this chapter and the next, as the detail provided at business unit level forms the foundation for corporate analysis.

DECIDING WHICH TECHNOLOGIES YOU NEED

In developing technology strategy, and deciding which technologies matter and how much development effort is required, managers have a natural tendency to start with the technologies. Taken to extremes, doing it this way may lead to decisions such as those taken by the small electric motors company mentioned in the last chapter, when it invested in R&D in warm temperature super-conducting materials. Even when not taken to extremes, managers who start with the technologies run the risk of devoting too much attention to 'interesting' technologies and technologies in which the business is already investing, rather than those which the business really needs.

Nonetheless, many technologists, and indeed many marketing managers, argue that this is the right approach to take and that focusing on technologies is the only way of effectively looking forward. They point out that, since market trends can seldom be predicted more than a year or so ahead, while technology trends can be predicted for five or more years, starting with the technologies makes sense. However, the counter argument is stronger. A focus on technology may well lead to functionally successful products or components, but is no guarantee of commercial success. In the absence of market knowledge, technologists concentrate on getting technologies to work, but in doing so may not take due account of customer needs for maintainability, size, weight, product flexibility and so on. And problems cannot always be remedied when you collect feedback from a working prototype. Technical decisions made early on may be irreversible at this point. For example, using platinum for heating elements in electric cookers may make technical sense in terms of improving thermal efficiency, but its cost is likely to make it commercially unacceptable. If this realisation comes late, not only does the platinum need to be replaced by a lower cost material, but the bonding materials, the electric hob sheet material, the controls and sensors will need to be modified too. In short, the development team will need to throw away the prototype and start again.

Since many products have numerous components, each embodying numerous technologies, technology developments will be interdependent. Getting better products that customers will buy cannot result from technology push alone. If you want to make effective technology decisions leading to successful product and process innovation, you need to focus technology effort on market needs. Difficult though it may be, there is no option but to start with the market, and to use market and business needs to determine technology needs and so provide the information needed to develop technology strategy.

How can it be done? For a business unit or a product group within a business unit, there is a structured five-step process which local managers can follow to identify the technology needs of the business (Figure 3.2, p. 36):

O   Identify current product / market segments.
O   Identify the bases of competition.
O   Assess the implied key factors for success.
O   Identify relevant technologies.
O   Select the strategically important technologies.

The process, as detailed below, provides the information needed by local managers to help them identify those technologies which are strategically important at business unit level. The next section of this chapter then looks at the business unit competitive position in those technologies, and where actions are needed to strengthen that position.

In a large corporation, you can repeat these processes for deciding technology strategy in every business unit and then add the resulting action plans together to give the corporate action plan. This bottom up approach, however, does not capture any technology benefits that might result from synergies between business units. Neither does it allow you to allocate priorities to the business unit needs. To ensure that these synergy benefits are captured and to allow priorities to be set, you will need to supplement the bottom up business unit view with a top down corporate view. One way of doing this is discussed later in the chapter.

IDENTIFY PRODUCT / MARKET SEGMENTS

The first step is to identify the product and market segments. Techniques for market segmentation are outside the scope of this book, but in essence what you have to do is to separate out market segments that are distinct in terms of:

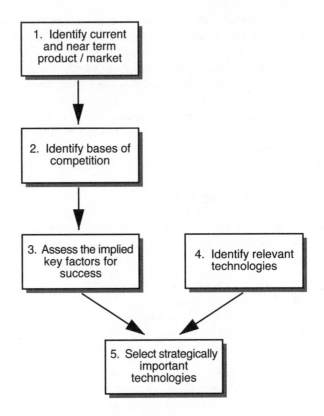

FIGURE 3.2   Identifying the Technology Needs of Your Business
Source: Arthur D. Little

O   Customer base
O   Competitors
O   Distribution channels
O   Geography.

For example, consider a business unit manufacturing precision mechanical parts, such as small gear wheels and mounting brackets. With a £30 million turnover, the unit supplies primarily the automotive, domestic appliance and machine tool markets. Since a first cut at market segmentation would give just these three markets, further segmentation is probably necessary. In the automotive market, for example, it may be desirable to segment into high volume and low volume parts. High volume parts are likely to include such items as standard sizes of small flanges and pulleys. Low volume parts, in contrast, are likely to be custom designed in conjunction with the automotive companies to perform specific functions. These two product segments are therefore sold differently, via different channels, and are likely to have different groups of competitors.

Precisely how you segment the market depends on which market features you perceive to be critical. In this example, you could segment on the basis of the loads the parts will be subject to. Highly loaded parts will compete with turned steel components. Low loaded parts will compete with plastic components. If the nature of the competition is more critical than the nature of the distribution channels, this type of segmentation may be more appropriate.

IDENTIFY BASES OF COMPETITION

The next step is to identify the bases of competition for each of the product market segments. These reflect the purchasing criteria that customers use in making their choice of supplier. A list of the principal bases of competition is given in Figure 3.3. Only a selection of these will apply to any specific product/market segment.

In most product/market segments, some purchasing criteria will be entry hurdles rather than bases of competition. For example, adequate

Product performance

Price

Quality

Reliability

Maintainability

Availability and delivery response

Flexibility (e.g. customisation options)

After-sales service

Compliance with international standards

FIGURE 3.3   Principal Bases of Competition
Source: Arthur D. Little

quality assurance procedures, evidenced by compliance with ISO9000, are now often a prerequisite for consideration as a supplier. If the customer has specified ISO9000 compliance, this is one of the purchasing criteria. However, it is not a basis of competition. You either comply with ISO9000 or you don't. It would be difficult to demonstrate that you were better than the competition because you complied better than they did.

Being aware of the hurdle purchasing criteria is important; understanding the criteria the customers use to distinguish one supplier from another is even more important.

In the case of our precision mechanical components business, the likely purchasing criteria are:

O   Price
O   Delivery schedules
O   Design ability
O   Design response time.

The relevant criteria may well be different for each product market segment. For high precision machine tool components, product performance, quality and flexibility may be the most significant bases of competition. For automotive high volume parts, price, quality and delivery response are likely to dominate.

The bases of competition are likely to evolve as the product/market segment matures. In most cases, product performance gradually decreases in importance and price, delivery and other quality parameters increase in importance. You could argue that there are only two bases of competition that matter: quality per cost and customer response time. Other bases of competition, such as reliability, maintainability and product performance are really just subsets of quality. In the long run this may be true, but in the shorter term, the average imperfect business has to decide *which* aspects of quality and time matter most in its sphere of activity. Hence the need to establish a list of bases of competition.

ASSESS KEY FACTORS FOR SUCCESS

Once the bases of competition are clear, you can determine the key factors for success. These are the things that the business must do well in order to compete effectively on these bases. Superficially, it appears that these often correlate directly (Figure 3.4). However, it is often worth going further in the analysis, as your set of priorities is likely to be unique.

Because you and your competitors may be following different strategies, the key factors for success which you must do well on to succeed will not be the same as your competitors'. The mechanical components company in our example could choose to compete by targeting the

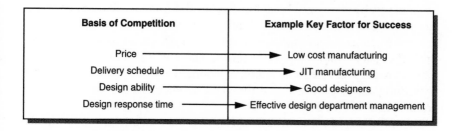

Basis of Competition	Example Key Factor for Success
Price ———————————————▶	Low cost manufacturing
Delivery schedule ———————————▶	JIT manufacturing
Design ability ———————————▶	Good designers
Design response time ———————▶	Effective design department management

FIGURE 3.4   Determination of Key Factors for
             Success
             Source: Arthur D. Little

difficult applications and selling higher value, more differentiated products than its competitors. With a reputation for tackling the problems
others could not solve, the one key factor for success is good design
engineers. The other factors, though important, are unlikely to have as big
an influence on the customer's choice of purchase.

A second reason why it is worth spending time assessing key factors for
success is that they are rarely as straightforward as in this example. The
ability to compete through good design will depend on more than just the
availability of good designers. It could also be a function of many other
factors including:

O   Broad applications experience
O   Good development and test facilities
O   Good working relationships with materials suppliers
O   CAD/CAE facilities.

Each of these may in turn depend on several other factors. You recruit and
keep good designers by paying them well, offering challenging jobs,
ensuring working conditions are good, and encouraging a company
culture that is not repressive and dictatorial. That is one of the reasons that
many companies who depend on quality design locate on science parks,
such as the ones in Cambridge, Oxford and York. Such environments can
offer a pool of skilled scientists and engineers, and the presence of a large
number of small flexible high technology companies in the area also
provides a ready source of rapid prototyping and testing services. In
addition, the pleasant environment, egalitarian working practices and
multi-disciplinary workforce leads to high levels of creativity.

Idyllic science park locations are not the only way forward though.
Pace Microelectronics, the fast growing UK electronics company, makes

satellite receivers in an old mill building in Bradford, a Victorian industrial city in the north of England. The mill is a famous architectural landmark, and Pace shares the premises with a book shop, an art gallery and some upmarket fashion and accessory shops. The environment is therefore an extremely creative one, which attracts young design engineers looking for something a little different than the giant defence electronics firms which are the main alternatives.

The influence of location illustrates the need to explore key factors for success in some detail. You need to understand the key factors for success for your business, and the factors which underpin them, if you are to gain maximum strategic value from technology.

Having got this far, with a list of the key factors for success, the next step is to identify which of those are primarily technology-dependent, and therefore what technologies you will need to meet your strategic objectives.

IDENTIFY RELEVANT TECHNOLOGIES

The most obvious way to identify relevant technologies is to look at each key factor for success in turn and assess which technologies could be relevant. This is actually quite difficult to do. Knowing the key factors for success provides few clues as to which technologies might be important, and there is a high risk you will not pick up all the relevant technologies. You therefore need some sort of framework to ensure that your list of technologies is exhaustive. To achieve this and so make the strategy development process simpler to implement, it is necessary to step back for a moment and make a list of all the technologies that could be associated with the business. Putting this list and the list of key factors for success together on a matrix will allow you to see all the technologies that underpin the key factors for success. An example of such a matrix, for computer optical storage systems, is shown in Figure 3.5.

Separating and listing all the technologies relevant to a business can be a mind-boggling task. The approach presented here is the one developed over many years at Arthur D. Little. It works consistently and reliably and we use it in many industries. The objective is to develop a reasonably comprehensive list of the technologies used in the business. Before you start, remember the definition of technology. Technology is the *practical application* of scientific knowledge to give commercial products or services. Technology is all about application; knowledge of itself does not count. For example, metallurgy is not a technology, but knowing how to produce thin walled castings is. In fact, the 'knowing how to' phrase is quite a good test. If you can say we know how to *design, make or specify*

Important Technologies / **Key Factors for Success**

Important Technology	Price	Size	Power	Shock sensitivity	Erasable	Features	Reliability	WO	Integration	EMC	Assess Time	Data Rate	Storage Density	Data Integrity	Picture Quality	1995 Score	2000 Score
1995 Rank	1	2	3	4	5	6	7=	7=	9=	9=	11=	11=	13=	13=	13=		
2000	2=	1	2=	5	4	6	8=	7	12	-	8=	8=	11	-			
Physical support structure	✓✓	✓	✓	✓✓	✓		✓	✓✓	✓	✓		✓✓	✓✓	✓✓		87	87 (1)
Light path	✓✓	✓✓	✓✓		✓✓		✓			✓						58	56 (2)
Data signal processing	✓		✓	✓✓	✓✓	✓	✓	✓	✓			✓✓	✓	✓✓		50	47 (4=)
Tracking mechanism			✓	✓✓	✓					✓	✓	✓	✓			48	47 (4=)
Servo control	✓	✓	✓	✓	✓			✓			✓	✓	✓	✓		47	47 (4=)
System control	✓		✓	✓	✓	✓		✓			✓	✓		✓		45	40 (4=)
System architecture		✓	✓		✓✓	✓		✓	✓	✓	✓	✓				44	45 (6)
MO system	✓✓		✓									✓✓				38	44 (7)
Manufacturing	✓	✓✓							✓							35	38 (9)
Support (sourcing and purchasing)	✓	✓					✓									19	17 (10=)
Disc					✓			✓				✓	✓✓	✓✓		16	17 (10=)

FIGURE 3.5 Example Identification of Technologies Underpinning Key Factors for Success

Source: Arthur D. Little

41

a *product* or a *process* you have a technology. If you can't you probably don't. For example, we know how to:

O   Produce thin walled castings
O   Design for thermal shock
O   Design to eliminate power surge.

However, you cannot say we know how to:

O   Computer-aided design
O.   Thermodynamics
O   High temperature materials.

How do you develop the list of technologies? The best bet is to do it in an open discussion meeting with a small group of technical and marketing people drawn from across the business and facilitated by a neutral 'honest broker'. Start by dividing the business into technology categories. There are several ways of doing this, as shown in Figure 3.6.

These categories are deliberately broad, in keeping with the earlier definition of technology. There are two reasons for this. First, to ensure that all appropriate technologies are captured: in the production of precision powder metallurgy components, for example, a key requirement is to source the correct metal powders. It is not only the right material formulation, in terms of chemical formulation of steel and correct percentage of copper additives, but also the right statistical spread of powder particle dimensions that are critical for the production of defect-free high-strength sintered components. Materials sourcing is therefore much more than simple purchasing. It is a highly skilled technical activity requiring a good understanding of the underlying science and an awareness of how sensitive the process is to the different material parameters.

The second reason for adopting these broad categorisations is to stretch the thinking of those developing the list, challenging the conventional wisdom on how technology supports the business. In the paper making case, for example, most of the company's R&D was focused on the core process technologies of pulp drying, paper making and finishing. A broad technology listing identified the potential value of technology to the merchanting operations, in terms of developing more environmentally friendly packaging, better stock labelling and packaging systems, and computer based logistics management systems. The commercial advantage to be gained by incremental investment in these technologies was far greater than that gained by equivalent investment in the core process technologies. You therefore need to look at technologies with as open a mind as possible, to give the business the best chance of identifying those technologies which will give a real competitive edge.

With the basic category headings in place, you can begin to build a technology tree under each heading, cascading down as far as is required.

Scientific knowledge categorisation. For example, for a product such as a pump, the main categories would be:

- Materials selection (we know how to select appropriate materials)
- Mechanical design (we know how to design mechanical parts)
- Fluid dynamics design (we know how to design for efficient fluid flow)
- Electrical design (we know how to design electrical power and control elements).

Categorisation by process step. For a process such as paper making, the main categories would be:

- Growing trees
- Producing pulp
- Drying pulp
- Making paper
- Finishing paper
- Packaging and merchanting.

Value chain categorisation. For example, take the production of precision powder metallurgy components. The principal categories would be:

- Materials sourcing
- Component design
- Component production
- Component packaging
- Distribution and sales (i.e. we know how to distribute and sell components)
- After sales service.

FIGURE 3.6   Technology Categorisation
Source: Arthur D. Little

Figure 3.7 shows part of a full technology tree for paper making to illustrate the principle. In this example, the shaded boxes give one technology; we know how to apply infra-red heating, to remove water from paper in the paper making process.

It is essential that you do not limit yourself to the technologies you currently use or have under development. Put in all or most of the technologies that your competitors use or could use. If your paper making company uses infra-red heating for water removal, you should still include RF heating, hot cylinders and other thermal drying technologies in the list,

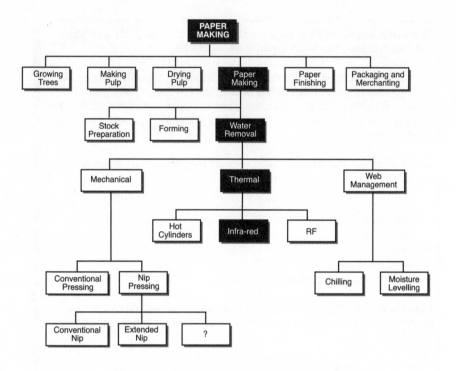

FIGURE 3.7   Part of a Technology Tree for Paper Making
Source: Arthur D. Little

for subsequent evaluation. Depending on the technologies, you may also want to do a little brainstorming at this point to stretch the definitions and include new untried technology alternatives.

The number of distinct technologies that you generate will depend on the degree to which you separate the technologies. For example, at a high level, a pump manufacturing company might regard 'the design and manufacture of boiler feed pumps' as a distinct technology in its own right and consider further unbundling unnecessary. However, in deciding how to apply technology development resources, it may be necessary to unbundle further to home in on specific areas where technology could give competitive advantage. For example, you could break the pump down into its constituent parts, identifying the 'design and manufacture of a high efficiency impeller' as one of the constituent technologies. At the next level down, you could look at the mechanical design of the impeller, the fluid dynamics design of the impeller, and the manufacture of the impeller as discrete elements of impeller technology. Mechanical design could then be separated into stress design, materials technology, vibration assessment and so on. These can be subdivided almost ad infinitum.

Where you call a halt depends on what you intend to do with the unbundled list. At a corporate level, you are probably only interested in the few technologies at the top level of the tree, so that you can draw comparisons between business units and identify common themes. The business unit manager, on the other hand, is interested in the 30 or so technologies which underpin his business. At a finer level of detail, the R&D manager of the business unit may want to unbundle technologies further to a couple of hundred or so to be sure that he is not missing a trick in nurturing some valuable new technical development.

Experience suggests that unbundling into more than 200 or so technologies is unlikely to be worthwhile. Don't forget that you can always revisit part of the picture and develop it in more detail later if need be. Two hundred technologies is, for most business units, a fairly all encompassing list, providing a good picture of the technologies used. A list is all it is though. On its own, its usefulness is limited. It provides a view of the technologies used, and can act as a check that technology development resources are spent on technologies relevant to the company, but it gives no sense of priorities or strategic direction.

This type of technology listing exercise is not always as straightforward as it might look. Many people end up having an 'other' or 'support' technologies category as a catch all for all the strange technologies that everyone intrinsically recognises as important but that do not fit comfortably in one of the agreed categories. Confusion over the hierarchy of technologies is also common. In Figure 3.7, you could argue that pulp drying is a subset of making pulp and should therefore be under it. You could equally well argue that web management is quite distinct from the water removal technologies and so should be placed alongside water removal as a distinct paper making technology. This confusion and lack of rigour is not necessarily a problem, provided you recognise that it exists, spend enough time in discussion to minimise it, and ensure that all the technologies are covered somewhere within the tree.

SELECT STRATEGICALLY IMPORTANT TECHNOLOGIES

To obtain real value from the list of unbundled technologies you need to refine it, identifying the strategic implications you can deduce from it. The first step is to identify which of the technologies are the most strategically important, and so which are the ones you need to concentrate on. Then for those which are strategically important you need to look at how good the business is relative to its competitors.

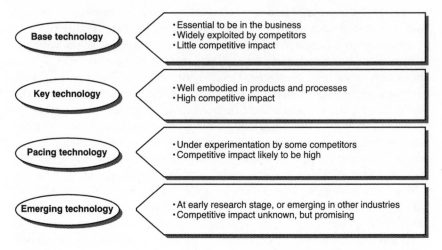

N.B. This classification is industry-specific

FIGURE 3.8   Definition of Technology Categories
Source: Arthur D. Little

Determining the level of strategic importance and the competitive position of technologies is inevitably a matter of judgement, but it is possible to inject some analytical rigour into the process.

To get a sense of the strategic importance of technologies, they can be divided into four categories: base, key, pacing and emerging, indicating the scope of competitive advantage the technology offers and its level of maturity. The definitions for these categories are given in Figure 3.8. A more detailed description of this technology categorisation is given in *Third Generation R&D*, Arthur D. Little's book on research management (Ref. 3.5).

Base technologies for a typical consumer electronics product, such as a CD player, include printed circuit board design layout and assembly, IC design, and casing design. None of these technologies now gives any significant competitive advantage, but all are required to produce a CD.

Such base technologies will account for a large proportion, typically 30 to 50 per cent, of the technology list. Many of these, once identified, need only be assessed in a cursory fashion. If a straw poll of your managers suggests that your business is either competent enough on its own or can source from a competent supplier, it is not necessary to consider a base technology any further. This simplifies the strategy process and makes it more manageable. Base technologies are commodity items which do not give significant competitive advantage but which are entry hurdles. Provided you have got them, you do not need to worry.

Key technologies are those that give significant competitive advantage. One of the key technologies for a CD player is the design of the tracking mechanism that moves the laser/lens assembly across the disc to read the signal. Only two companies, Philips and Sony, are strong in this technology, and they and their licensees dominate the market. This tracking mechanism is one of the principal sources of competitive advantage in this industry. The company that is able to make the mechanism thinner, cheaper, more shock resistant and better able to play warped or damaged discs, is likely to gain valuable extra market share.

Pacing technologies are, or may be, tomorrow's key technologies. They are technologies that are emerging from the R&D labs and beginning to be incorporated into niche products as a prelude to incorporate into the core product range if they prove successful. A representative pacing technology for a CD player is the LDGU, an integrated laser diffraction grating unit. As an integrated solid state component, its small size, robustness and low unit cost will improve the tracking mechanism, giving significant competitive advantage to whichever company adopts it first.

Interestingly, the company strongest in LDGU technology is not Philips or Sony but Sharp. This situation arises more often than one would expect. Well established players, strong in the base and key technologies can be caught out by other companies developing new substitute pacing technologies. It is very tempting to assume that your technology approach is the only viable one, and to fail to anticipate the threat of substitution posed by alternative technologies. Techniques for anticipating such technology threats are discussed further in the next chapter.

Pacing technologies may become tomorrow's key technologies, but do not always do so. Gallium arsenide is a good example. Thought by many in the industry to be close to being adopted as standard for high performance microelectronic chips, it has so far failed to displace silicon, the established key technology, except in a few niche areas.

Finally, *emerging technologies* are those which may become tomorrow's pacing technologies. Still in the research stage, emerging technologies show promise, but are not guaranteed to become valuable. In the CD player example, emerging technologies include blue lasers and multi-layer discs, both offering the promise of much higher disc storage densities. Taking a broader view, you could argue that high capacity, low cost, solid state memories, which offer the potential for storing a CD's worth of music on a piece of silicon less than the size of a fingernail, should also be included as an emerging technology for CD players.

With these four technology classifications in mind, you should return to the technology list and run through it deciding whether each technology is base, key, pacing or emerging. This is a rough and ready process, and it is not worth agonising for hours over each decision. If in doubt you should always opt for the higher category; for example between base and key, opt for key. Remember, though, that not everything can be key, even though some of the technologists in your company are likely to argue so. If a technology is not in *widespread* use in the industry, it is probably pacing or emerging. Equally, if it can be readily sourced externally, then it is a base technology.

At this stage in the process of developing a technology strategy, you will have a good understanding in four areas:

O   The bases of competition for your business
O   The key factors for success
O   The technologies which underpin those factors
O   The strategic importance of those technologies.

Armed with this information, you can now assess how good your business is in the technologies which matter, and so find out where you need to take action to strengthen your position.

If required, you may want to extend the assessment of strategic importance to look at the relative commercial impact of the technologies. Particularly in multi-technology, multi-product businesses, there can be a lot of variation in the relative significance of technologies within each product category. Some key technologies will impact heavily on only one product: others may have less impact, but on a greater proportion of the product range. Similarly, for a given product, some technologies will impact on all the key factors for success, whereas others will only impact on one. This additional dimension to the analysis can be valuable in further prioritising the technologies and so making strategic choices easier to make.

DETERMINING COMPETITIVE STRENGTHS AND WEAKNESSES

Once you have a good understanding of what technologies are important to the business, and how they rank in terms of strategic importance, you can assess how good your business is at each of these technologies.

With this information, you can pinpoint the strategic actions needed to strengthen your technology capability, and how much effort is required. Simplistically, technologies which are strategically important but in which the company is competitively weak need attention and investment.

Technologies in which the company is strong, and which are not of great strategic importance, need less attention.

The best way to assess how good you are at the various technologies is to compare yourself with your main competitors. If instead you try to stick to absolute measures, there is a danger of viewing your state of technology competence unrealistically. All your technologists may justifiably claim to be very good at the technologies involved in sintering powdered metals. However, if the principal competitors are much better, you have a competitive weakness. To avoid acrimony and mud slinging in deciding on strengths and weaknesses in a specific technology area, you can use standard criteria. Dividing competence into five categories gives the following:

- O   Clear leader
- O   Strong
- O   Favourable
- O   Tenable
- O   Weak.

Figure 3.9 gives definitions for each of these categories. The definitions for the two extremes are straightforward.

Clear Leader	Sets the pace and direction of technological development and recognised for such in the industry.
Strong	Able to express independent technical actions and set new directions.
Favourable	Able to sustain technological competitiveness in general and / or leadership in technical niches.
Tenable	Unable to set independent course. Continually in catch-up mode.
Weak	Unable to sustain quality of technical outputs versus competitors. Short-term fire-fighting focus.

FIGURE 3.9   Definition of Level of Technology Competence
Source: Arthur D. Little

A *clear leader* is well ahead of all the competition. There can be only one clear leader for any one technology, but in many technologies there may be none. Many businesses start by thinking themselves clear leaders, but on reflection recognise that competitors are not far behind. Arguable clear leaders include 3M with its Post-it® adhesives technologies, Raychem with its heat shrink polymer technologies and Pechiney with its high current aluminium smelting technology.

If you are *weak* you are vulnerable, and probably dependent on competitors for the technology competence. For example, at the time of writing, Alba, the aluminium company of Bahrain, has little in-house smelting technology, and relies on Pechiney and others for the necessary skills. Being weak in a technology does not necessarily mean being weak in business terms. For Alba, weakness in smelting, which is a base technology, is a reasonable strategic position to adopt. It does not have the critical mass to sustain its own smelting R&D, and adequate technology can be readily sourced from the major world players. However, if Alba were weak in one of the *key* technologies, such as understanding how to use sensor and control systems to improve smelter-operating efficiency, then it would have cause for concern.

The three middle positions, *strong, favourable* and *tenable*, are all shades of grey. Again, there is a tendency for businesses to overrate themselves, and to put themselves and all their competitors as equally strong. This is not a valid position. Everyone cannot be strong; usually no more than one or two players can be rated strong in any one technology.

For some technologies, you may find it worthwhile to assess competitive position quantitatively by assessing performance against standard criteria, number of patents, or similar quantitative measures. The difficulty is that for many technologies, and particularly application technologies in mature industries, useful quantitative data can be hard to come by. How, for example, can you collect data to show whether a company is stronger than its competitors in the technology of selecting the best alloys for high stress components? You can't, and needn't try. For such technologies, a consensus view of senior technologists and managers supported by customer input will give an adequate response. If your customers are very satisfied and say you are the only supplier who can cope with their problems, your competitive position is clearly at least favourable and probably strong unless your customers have not looked hard at competing suppliers. Conversely, a sales manager's report that your principal competitor won a contract because it could do the job more cheaply and using less material does tend to suggest that it is more competent than you are.

For businesses producing stand alone products, purchasing and stripping down competitor offerings can give good clues about technology position. One company manufacturing small high performance pumps, bought the offerings of three of its principal global competitors to compare with its current product range. Some technology parameters could be quantified, such as noise generated, pumping efficiency, and power consumption. Others could be derived indirectly. The parts count was one measure of the effectiveness of design for manufacture. Materials analysis indicated the level of chemical resistance of the product. Time to strip down and replace a key component indicated maintainability. A third group of technologies could be assessed only qualitatively. The quality of the design for use in harsh environments, the technology for minimising the risk of fatigue failure, and the quality of the aesthetic design of the product, all belonged in this third group. However, whether analysed quantitatively or qualitatively, such competing product dissection activity will give a good picture of the current competitive strength of your own offering.

In some businesses, there is no competitor against which to measure your strengths and weaknesses. In the telecommunications industries or the utilities, for instance, there are often no direct competitors and comparisons with indirect competitors can be misleading as the competitive battlegrounds are rarely equal. Nonetheless, even in a monopoly, you can still assess you own technologies, either against other players in the world or against suppliers and customers. For example, a UK water utility could assess its technology competence in, say, sludge dewatering, against one or more of the other UK water companies, against non-UK water utilities, such as Compagnie Lyonnaise des Eaux, or against the leading world suppliers of sludge dewatering machinery, such as Alfa-Laval, Envirex or Passavant.

With an understanding of both competitive position and strategic importance, you can map all the technologies onto one matrix and make broad brush judgements on the strategic implications for the business unit. Figure 3.10 shows what these implications are.

Look first at the base technologies. If you are strong or a clear leader in a base technology you may well be wasting resources. The strategic impact of investing to strengthen your position in such technologies is likely to be small, and money would be better spent elsewhere. If you are weak or just tenable in a base technology, raise the alarm. You have to have base technologies to compete in today's business, so if you are weak you need either to build your in-house competence or to source externally.

Strength in key technologies provides opportunities for leverage. Weakness in key technologies implies weakness in business competitive position and must be addressed. This is where you are the most vulnerable, and remedying any weaknesses here should be top priority.

Technology significance	Level of Technology Competence				
	Clear leader	Strong	Favourable	Tenable	Weak
Base	Alarm signal for waste of resources		Industry average	Alarm signal for survival	
Key	Opportunities for present competitive advantage			Alarm signal for present	
Pacing	Opportunities for future competitive advantage			Alarm signal for future	
Emerging					

FIGURE 3.10   Strategic Implication of Competence Levels
Source: Arthur D. Little

Strength in the new pacing or emerging technologies provides scope for growth, provided that technology strength can be matched by strengths in the other capabilities needed to grow the business.

Weakness in these new technologies is an alarm signal. This is a not uncommon position. Emerging technologies often develop in other industries, and it is therefore natural for the incumbents to be weak in these areas. Automotive companies are strong in the manipulation and production of steel body panels (base technology) but weak in plastic body panels (pacing / emerging technology). Industrial motor drive companies were strong in analogue drive systems (base) but had to adapt to digital-processor-based drive systems (pacing / key). Slide rule companies were strong in the precision machining of plastics (base) but were unable to adapt to electronics technology for calculators.

These three examples show the three most common routes out of a weak position in new technology. Many automotive companies entered into joint ventures or alliances with plastics companies to access plastic body panel technology. The automotive companies reasoned that their prime business was assembly not manufacture, and that their position was so weak that the investment needed to become competitive in plastic body panels was too great. Alliances with plastics companies provided a good route out of the dilemma, since the plastics companies were complementary rather than competitive and so such alliances were mutually beneficial.

In the motor drive example, the companies concerned had little choice but to develop their own capabilities. The alternative was to go out of business. Developing their own capabilities was a viable option as the entry barriers were low, time to catch up was short and investment were low.

In contrast, in the slide rule case, the new technology was so different and would have required such different production technologies, that adaptation was almost impossible. The slide rule companies withdrew from the business. The substitution of slide rules by calculators is a familiar example of how a emerging technology can change the structure of the industry. Many emerging technologies that appeared less than radically different at first sight have had a similar devastating impact. 'The Material's Substitution Dilemma' illustrated below is an example of this, with the management trapped in a business crisis by a new group of emerging technologies.

The Materials Substitution Dilemma

Consider a company making bronze synchromesh rings for automotive gear boxes. A profitable steady niche business, with two main bases of competition: the ability to work with the automotive gear box companies to develop a good component specification, and the ability to cast and machine precision components in bronze quickly and cheaply. Over time, bronze synchromesh rings became almost a base technology, from the viewpoint of the gearbox manufacturer, and grey cast iron rings with bonded paper coatings became the pacing technology, offering better performance at lower material cost. From the point of view of the bronze synchromesh ring company, grey cast iron rings represented a threat. The company was technically weak in casting iron, and lacked the technologies to bond paper coatings to the iron. Even worse, the cast iron rings rendered the company's technical skills, production experience and manufacturing assets of little value. An incremental technology change had therefore led to a business crisis: should the company invest in (or acquire) iron casting capability, or should it abandon the automotive industry and try to market its bronze component production skills to other industries? In the event, the management chose to do both, acquiring a grey cast iron component company, and diversifying the bronze business into domestic appliance components and other non-automotive markets.

Source: Arthur D. Little

Decisions needed to correct weaknesses in emerging or pacing technologies are often complex and have far reaching consequences for the business as a whole. Although you cannot prevent new technologies emerging, you can build the capability to anticipate long term technology trends and detect the emergence of new substitution threats at an early stage, so that they can be addressed before they matter. Techniques for doing this are covered in Chapter 5.

4

DEVELOPING TECHNOLOGY STRATEGIES

❖

THIS chapter is concerned with developing technology strategies based on the technology position assessment covered by the previous chapter. The main emphasis is on corporate level strategy, but the approach outlined here can also be used at business unit level to identify technologies that have a clear strategic linkage with business success, and to develop local technology strategies. You can identify the technologies that are relevant, determine which ones have the greatest strategic value, and assess what you need to do to be better at them. All the basic information needed to make decisions on what to do is here, and decision-making should be relatively straightforward, as discussed later in this chapter.

SETTING CORPORATE TECHNOLOGY PRIORITIES

This book is concerned primarily with the importance of technology at corporate level. As discussed in Chapter 2, those managing large corporations often argue that technology synergy between business units is one of the key parenting advantages that the corporation can provide. For such technology synergy to be effective, it must build on some technology core competence that underpins several aspects of the corporation. Much has been written about the core competence idea, first crystallised by Hamel and Prahalad (Ref. 4.1). Essentially it is a belief that corporations can develop one aspect of their business to be a sustainable source of competitive advantage. The example often quoted is Honda, which developed a core competence in the technologies of small lightweight high speed internal combustion engines, and used this competence to build businesses in motorcycles, automobiles, lawnmowers, small generating sets and so on. Another example is 3M, with a core competence in adhesive coatings that underpins most if not all its business units.

So, before agreeing on a set of technology strategies for the individual businesses, you need to take a corporate overview, identifying those underlying core competences which need to be reinforced at a corporate level. You have to look top down as well as bottom up, because the core competencies may not be the top level technologies at individual business unit level.

A good example is provided by consumer electronics. The key technologies in individual products, such as camcorders, TV sets, CD players and so on, vary considerably. In camcorders, tape head technology, battery technology and judder-free software are the driving technologies. In TV sets, picture tube technology is critical, and in CD players the laser and associated drive system are critical. At business unit level, a tenable or favourable position in miniaturisation technology would not be a particular cause for concern for the camcorder or audio business unit managers. After all, although miniaturisation helps compete in camcorders and CD players, it is not the differentiating factor. However, from a corporate viewpoint, a core competence in miniaturisation is critical. All consumer electronics products are evolving down a path characterised in the industry as LTSS: Lighter, Thinner, Smaller, Smarter. Business units that lack miniaturisation skills will find their competitive position slowly weakening. More seriously, corporations which lack such skills will find that across the board their competitive position is weakened. Furthermore, miniaturisation skills are difficult to acquire except by experience. Consequently, the corporation that recognises miniaturisation as an underlying core competence is more likely to succeed than one that does not. Recognising miniaturisation as a core competence means that the corporation will support the development of miniaturisation technologies in the business units where such technologies are important, such as portable personal cassette players, and will make a conscious effort to exploit that technology strength by transferring the skills across other business units in the corporation. The technology skills are therefore developed first where they are needed, but with corporate recognition that some corporate help in technology development will yield significant dividends across the corporation.

Miniaturisation technologies are a clear candidate for recognition as a core competence. Others in consumer electronics include flat panel displays and digital signal processing. Core competencies can be identified in most industries, and fall into three main categories (see Figure 4.1).

**Categories of Technology
Core Competence**

Key component technologies:

Differentiating products in several business units.

Enhancement technologies:

Increasing business effectiveness in several business units.

Foundation technologies:

Underpinning many aspects of the business and providing scope for product or process improvement.

FIGURE 4.1 Categories of Technology Core Competence
Source: Arthur D. Little

○ *Key component technologies* are those which are critical for a key component or sub-assembly that acts as a differentiating feature for products in several business units. Honda's internal combustion engine technologies, Toshiba's flat panel display technologies, and 3M's adhesive technologies are good examples. Corporate coordination of such technologies allows the company to build a mutually reinforcing product portfolio, feeding on its own product improvements.

○ *Enhancement technologies* are those that enhance production or management processes across the corporation, allowing each business unit to compete more effectively. Stock tracking technologies for retailing groups such as Burton, process control technologies for chemicals groups such as ICI or BASF, and project management technologies for electrical engineering groups like ABB and GEC all fall into this category. Corporate coordination here is primarily aimed at sharing resources and achieving greater economies of scale and cross-learning of best practice.

O   *Foundation technologies* are those that appear in the lists of technologies for every business unit within the corporation. Individually they may not be critical, but viewed at a corporate level they are valuable foundation competences that underpin the effectiveness of the business and merit corporate attention. Miniaturisation technologies and most materials technologies fall into this category. Foundation technologies are probably the most critical of all. They are also the most difficult to build, as effective core competence in this area relies on the pooling of know-how across business units in technologies which have broad application and where there are few obvious 'anchors' to help the transfer of know-how.

In all three cases, a core technology competence is more than just technology know-how. It is a fully integrated set of technological and managerial capabilities, covering not only technical knowledge and applications experience, but also related business process management and strategic leadership. Because a core competence is such a mixture of explicit know-how, embedded experience and softer cultural behaviours, it is very hard to imitate. Get it right and you have a significant competitive edge:

O   Highly differentiating, and able to set the company apart from the competition in market perception as well as product capability

O   Durable, because it is difficult for competitors to replicate the mixture of technology capability and in-depth experience and expertise

O   Strategically significant, because it both helps to define the company in the eyes of the marketplace and the shareholder, and provides a potential springboard for creating new business.

For these reasons it is vital that, at the corporate level, you know what the technology core competences of the corporation are, can assess in which business units they have the biggest strategic impact, and hence decide where they should be given maximum corporate support.

Reviewing the technology core competences like this provides one reason for putting apparently disproportionate resources behind certain technologies and into specific business units. There is another, commercial, reason for setting resource priorities across business units. Quite simply, growing business units dependent on key and pacing technologies will need to spend proportionally more on technology than mature

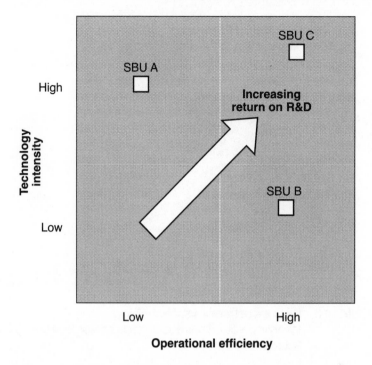

FIGURE 4.2 Comparing Business Unit R&D Investment
Source: Arthur D. Little

business units primarily dependent on base technologies. Although this may appear self evident, many corporations still do not differentiate between the technology expenditure needs of different business units. The largest most mature business units are often allowed to spend the same percentage of sales on technology development as the smallest emerging business unit, with the result that the emerging business unit is starved of investment.

Can you set clear corporate guidelines to ensure that resources go where they are needed? In theory, it should be possible to define a rule based on technology intensity and business operational efficiency (Figure 4.2). The more technology-intensive the business and the greater its operational efficiency then the greater the return you can expect on R&D investment. An alternative approach is to look just at technology-intensity. Figure 4.3 shows an example, highlighting which business units appear to be overspending and which underspending. Some of the volume businesses, such as office stationery and photocopy paper, have the scale and

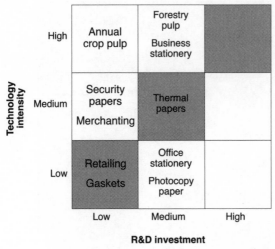

FIGURE 4.3   R&D Investment vs. Technology
Intensity – Illustrative Comparison of Business Units
Source Arthur D. Little

political muscle within the corporation to demand more technology development expenditure than they need. In contrast, some smaller, higher technology businesses, such as annual crop pulp and security papers, spend less on technology than they should.

Both approaches are qualitative and inherently subjective and so cannot be applied rigorously. However, both provide a starting point for negotiation between the centre and the business units. The problem can also be fixed either by setting different financial controls on different types of business or by direct corporate intervention in favour of the most important emerging business units. Precisely how you do it doesn't matter, as long as the problem is explicitly addressed by all the management involved.

With this corporate part of the jigsaw in place, supplementing the business unit technology evaluation discussed earlier in this chapter, you now have a comprehensive picture of the state of technology across the corporation and a good idea on where you should focus resources to build the competitive strength of the business. What you need to do this is discussed in the next section, and how to manage it is discussed in Chapter 9.

DECIDING ON STRATEGIC ACTIONS

No company can afford to develop all the technology it needs. So how do you decide what to try to keep in house, and how much to spend on making those in-house technologies competitive? A good starting point is to look at what you need to do, rather than what you think you can afford to do. Work out which technologies you want to develop, how much you need to invest, and what the total cost will be. *Then* check whether the business cash flows can support the investment and iterate until it looks as if they can. Figure 4.4 (page 62) shows the flow chart algorithm you need to follow.

DECIDING ON TECHNOLOGY PROJECTS

To start then, return to Figure 3.10, showing the current state of the business unit's technologies. Consider the business unit strategy and decide what an ideal distribution of technologies would look like. Be realistic, accepting that you cannot expect to be in a dominant competitive position in all the key technologies. Indeed, you may not want to be. For example, if you are running a small custom manufacturing business competing primarily on the basis of fast response and applications engineering skills, it may well be that your target competitive position should be no more than favourable in any of the technologies.

So, clustering the technologies to make the process manageable, list each cluster's current competitive position and desired competitive position. Next go through each cluster and identify what you need to do and what resources you need to get you from where you are now to where you want to be, and when you want to be there. The template in Figure 4.5 (page 63) gives generic strategies for each principal technology category. Building on these generic strategies, define explicitly what you are proposing to do in each technology area. Vague statements about wanting to move from a favourable to a strong position in die casting technologies are not enough. You need to define what you mean by a strong position: for example, 'we want to be able to produce thin walled castings of a given strength' or 'we want to be able to handle difficult to cast alloys'. In the *invest selectively* group, you need to select which of the technologies you are going to focus on as it is unlikely that you will have adequate resources to build a strong position in all of them.

EVALUATING INDIVIDUAL PROJECTS

At this stage, you need to begin to evaluate the costs, returns and risks of the individual projects. You may not yet be able to take this evaluation to the detailed level outlined here, but you can begin the first iteration.

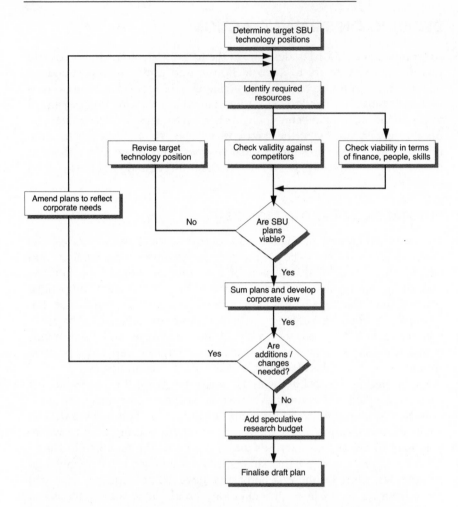

FIGURE 4.4   Development of Technology Investment Plans
Source: Arthur D. Little

For most capital investment projects, you would apply a form of Net Present Value (NPV) analysis. However, for investment in technology development, more complex evaluation is needed:

○   Because of the technical and commercial risk attached to technology development. The relative attractiveness of two projects with identical NPVs, but different risk profiles, will depend on how risk averse your business is. Consider a fast moving consumer goods business, producing shampoo, toiletries, and other personal care products. The board has to choose between two projects, since it

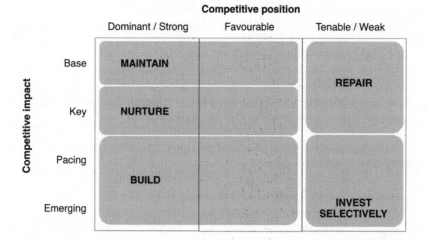

FIGURE 4.5 Generic Strategies for Technology Development
Source: Arthur D. Little

has resources for only one. The first project is to refine a core shampoo, reformulating it slightly to create a creamier consistency. The increase in sales and profits will be low, but so will the risks. In fact, *not* proceeding and allowing competitors to catch up may be riskier than going ahead. The other project is to develop a hair growth inhibition cream for use by men and women to extend intervals between shaving or depilation. If the cream could be developed and the consumer benefits sold, this breakthrough product would generate high returns. However, both technical and commercial risks are high, giving a high discount rate and an overall NPV similar to the incremental shampoo development. The choice between these two projects is clearly *not* just a function of discounted financial value.

O   Because development projects take different lengths of time to deliver commercial results. As for risk, the NPVs for short term small changes and longer term more radical developments can be similar, and priorities cannot be set solely on the basis of financial value.

O   Because projects have different objectives: to support existing businesses, to launch new businesses and technologies, or to broaden and deepen underlying technology capabilities. Once again, their priority will depend as much on strategic intent as on financial gain.

Investment in technology development must therefore be assessed on a portfolio basis, where the portfolio is balanced to give the mix of strategic objectives, reward and timeframes you need to support the business. This is discussed later.

With this caveat in mind, the quantitative evaluation of individual projects is still the right starting point. First, we need basic data on the project, covering cost, timing and expected benefit. Figure 4.6 gives an illustrative project plan, covering all the principal data parameters.

Objective of project
- Develop robust piezo-electric pressure sensors
- Start date and planned finish date:
  - Start 1st January 1992
  - Finish 20th September 1992
- Budget (manpower and other costs): 8.5 man-years plus £400,000 equipment

Nature of project
- To develop a commercial product based on our new piezo-electric sensor technology. The project will develop the sensor element to commercial product level, and then develop a product design with local IC-based calibration and data error correction.

Key milestones
- Prototype product (bread-boarded) 1st May 1991
- Pilot production of sensor element 31st December 1991
- IC design 31st December 1991
- Pre-production prototype 30th June 1992
- Pilot production 30th September 1992

Expected benefit
- Sales of £1 million in 1993, rising to £4 million per annum by end 1994
- Knock-on benefits in sales of data loggers

Linkages to other projects
- IC design is dependent on acquisition of new CAD system

Principal hurdles and risks
- Yield of sensor production process
- Shock resistance of sensor elements
- Cost of product assembly

Sponsors

Commercial	*Technical*
J. Smith	P. Brown
Marketing Director	Sensor Laboratory
Sensors and Instrumentation Division	

FIGURE 4.6   Illustrative Technical Innovation Project Plan
Source: *The Innovation Plans Handbook* This, and other figures from *The Innovation Plans Handbook* elsewhere in this book are Crown Copyright, reproduced with the permission of Her Majesty's Stationery Office.
(Ref. 4.2)

With these data in place, you can assess the project's financial costs and returns and calculate the overall present value. This is easier said than done. To determine NPV, you need precise numbers for costs, returns, and timing and the discount rate to be applied. Each of these is subject to interpretation:

O   Costs can be difficult to quantify, particularly if development is viewed as an overhead department and resource utilisation is not tracked by project.

O   Returns are also difficult to quantify, especially if a project leads to incremental improvements to several products.

O   Timings should be known, but sensitivities to timing need testing. Bringing a project forward three months may cost more, but may then allow you to realise a much greater benefit by beating the competition to the market.

O   Discount rates need to reflect both the usual discount rate in the organisation, and the premium attributable to the risk inherent in the project. Since you can reduce risk by tracking project progress against agreed milestones, the discount rate may vary over time.

Elaborate valuation systems that attempt to cover all eventualities are rarely useful. It is far better to apply simple, pragmatic rules. An example is shown in Figure 4.7. Remember that your objectives are first to determine whether the technology investment is worthwhile, and second

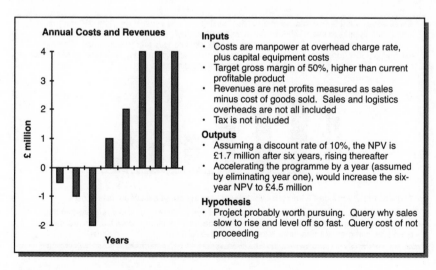

FIGURE 4.7   Assessment of Project Benefit
Source: Arthur D. Little

to enable yourself to set priorities. So long as the numbers are of the right order of magnitude and the approach is consistent, further analytical detail is unnecessary. In fact, further analysis is probably detrimental, conferring a false sense of numerical accuracy and inviting in-depth review from financial analysts of data that won't bear scrutiny.

You need to be pragmatic in assessing project value. You also should remember that you cannot evaluate a project in isolation. A development project does not just lead to a single result, but also helps develop the organisation's capabilities, possibly increasing the chances of success of other projects. A particular project may also have an ongoing value far in excess of the immediate project outcome because it provides a springboard for generations of new products, or strengthens underlying competitiveness. Conversely, you need to consider the costs associated with *not* going ahead with a project. Typically, the base case against which to assess a project is not neutral, but rather a gradual decline of competitiveness. So, if a project will lead to a product that will do no more than hold the current market position, despite considerable development cost, it may still be worth proceeding if the alternative is to lose market share to a competitor. Consider the household cleaner case outlined in Figure 4.8.

You do need to discuss the costs and merits of every project before it starts, but you also need to consider the strategic implications of the project before making a go/no go decision.

A well-established household cleaner product selling steadily world-wide. The brand name is strong and applies to many other products in the company's portfolio. Recently, competitors have launched products with less abrasive creams, delivering higher performance. The existing product generates £15 million a year net revenues world-wide. Sales are expected to decline at 20% per year from next year at constant margins.

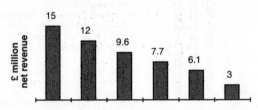

The loss of NPV will be £24 million over the six-year period, at a discount rate of 10%.

If it is strategically important to hold the brand position, a project that delivers a product that could maintain market share will almost certainly be worth pursuing, even if an assessment based on incremental sales gives a zero or negative NPV.

FIGURE 4.8   The Moving Base Case
Source: Arthur D. Little

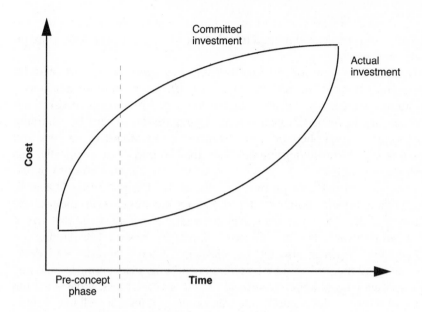

FIGURE 4.9   The Importance of Decision-Making in the Pre-
             Concept Phase
             Source: Arthur D. Little

Remember also that costs and impact differ at different stages of the
product development process. As you move from the pre-concept technology development phase into concept design and design for manufacture, costs roughly triple each time – this is the Pi rule discussed in
earlier chapters. Pre-concept work accounts for only about seven per cent
of the total development cost, and yet is fundamental to getting the
product cost right and to designing a product that people want to buy.
Costs in the early stages are not therefore critical to commercial survival,
but effective development decision-making is (Figure 4.9). Keep this in
mind when justifying the cost of a development project to a sceptical
internal audience.

With a reasonable idea of what you plan to do with each technology,
you can pull together the components of the technology plans and
summarise the total resource needs: money, facilities, people and specific
expertise. You can then review the overall portfolio of activities.

EVALUATING THE PORTFOLIO

Does the overall investment in development give the best mix of risk,
reward and fit with strategic objectives?

You need to take a view of the portfolio as a whole, ensuring that the balance of projects is right and that the portfolio is not over dependent on any one project.

At business unit or divisional level, management should start by examining the risk/reward map (Figure 4.10). You want to see a balanced portfolio, with not too many projects and a good mix of high risk/high return and lower risk/lower return. Aggregate the reward by summing the projects multiplied by their estimated probabilities of success and comparing the resulting figure with total spend. Mathematically this approach is nonsense: projects either succeed or fail. The return from two projects of 60 per cent probability will not be 1.2, but rather 0, 1 or 2. Aggregate reward numbers are therefore meaningless in themselves. However, the aim of the analysis is to develop a picture of the patterns of risk and reward. For this purpose, aggregate reward calculations are acceptable. You can also test the elasticity of the aggregate reward, by reducing all the probabilities by ten per cent or by discounting to zero any project with a probability of success of 40 per cent or less. What is the net rate of return of the portfolio after discounting? If it's not well into double

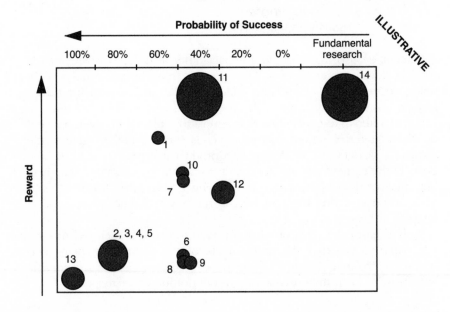

FIGURE 4.10   Risk/Reward Assessment of Project Portfolio
Source: Arthur D. Little

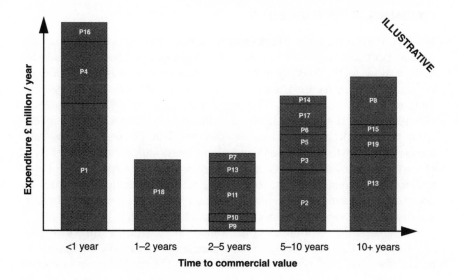

FIGURE 4.11   Time Distribution of Projects
Source: Arthur D. Little

figures, something is wrong – you have the wrong projects or the wrong market. The first problem you can fix; the second you have to adapt to, accepting that fierce competition and pressure for low margins will limit returns.

Look also at time to commercial impact (Figure 4.11). You would normally expect to see a bath tub distribution: short and long term peaks with a dip in the middle. This shape occurs because businesses typically do not have well formed technology and business strategies. As a consequence, development work polarises into long term non-product-specific work and short term reactive measures. The business culture can compound the problem. Short term work is low risk – the objectives are clear, so developers can feel confident of success. Long term work is more glamorous and, despite the high risk, developers can feel confident that failure will not be seen as personal failure. In the medium term, however, the objectives are clear but risks are high, so failure is both visible and likely. No one wants to work on such projects, hence the bottom of the bath tub. Correcting the profile so that medium term work anticipates competitive threats and removes the need for panic reactions will have a big impact on the business.

EVALUATING AT CORPORATE LEVEL

You can then review the plans from a corporate perspective, pulling the various portfolios together to assess the aggregate position. You can also look at how technology investment is distributed across the businesses within the group. As already discussed, you can categorise businesses by their need for technology. The need may not be related to size of business; large mature businesses usually require less technology investment than small growing ones, as discussed in Chapter 3. New high technology growth businesses within large corporations are often starved of cash by their bigger, more mature siblings. One of the main roles of technology management at corporate level is to tackle this issue, by comparing investment and return in the different businesses and rebalancing the distribution to maximise net corporate benefit.

You also need to look at core competences from a corporate perspective. For the core competences identified in the previous section, more effort may well be needed to strengthen the capability and improve the competitive position. For many core competence areas it may be necessary to ensure technology success by backing several possible developments. For flat panel displays, for example, maintaining a strong core competence is likely to require investment across most of the relevant technologies including active matrix, super twist nematic, micro diode, electropolymer and ferroelectric display technologies.

Finally, you need to remember to allow adequate resources for longer term speculative research in selected emerging technologies which appear to show commercial potential. How you manage this, whether by allowing each developer some free time or by dedicating some people to futuristic research is discussed further in Chapters 8 and 9. You need to leave some time and resources free for such speculative work, not just because it can pay enormous dividends, but also because it provides a creative safety valve for the development staff, so helping to foster a more innovative climate in the company.

FINALISING THE PLAN

With a first draft of the technology plan complete, it is worth pausing and reflecting on its feasibility. Revisit each cluster of technologies and evaluate the costs, returns and risks of your plans in more detail. Compare what you are proposing to do with what competitors and others active in the technologies are doing or planning to do. Take an objective standpoint and consider:

O   Is the objective realistic, or is it predicated on making a breakthrough where countless others have failed?

O   Does the plan assume that your research staff are somehow
         cleverer or better than those of your competitors? Are you assum-
         ing that your team of 20 can achieve what your Japanese com-
         petitor has 100 people working on?
O   Will you need to circumvent some patent on a crucial part of the
         technology, and if so, how do you plan to do it?
O   Are you too far behind to catch up? Remember that in the three
         years it will take you to lift your competitive position from tenable
         to favourable, the competition will be developing its technology,
         pushing you back to a tenable position again unless you either
         throw more resources at the problem, or buy in some of techno-
         logy skills you need.

Realism is critical at this stage in the planning process. All corporations are
constrained by resources, and successful ones are the ones that focus their
resources where the chances of large commercial impact are greatest,
rather than those that spread resources across all technologies in a futile
attempt to stay competitive across a broad front.

There is one exception to the rule. It may be that, although you are far
behind the competition and unable to devote adequate resources, competitive strength in a particular technology is crucial to the business
corporate strategy and that no other routes forward are available. In this
case, you have no choice but to invest the resources to acquire the
technology you need, even though this may weaken the corporation
elsewhere. This is not a satisfactory position, as it is tantamount to 'betting
the company', but it may be the only option. For the synchromesh rings
business, for example, developing a technical competence in grey cast
iron rings was critical for survival in the automotive business. In such a
situation, there is no choice but to buy in the technology, since developing it in-house from scratch will always take too long. Buying in can be
done by acquisition, licence, or contract R&D; which you choose depends
on what is available and what the cost benefit trade-offs are. This topic is
addressed in Chapter 6.

Once you have reviewed your plan against knowledge of competitors'
capabilities, and revised the plan to reflect the points raised above, you
can summarise the total resource needs of the plan at corporate level, in
terms of money, facilities, people and mix of skills. Starting with the total
budget, compare this with previous years and with the levels of activity of
competitors and comparable companies. As discussed in the previous
chapter, there are no hard and fast rules about how much a business
should invest in R&D and technology development. The amount will be a
function of the strategy of the business and its starting competitive
position, and so the figure developed by the bottom-up process described

above should be the correct one. Having said that, a common sense sanity check is clearly beneficial. If the business spent two per cent of turnover on R&D last year, and the plan calls for 12 per cent this year, then it is unlikely to be acceptable to the board, and unlikely to be financially viable. If a spend of 12 per cent is really needed for the strategy to succeed, then it suggests that the strategy is itself not viable and that you should have a fundamental rethink about the strategy. For this to happen is not unknown. For example, an electronics subassembly business unit went through this technology strategy process and identified three principal technology objectives:

O   Reducing the cost of a key component to strengthen competitive position in the core market

O   Increasing the performance of the product so as to enter a new growth market

O   Developing a miniaturised version of the product to maintain a favourable competitive position in a niche segment of the core market.

Once the technology plan had been developed, it became clear that these three objectives were not tenable. There was simply not enough cash to go around to allow all three to proceed as desired. After much debate, it was agreed that the basic strategy should be changed. The business would focus on cost reduction and on entering the new market. Based on the results of these two initiatives, it would then be possible to develop a cheaper part-miniaturised version of the product aimed at the niche market segment. This part-miniaturised version would give some loss of market share in that niche, but would at least maintain a presence which could be reinforced at some future date when finances permitted. This revised strategy may not have been ideal, but it was achievable.

Although it is more likely that the plan will exceed current resources, it is also possible for the planned budget to undershoot past expenditure. There are two possible explanations for this: past expenditure may have been wasted on R&D that was unlikely to be fruitful, or the current plan may be too conservative and underrating the business relative to competitors. If the first is the case, look at the merits of redirecting effort rather than simply cutting.

Comparisons with competitors are also worthwhile, but need to be treated with caution. It is worth looking at competitive R&D spends, but it is also then worth trying to explain the differences rather than jumping to conclusions on what is the 'right' R&D spend for your business. Competitor comparisons not only give you peace of mind, but also provide some of the information you will need to justify to the board and to shareholders and their advisors why your business is following this plan.

Shareholders and analysts are becoming increasingly concerned about how much effort businesses are devoting to future growth opportunities and will look for explanation as to the course you have taken. This is discussed further in Chapter 11. If the main competitor appears to spend considerably less than you, ask yourself if this is because:

O   They compete more on service and less on technology.
O   The spend is hidden in purchase of capital equipment which incorporates new technology.
O   They have a strong competitive position based on historically higher R&D spend.
O   Their accounting methods are different.

Similar explanations could apply if they spend more.

If there are no good explanations for wide discrepancies in R&D expenditure, then either the competitor's strategy is wrong or yours is. At this point, all you can do is recheck that your plans are consistent and sensible and then cross your fingers and hope that your management skills are better than your competitor's. Time alone will tell.

With the budget clear, the next step is to check the fit with existing capabilities in terms of facilities, people and skills mix. The technology development world is relatively slow moving, in that it can take several years to build specialist teams and establish specialist test facilities. You can't switch overnight from photographic chemicals research to electronic imaging research, or from powder metallurgy research to plastic injection moulding. By the same token, you can't redirect a group of research metallurgists from work on fundamental grain structure and alloying to work on improving material machining properties. Once, again, be realistic. If the plan demands a major shift, you need to allow time for redirection, retraining and, if necessary, redundancy and recruitment.

5

PLANNING FOR THE LONGER TERM

B Y starting with business strategy, digging down into the details of individual technologies, their importance to the business and the strength of the business in them, and then by building up again to a comprehensive technology plan, management will have a first idea of how much to spend and what to spend it on. This development of an outline technology strategy provides a firm foundation for organic growth in the business, building incrementally on the current position. For most businesses, most of the time, this will be enough. However, in every industry there is always a threat of substitution by a completely different technology. It therefore makes a lot of sense to try to look ten or more years further into the future to identify the likelihood of a substitution threat, where such a threat might come from and what businesses can do now to be ready for it.

Industrial history is littered with businesses that failed because they did not adapt to new technology. Steam locomotive companies, electronic valve companies and slide rule companies, along with countless others, have all gone the way of dinosaurs and dodos. Why did these companies fail to respond to the major shifts in the technologies of their industries? Was it that they were too slow to realise what was happening? Or that they knew what was coming but were somehow unable to adapt? This chapter explores these issues. It starts by looking at how you can track trends in technologies and anticipate substitution threats early. It then looks at what you can do to reduce the vulnerability of business to technology change, and discusses the barriers you face in trying to turn technology change to your advantage.

To plan for the longer term, the first thing managers need to do is to track trends in technologies and predict the trends ahead. The last two

75

chapters covered the development of technology strategies and the identification of emerging or pacing technologies that are likely to become competitively critical. The first questions to ask now are how quickly are the pacing technologies evolving and when will they become key to competitiveness? Will metal matrix composite pistons be in common usage in motor car engines in two years or in twenty? Will electronic controls be used for domestic door locks next year or not for another ten years?

Pharmaceutical treatments for arthritis and other degenerative conditions, digital broadcasting, edible packaging films and genetically engineered fruit and vegetables are other technologies which are all possible today and under commercial investigation. Some of these new technologies will be in widespread use within the decade while others may take a further ten years to happen. Knowing whether a technology is base, key, pacing or emerging is not enough. You need to determine the *rate* of evolution of the technology from one category to the next.

TRACKING THE RATE OF CHANGE

Three techniques for assessing the rate of change of technology and predicting how critical technical parameters are likely to evolve merit attention:

○   Extrapolation of trends
○   Delphi forecasting
○   Market pressure forecasting.

Each technique has advantages and disadvantages and is best suited for a particular industry dynamic, as discussed below.

EXTRAPOLATION OF TRENDS

Reviewing past technology development and extrapolating on the assumption that trends will continue ad infinitum can be surprisingly effective. There are limits, and technologies will not develop indefinitely, but this approach works well for aggregate technologies at the top of the technology tree. Trends in power per unit weight of internal combustion engines, or memory density on silicon, are typical examples where trends have been consistent for many years.

Work in this area builds on the 'experience curve' developed by the Boston Consulting Group, which carried out research in the 1970s into the cost of a variety of commodity materials (Ref. 5.1). They discovered that costs declined logarithmically over time, as the cumulative experience of producers enabled them incrementally to improve the way they did things

Cost of the three-minute telephone call New York to London, 1990 $

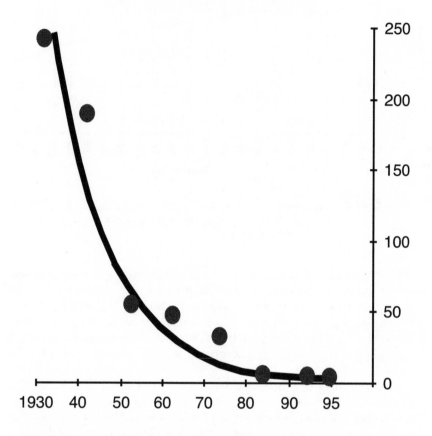

FIGURE 5.1   The Declining Cost of Telephoning
Source: ©*The Economist*, London, 28th September 1996
(Ref. 5.2)

and so realise efficiency gains. Just as in commodity materials, producers realise successive incremental productivity gains by fine tuning individual process steps, so the technology of complex products can be progressively improved by a series of small enhancements. Particularly in technology areas that are long lived and stable, the same trend is usually apparent. Figures 5.1, 5.2 and 5.3 show representative examples: long distance telephony (Ref. 5.2), fibre optic connectors (Ref. 5.3) and Japanese motorcycles (Ref. 5.4).

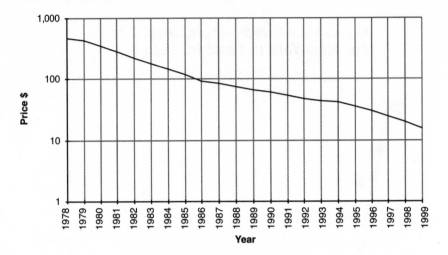

FIGURE 5.2   Experience Curve for Fibre Optic Couplers
Source: Arthur D. Little, derived from data
from Webb (ref. 5.2)

The advantage of this approach to forecasting is that, provided past data can be obtained, predicting what technology developments can be expected and when is straightforward. So, particularly for overall perform-ance trends, this approach can be very useful for setting goals. It cannot tell you how to achieve the goal, but it does tell you what goal you should be aiming for. As a guide to determining strategic objectives this can be very useful.

Extrapolation of trends is also helpful for comparing the progress of different technologies. In computer disk storage costs, for example, plotting magnetic technologies against optical technologies suggests that optical technologies are at the time of writing, close to capturing the mass market within the next five years. However, as Figure 5.4 shows schemat-ically, solid state memory storage technologies are developing faster than optical technologies and are likely to be competitive within 10–15 years. This could be bad news for the optical technology based companies, suggesting that the mass market potential of their products will be limited by the arrival of solid state memory products.

There is a danger, though, in taking this type of extrapolation too literally. Extrapolation is always risky, particularly when, as in this case, you are trying to predict the crossover points of three sloping lines ten years out. Slight changes in the gradients of the lines can shift those crossover points dramatically, and shifts are not only possible but likely. Magnetic storage technologies are relatively mature and treated as such by

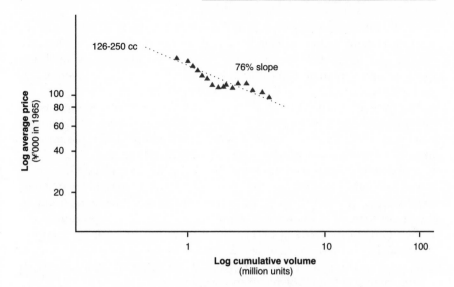

FIGURE 5.3   The Price of Japanese Motorcycles
Source: Reprinted with permission from the *Journal of Marketing*, published by the American Marketing Association, Vol. 47, Spring 1983 (Ref. 5.4)

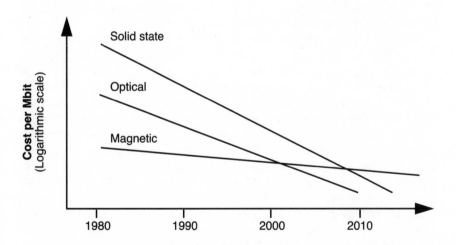

FIGURE 5.4   Trends in Competing Data Storage Technologies
Source: Arthur D. Little

magnetic storage businesses, which have scaled down R&D investment to the point where it just covers incremental development. With threats from optical and solid state technologies in sight, magnetic companies are likely to step up their R&D effort, leading to a faster improvement in performance. Gradient shifts can also be caused by limitations on individual technologies. Trend lines such as these assume that the cumulative effect of numerous incremental developments across many technologies will average out to give a steady overall trend. Although this assumption may be correct most of the time, at any one time the bulk of the improvement is likely to come from developments in only one or two of the technologies. As these fruitful seams peter out, development switches to new areas. The switch-over points cause hiccups in the overall trend. In the grand scheme of things over many years these hiccups go unnoticed. If they happen in the next two or three years however, they can upset dramatically the expected trade-offs between competing technologies. They may even cause developers to shift the focus of their efforts, so further changing the gradients of the trend lines.

The physical laws of science are another cause of shifts in gradient. Extrapolation of current trends in miniaturisation in silicon, for example, soon leads to components less than one molecule across. This clearly contravenes the laws of science, showing that miniaturisation cannot continue for much longer at the same rate. In a similar vein, optical components are limited by the properties of light, magnetic components by the size of the magnetic particles, and structural components by the theoretical limits on material strength.

This is not to say that extrapolating trends is a waste of time. Far from it. It is useful for setting goals, for comparing technologies and for gaining a sense of what may be achievable in the future. However, the danger of extrapolation is that the accuracy of past data lends a spurious credibility to the prediction. Extrapolations on their own are not enough, since they do not take into account deviations likely to occur because of changes in industry conditions or in what is technically possible. Even in aggregate high level technology areas, extrapolation needs caution and judgement. How to input that judgement has been a challenge to technology forecasters for years. Objective analysis of the future is not possible, and subjective views are always diverse and usually wrong. In 1989, Steven Schnaars published a detailed review of the success or failure of past forecasts under the title *Megamistakes* (Ref. 5.5). He found that, in general, the results were dismal. In a major forecasting exercise in 1967, the Top 100 innovations for the rest of twentieth century were picked. So far 15 have proved correct with a further ten counted as near misses. Not a very good performance, and not untypical. Figure 5.5 gives some more quotations taken from *Megamistakes*. The conclusion is clear: the expert

"Within ten years, the internal combustion engine will be a collector's item"	1971
"The picture telephone will be in widespread use by the 1980s"	1969
"There will be limitless supplies of nuclear power"	1966
"Plastics will be the primary structural material in buildings"	1969
"Books and newspapers will be replaced by computers"	1959

FIGURE 5.5   Predictions for the Future
Source: *MEGAMISTAKES: Forecasting and The Myth Of Rapid Technological Change* by Steven P. Schnaars. New York: The Free Press, a Division of Simon & Schuster, 1989

of today cannot be relied on to make valid judgements on the availability of and need for technology in the future. Inevitably, people's ideas are constrained by their own interpretation of the world and the technological possibilities open to them.

One of the noticeable features of most of the predictions reported in *Megamistakes* is that they are overly optimistic, viewing technology as the solution to all the problems facing the world. This is to some extent because the 1960s, when most of these predictions were made, was a decade of technological hope. Since then, the impact of an energy crisis in the 1970s and a financially-driven boom in the 1980s have reduced society's faith in technology considerably. Equivalent forecasts, if made today, would be a lot less optimistic.

If one looks at predictions made centuries rather than decades ago, societal bias becomes even more apparent. The 1991 Cambridge Darwin Lectures on *Predicting the Future* (Ref. 5.6) covering predictions back to early mediaeval times make this clear, as does *Science and the Retreat from Reason* (Ref. 5.7), a study on trends in scientific philosophy.

To some extent, this is a problem that cannot be resolved. If we interpret the world according to our preconceived set of values, then we will simply not recognise future opportunities when we see them. One solution that has been tried is to bring together a group of people to forecast the future, in the hope that their individual value sets will be different, so maximising the chances of identifying new opportunities. Unfortunately, putting a group of individuals together to discuss technology trends is rarely the answer, as peer pressure leads to a consensus view driven by the dominant personalities in the group. What tends to happen is one of two extremes. Either the group becomes very cautious, as optimistic people are made to feel that their views are outrageously unrealistic, or the group is swept along by shared technological enthusiasm, and ends up forecasting imminent breakthroughs, sweeping rational objection aside. One technique that is useful in overcoming these problems is the Delphi forecasting technique.

DELPHI FORECASTING

The Delphi technique is designed to generate a consensus view without the limitations of individual or group thinking. It works as follows. A briefing document that sets the scene and summarises past trends and current position is sent to a group of people. They are asked to respond to one or more questions and where possible to provide supporting evidence. The individual responses are then analysed, and a first cut consensus is developed. This viewpoint, with the collated evidence, is sent back to participants, who are asked to respond again. Anonymity is maintained throughout the process. If considerable divergence still exists, the process is repeated. The Delphi technique works well because it both minimises individual bias and avoids 'group think'. By turning technology forecasting into a quasi objective exercise and removing the impact of personalities, the technique is one of the best ways of getting technologists to think deeply about where the future lies. However, the Dephi technique is not without problems. Most seriously, it still does not eliminate the effect of a bias shared by all the participants. For example, a Delphi group on commercial air transport in the early 1960s would have focused on the expected development of ever faster supersonic and hypersonic jets. The idea of aircraft as buses in the skies, travelling subsonically at lower unit costs, was just too extreme to be accepted. Similarly, in the early 1970s, an automotive Delphi group would have predicted the imminent demise of large, petrol-engined motor cars and the rapid development of small electric-powered 'people movers'. As for individuals, Delphi groups tend to be conditioned by the mood of the times, with each member consciously or subconsciously reflecting society's views and attitudes.

Delphi groups also have practical disadvantages. They take a lot of time and effort to organise, and it is often difficult to find a group of people who are each expert enough to make a valuable input, but who together have a broad enough spread of experience to reduce 'group think'. A quasi Delphi group, in which people in a company are brought together for a structured discussion, eliminates some of the practical disadvantages. If an external facilitator is used to prevent individuals dominating the proceedings, the results will be nearly as good as for a full Delphi approach. The addition of a few invited experts to provide an external perspective can further enhance the outcome. This company-led approach is akin to structured brainstorming and builds on many of the group dynamics used there (Ref. 5.8).

In many businesses, Delphi is the best of the options available for predicting the rate of change of technologies. Consider for example, a company manufacturing ceramic-reinforced aluminium, which offers better stiffness and high temperature properties than plain unreinforced aluminium. How should the company decide where to focus its technology development? Do particulate reinforcements offer more or less potential than powder reinforcements? Will extrusions be accepted by the high volume customers before or after castings? A full or quasi Delphi approach will begin to answer these questions, identifying the priority areas for technology development and giving an indication of timing. These views can be validated subsequently. If the Delphi group identifies particulate reinforced connecting rods for engines as a priority area, market research can focus on the likely speed of take up by the automotive companies and on the precise performance needs.

For the aluminium company, Delphi is more reliable than trend extrapolation or the market pressure forecasting approach described below. More generally, Delphi is appropriate to industries where technology development is driven by the evolution of applications for the technology rather than by evolution of technology performance alone.

MARKET PRESSURE FORECASTING

Market pressure forecasting is the third common approach for predicting the rate of change of technology, used in businesses where technologies are adapted, modified and assembled in new combinations to tailor products to market needs. It is applicable to nearly all businesses, especially those producing fully assembled products for end customer use. It presumes that market pull is the driver for development and that technology push either does not occur, or has little impact. In essence, it is an extension of the first step of technology strategy development discussed in the previous chapter. Customers and potential customers are asked about how they make their buying decision and about the factors that they consider in making a purchase. They are encouraged to be wide ranging in their thoughts and to describe the 'ideal' solution. The assumption is that the customer is king, and that sooner or later companies will adapt their products to meet customers' needs, setting technical trends. In washing machines, for example, the current pressure is for machines that are quieter in operation and use less water and detergent than existing models. Armed with this knowledge, and the evidence behind it, the manager can begin to identify the higher priority areas for technological development, such as dirty water sensors, new self-dampening structural materials and so on.

Market pressure forecasting does not replace the extrapolation of trends or Delphi or other think tank approaches. What it does do is to provide a check against the wilder excesses of technological forecasting. In the commercial aerospace business for example, whereas Delphi techniques in the 1960s led to expectations of supersonic and hypersonic transport, market pressure forecasting would have picked up the embryonic package holiday business. This analysis might well have identified the changing nature of the commercial air passenger business, encouraging companies to switch focus more rapidly from speed towards comfort, low unit cost and frequent flights.

Like the other techniques, market pressure forecasting has advantages and disadvantages. On the plus side, it gets companies talking to their customers and listening to their needs. On the minus side, customers do not always tell the truth about what they want. Some research into the validity of market research undertaken by Hitachi's consumer electronics business (Ref. 5.9) identified the five pitfalls you face in asking customers what they want:

O   *Indifference.* Customers are typically indifferent to a new product until its relevance to their needs has been proven. They are therefore unable to articulate clearly all of their unmet needs.

O   *Absence of responsibility.* The consumer is unlikely to lie deliberately, but equally does not feel responsible for the consequences of what he or she says. Flippant, insincere and 'wish-list' comments are as likely as useful ones.

O   *Conservative attitudes.* Customers will usually prefer conventional approaches to innovative ones initially, but over time will come to see the benefits of the innovative approach and change their purchasing patterns accordingly. Initial perceptions are therefore misleading.

O   *Vanity.* Customers will describe what they would like to buy to reinforce a positive self-image, rather than what they need to buy because of cost and other constraints. Even with industrial products, potential customers connive in the hype around new innovations, but often actually buy inferior but cheaper products.

O   *Insufficient information.* Whether or not a new technology development is adopted by the market depends not only on the performance of the new technology compared to the old, but also how it is packaged and presented to the customer. In the early days of deciding which technology development route to pursue, performance features are much easier to articulate than other product attributes which may follow. This lack of information about how a product will actually function in practice makes it difficult for the customer to be precise about his or her intentions.

Even if you can get around these problems, you still face the difficulty that customers are talking about today's needs which may be much less important in 10 or 20 years' time. Like all of us, customers rationalise their product needs in terms of current priorities. If customers like driving fast cars, they will claim that they will want fast cars in 20 years' time, although they might accept the need for fast cars that are small, recyclable and with low fuel consumption. However, in 20 years' time the road network may be so congested as to limit the scope for fast driving, with the result that outright performance may no longer be an issue.

To avoid too strong a focus on today's needs, market pressure forecasting can be refined to take into account underlying changes in market structure. For example, demographic trends will predict the number and geographic distribution of the population, work patterns and the range of family structures of potential car purchasers. Combined with knowledge of the road network, and some intuitive assessment of experiments on road traffic pricing in cities, automotive manufacturers can forecast how we will live in 20 years, and so what sort of car we are likely to need. Armed with such information, managers can then focus your detailed customer research, assign priorities to product attributes and set technological priorities.

As with all forecasting techniques, realism is important. It would be easy to take a Malthusian view of gridlocked cities with millions spending hours each day stuck in traffic jams. It would be just as easy to foresee a country in which everyone worked from home, linked by computer and telecommunications networks, spending hardly any time travelling. What actually happens will lie somewhere between the two. Market pressure forecasting is therefore an inexact science, building on solid data and analysis but relying heavily on intuition and judgement.

For some companies, long term forecasting is not just useful in guiding strategy but fundamental to business success. Most of the materials processing industries, petrochemicals, steel, non-ferrous metals and aggregates, operate with 10 to 20 year time horizons for capital expenditure planning. New process plants typically take 10 years or more to design and build and then have operating lives of 20 years or more. The right decision at the right time can make the difference between commercial success and failure. Increasingly these companies are adopting a scenario approach to market pressure forecasting. Starting with global issues such as the economic consequences of shifts in the world political power balance, global warming and population trends, forecasters home in on three or four scenarios for their business. For each scenario, managers can develop a strategy. Senior managers then agree on the best combination of strategic actions to ensure the best possible outcome and minimise the downside. This approach is surprisingly robust. Arthur D. Little conducted a study ten years ago to look at trends in materials usage to identify technology and market priorities for the next 30 years for a diversified materials company. The study started with the political world order and worked down from there. Although the study failed to predict the disintegration of the Soviet bloc, it did get other political and economic trends about right so far. More important, it identified a set of target product/market opportunities that are still valid and look set to remain valid, and designed a technology strategy to equip the business to develop those opportunities.

More recently, a study on the future of medical devices highlighted the opposing trends of increased elderly populations and growing constraints on healthcare costs. Coupled with economic growth in the developing world and shifts in patterns of care towards earlier diagnosis, less intervention and reduced hospital stays, these trends present a confusing picture of the future market for medical products. By undertaking systematic analysis of these trends, with the development of alternative scenarios and sensitivity testing around them, you can cut through the confusion to develop a clear view of where the market is going, which segments offer the greatest potential, and what is likely to be required in terms of products. Based on this information, you can begin to set technology development priorities to build your future competitive position.

ANTICIPATING SUBSTITUTION THREATS

One of the big problems in trying to forecast the future is that you cannot use the techniques above to forecast the arrival of a major new technology: all forecasting techniques are inherently incremental, creating a map of the future as a logical extension of the past. The problem is compounded by the fact that new technologies often emerge in completely different industries, and go unnoticed until it is too late. Moreover, new technologies tend to start as worse performers than current technologies. Even if forecasters do identify them, they tend to see them as second rate technologies of little significance, failing to realise that it is the new rather than the old technology which has the greater long term potential.

Take, for instance, a prosaic example such as the development of laser measurement devices to replace tape measures. These devices are in widespread use by professional users such as estate agents and surveyors as they are quick and accurate and can be operated with one hand. Ten years ago they did not exist. As a tape measure manufacturer, you would have been concerned with the introduction of low cost materials, dual metric and imperial measurement, and differentiating features such as tape locking devices. None of the forecasting techniques would have been likely to predict anything other than incremental developments. Laser range finders were being used for defence applications, but were perceived as too esoteric and too expensive for volume use. The early range finders that were developed for the civilian market were indeed expensive and not very robust, and did not even confer any accuracy benefits. Quite reasonably, they were viewed as unlikely ever to be a real threat. Ten years later laser range finder technology has developed rapidly. Prices have tumbled and performance has improved, driven by the ready availability of very cheap semiconductor lasers, arising as a side benefit of the growth in use of semiconductor lasers in consumer electronics, and by the introduction of low cost low power liquid crystal displays, again from the consumer electronics industry. For many professional applications, laser range finders are now the preferred product. As the product continues to evolve, it is beginning to make significant inroads into the consumer market.

So if forecasting techniques are unable to predict these technology discontinuities, how can you find out when a substitute technology is threatening your business, and what it might be? The simple answer is that you cannot, at least not with a high degree of certainty. This issue was explored in detail recently by Ellinor Ehrnberg and her colleagues at Chalmers University in Sweden (Ref. 5.10). She looked at several cases where technology substitution had occurred to see if the substitution could have been predicted in advance, and found that commercial usage of a new technology was preceded by a marked increase in patents and publications. Figure 5.6 gives the example of laser systems. However, the picture was often less clear and the time delay between research activity and commercial exploitation was highly variable. The use of robots in flexible manufacturing systems, for example, gives a much more confused picture (Figure 5.7). The conclusion seems to be that, even if you can identify the substitute technology that is emerging, you cannot readily predict when it will impact on your business.

With the mechanistic approach to forecasting substitutes discounted, we need to look at alternative approaches which build on internal knowledge of trends in technologies and markets. The objective is to identify which technologies are likely to be vulnerable to threat, and then search proactively for substitutes.

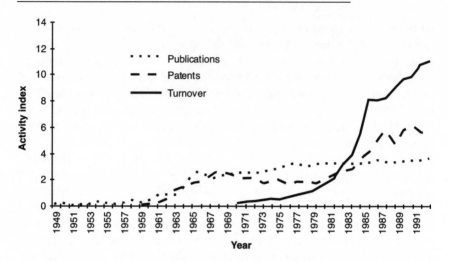

FIGURE 5.6   Indicators of Activity Related to Laser Beam
Sources
Source: Ehrnberg (Ref. 5.10)

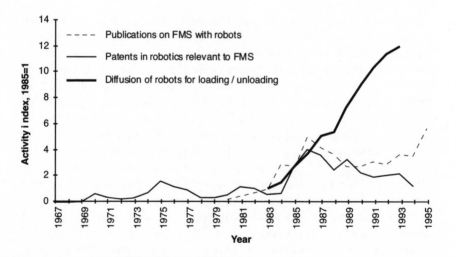

FIGURE 5.7   Indicators for Robots Used in Flexible
Manufacturing Systems
Source: Ehrnberg (Ref. 5.10)

How can you identify the point at which existing technologies are likely to be vulnerable? As discussed in the previous chapter, all technologies have a lifecycle, moving from emerging through pacing and key to finish as base technologies. As they evolve, their competitive impact grows and then declines as their use becomes widespread and their differentiation ability decreases.

When technologies first develop, the market is uncertain of their potential and adoption is slow and haphazard. Once their worth has been proved, the rate of adoption increases rapidly, providing the market feedback and impetus for development. The technologies then evolve more rapidly, increasing market adoption. Ultimately, however, the process slows down. The technology approaches physical or practical barriers, the market becomes saturated, and the pressure for development disappears. At this point, the substitution threat becomes visible, with new technologies unconstrained by the same physical barriers offering novel market attributes.

Technology evolution therefore typically follows an 'S' curve, with new technologies overtaking and replacing existing ones (Figure 5.8). This concept has been aired widely in the management press, particularly by Richard Foster (Ref. 5.11) who has documented 'S' curve technology evolutions in detail. The concept is powerful. The implication is that organisations can track what is happening to their technologies and anticipate when they need to move on. In this respect, this is a big leap

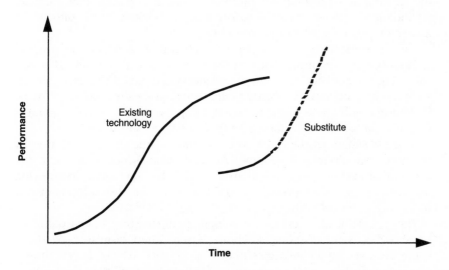

FIGURE 5.8   The Technology 'S' Curve
Source: Arthur D. Little

forward from conventional forecasting, because it makes explicit the view that technologies will sooner or later be replaced. How does the concept help companies to anticipate the threat of substitution?

You might expect that if you knew enough about what was happening to a technology now and what had happened in the past, you would be able to predict when evolution would level off. Sadly, this is rarely the case. First, technologies move in fits and starts, with a lot of scatter in real data points around the smoothed regression curve. Looking back at a long history with numerous data points this is not a problem, as the regression curve can still be fitted well to the data. Extrapolating forward from the last ten per cent of the data is risky however, as any scatter in the last few points is likely to have a disproportionate impact on the extrapolated curve.

Second, technologies do not evolve at the same rate. The rate depends on numerous factors including the macro-economic climate, competitive intensity in the industry and market pressures. Consequently you cannot predict at the start of an 'S' curve how long it will take to reach the end. Even worse, because 'S' curves typically last for tens of years, small errors in predicting the slope of the curve or the level of evolution at a given time are likely to affect significantly the predicted date and level of achievement at the end.

Third, substitution technologies evolve rapidly or slowly depending on the industrial climate, and on the perceived relative rates of evolution of the existing and substitute technologies. Even if it is clear that a critical technology is under threat of substitution, it is likely to be difficult to anticipate precisely when the substitution will occur.

Fourth, substitution can occur through an offshoot of the original technology. For example, with hindsight it is clear that Dolby B was a substitute for conventional audio cassette systems, and that steel radials were a substitute for rayon corded radial tyres. At the time, however, these looked like little more than incremental improvements, and it is unlikely that any one would have identified them easily as substitutes.

In most situations therefore, you cannot use the 'S' curve to predict when a technology will become obsolete. That is not to say that the concept should be dismissed as irrelevant. It has real value in showing that technologies have finite lives and that incremental development will ultimately yield diminishing returns.

The 'S' curve is also very useful in highlighting the threat of substitution, by showing why substitute technologies are often dismissed by those using the existing technologies until it is too late. As Figure 5.8 shows, new technologies usually start out performing less well than the existing technologies. The reasons are clear. Existing technologies have a critical mass of technology development and a large applications base providing commercial justification for it. New technologies lack both the committed resources and commercial justification. Their development is therefore a result of either an act of faith by management or a need for a niche application. Initial development and commercialisation are inevitably slow until a critical mass of resource and market need is reached, at which point the new technology begins moving up the 'S' curve, evolving rapidly to a point where it overtakes the incumbent technology (see panel on page 92).

It is hard for those involved in an industry to acknowledge that a new technology, currently underperforming the conventional technology, offers more long term potential and so poses a significant threat. The problem is compounded by three other barriers to acceptance of the threats. First, new technologies are often developed in industries which are different from those where they achieve their commercial potential and so tend to emerge unnoticed. Because new technologies are often driven by special performance needs, many such technologies surfaces first in the defence and aerospace industry, then transfer to civilian commercial applications. Technologies can also transfer from one industry sector to another. For example, many metal extrusion and forming processes are now used in the food processing industry; consumer electronics display technologies are now used in automobiles, and plastics processing technologies have been transferred to the ceramics industry. Second, even when a technology in another industrial sector is identified as offering possible potential for substitution, its significance is often then underestimated as the difficulties inherent in transferring technologies between sectors become apparent. These difficulties are often perceived as insurmountable barriers, whereas in reality their impact is more likely to be just one of delay.

Third, a 'not invented here' syndrome often prevails. If an electric valve company has been successful for decades, and senior managers have grown with it and nurtured that success, they may refuse to accept that a technology from a different industry could ever be a credible threat. Their past promotions were probably dependent on success in developing the current technology, and their current positions are concerned with backing the further development of the technology. It is hard in such a position to think the unthinkable and accept that new technologies provide a viable alternative for the future.

Consequently, substitute technologies, if they are identified at all, tend to be dismissed at first, with the justification that they are only for niche applications. Only later, as the limitations of current technologies and the potential of the substitution become more apparent is the threat taken seriously. By then it may be too late. In a few technology areas such as the development of fast computers, the limits on silicon technologies are

Flat Screen Display Technologies

Flat screen displays for consumer TV applications are an example of an emerging substitute technology that is still underperforming conventional CRT (cathode ray tube) picture tube technology. Flat screen displays are more than twice as expensive as picture tubes, are limited to small screen, and give inferior colour quality, resolution and reliability. In short, they pose no serious threat to conventional picture tubes. So far the only applications for which they have found a market are miniature portable TVs, in-flight entertainment systems, portable computer screens and industrial displays, as used in process control systems. Why then are the big electronics companies investing so heavily in developing flat screen displays? Because the conventional technology is at the top of its 'S' curve. Recent technology developments have been limited to producing flatter, squarer tubes with thinner higher strength glass. Important though these developments are, they are really minor tweaks to a mature well-established product. The problem is that, as screen size increases and wide screen formats are adopted, conventional TVs will become too large and too heavy to be suitable for home use. The advent of high definition TV will make the situation worse. The electronics companies have recognised this trend and are searching for alternative screen technologies. If flat screen technologies produce displays that cost less and perform better, the problem will be solved. Flat screens will then open up new potential for products as the technologies move up their 'S' curve. Indeed, some of this is happening already, as the development of flat screens and the explosive growth of lap-top and notebook computers go hand-in-hand. The challenge manufacturers face now is how to boost screen size, picture intensity and contrast up to current domestic standards. At the moment, none of the companies concerned knows how to improve the performance of flat screens to the degree necessary. Consequently, they are investing in a range of technologies. Canon is developing ferroelectric displays, Matsushita supertwist liquid crystals, Philips micro transistor network technologies. Some companies have already written off this generation of technologies and have leap-frogged to the next: light emitting polymers, although these are considered to be still many years from commercialisation. Choosing which of the various flat screen technologies to invest in is a matter of judgement based on knowledge of competitive position and perceptions of how the technologies are expected to evolve. The real challenge was to identify flat screen technologies as a substitution threat before the competitors did.

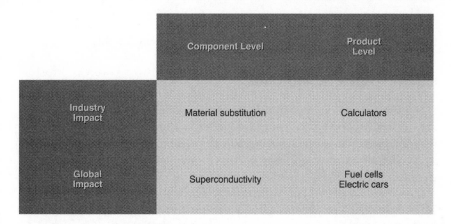

FIGURE 5.9   Categorisation of Technology Substitution by Level
of Impact
Source: Arthur D. Little

recognised and well understood, and rapid evolution is accepted as normal. Consequently, the industry is working hard to develop substitute optical and biological computing technologies. In most industries, however, the pace of change is slower and the limitations of conventional technologies are tolerated rather than treated as barriers to be overcome.

How then can you identify the threat posed by substitution technologies early enough to give yourself time to make a strategic response? The following guidelines can help:

O   Identify a wide ranging list of possible technologies.
O   Track technology maturity.
O   Identify industry sectors that could host substitute technologies.
O   Track the emergence of substitutes.

These guidelines will work whatever the level of the technology substitution. Some commentators have argued that there are significant differences in terms of impact of different substitutions and consequently that different approaches are needed. The first part of this statement is self-evident. Electricity, micro-electronics and the internal combustion engine are all examples of macro technologies which have changed the world. Push-button telephones may have replaced rotary dial telephones, but the impact on industry and society is clearly not in the same league. Trying to group substitution technologies according to whether they impact at product or component level, and whether the impact is industry-specific or global can help to focus strategic thinking. Figure 5.9 gives such a categorisation. At the end of the day, though, all substitutions require managerial attention and so must be investigated thoroughly.

IDENTIFY POSSIBLE TECHNOLOGIES

Using the technology unbundling and tree development techniques discussed in Chapter 3, you can pull together a wide ranging list of relevant technologies. The list will not include all possible substitute technologies, as by definition most will not yet have emerged and so will not be in people's minds. It is, however, a prerequisite. With the list of available technologies in place, you can start the process of identifying substitutes by brainstorming to identify possible alternative technologies, using morphological analysis techniques. Particularly with technologies related to materials, manufacturing processes and signal transmission and processing, some substitutes can be found just by looking at how else one could perform the function under study. At this stage, you have a slightly extended list of possible technologies to work with.

TRACK TECHNOLOGY MATURITY

The next step is to look at the maturity of the technologies on the list, to identify those which are new and therefore of interest and those which are old, and therefore under potential threat. Building on the concepts developed in Chapter 3, classify the technologies as base, key, pacing or emerging, to identify those that have significant strategic impact. As discussed earlier, key and pacing technologies give a company competitive advantage. Emerging technologies could give competitive advantage in the future. Base technologies are commodities; necessary but conferring no advantage. In the electronics industry, you need to be able to assemble printed circuit boards, or at least get them assembled to your specification. However, PCB assembly is a base technology, and does not have the strategic impact of digital electronics design skills or high speed processor chips. These are key technologies today, but likely to become commodity base technologies over of a number of years, as they mature. The new emerging technologies, including things like fuzzy logic software, neural nets and parallel processing systems, will become the key technologies of tomorrow.

Technology maturity and strategic impact tend to go together. Emerging technologies are likely to be at the bottom of the 'S' curve. Pacing or key technologies tend to be moving up the 'S' curve, and those that are base tend to be mature and at the top of the 'S' curve. But the correlation is not always perfect. Since it is directly related to competitive advantage, the strategic impact of a technology is industry specific. In contrast, technology maturity is not industry specific, as it is a measure of the evolution of a technology regardless of application. In practice, specific technologies are not readily transferable from the originating industry. So, although maturity is theoretically a measure independent of industry sector, it is normally determined by the sector that uses it most. The maturity of ceramic reinforced squeeze castings is driven by the market needs of the automotive components industry, the maturity of high speed video compression software by the broadcasting industry and the television and video cassette record manufacturers. Consequently, for most practical purposes, technologies are industry specific in their evolution. Maturity can therefore be regarded as synonymous with strategic impact.

Those technologies that are currently base in terms of strategic impact, and ageing in terms of maturity, can therefore be regarded as at the top of the 'S' curve and as candidates for substitution. In practice, most of these technologies will not be substituted, but will continue as base technologies, widely used and conferring no competitive advantage. However, some will be substituted and all offer the possibility of substitution.

At this stage you can match emerging and pacing technologies that fulfil the same or similar functions to the base technologies to develop a list of possible substitutions. To take a simple example, spot welding is a base technology, widely used for joining steel panels in the automotive and large domestic appliance industries. Emerging substitute technologies include adhesives, robotic seam welding using a variety of techniques, and new low cost, one-sided fasteners, such as derivatives of the pop rivet. At this stage, a review of the principal key technologies will show whether any of these are also under threat from the emerging and pacing technologies.

It is important not to lose all sense of proportion and see substitution threats around every corner. Although all technologies are continuously evolving as a normal feature of business life, the discontinuity posed by substitution is a rare and infrequent occurrence. When it happens, though, it can lead to wholesale change relatively quickly, so it is best to be prepared.

Reviewing all possible technologies and their substitution threats in immense detail is not necessary. However, managers need to know enough about what is going on to avoid investing large amounts in new spot welding plant just as all the competitors are switching to lower cost adhesives, or building an industrial business around ink-jet printing just when more effective substitute laser printing technologies are being developed.

It makes sense, therefore, to review technology maturity at two levels:

O   A broad wide-ranging review of all base technologies, flagging areas of possible concern

O   A more focused review of possible threats to the selected base technologies and those key technologies that underpin the company's competitive position.

IDENTIFY SECTORS OFFERING SUBSTITUTE TECHNOLOGIES

Most technologies evolve to meet a particular need in one industry sector. Once developed and proven, many can be transferred to other sectors, although such transfer almost always requires considerable adaptation and change. Because of this, identifying promising technologies in their 'raw' state is difficult. It is not surprising then that development engineers and chemists in the food processing industry do not turn immediately to the metals and plastics processing industries for inspiration. But that is just what they should be doing.

Companies need to focus on industry sectors that offer parallels to their sector. Consider the principal activities the company is involved in down the value chain, and look for comparable business models at each step. If a company cuts and shapes metal, it should look at technologies for cutting and shaping other materials; if it designs electronic circuitry, it should consider the design processes used in a range of other systems and networks, such as petrochemical plant pipework or roads. Managers must be creative. For alternative metal cutting and forming technologies, consider the possibilities offered by wire cutting of cheese, air and water knives used on paper, explosives for deforming rigid materials and so on should be considered, as should possibilities even further afield, such as techniques used in the plastics industry, textiles, even civil engineering. Brainstorming can help, as can exposure to other industries and markets. In one consumer goods company, for example, the new ventures group regularly visits exhibitions and reads journals in the chemicals, civil engineering, agricultural and building material sectors to seek inspiration and ideas for substitute technologies. Incidentally, not only has this group been successful in identifying potentially valuable new technologies, it has also managed to set up informal linkages with companies in other industries to share benchmarking information on wider business process and management issues.

TRACK THE EMERGENCE OF SUBSTITUTES

Armed with the list of possible substitution technologies, together with the list of possible relevant technologies used in other industries, you are now in a position to decide what needs to be done. Concentrate first on those technologies which will have a big impact soon. Review the list of emerging substitute technologies, in terms of both potential importance to the business and of the likely time before they will become significant, to agree some priority ordering.

The speed of evolution of the most important technologies can be tracked with a variety of indicators. The number of patents lodged by competitors, the number of researchers working in the field, and results published in the academic press all help to show how rapidly a technology is evolving, how much effort is being put into its development, and how important competitors perceive it to be.

If no evidence of development activity can be found, you may be the first to have identified the technology's substitution potential. You then have the freedom to decide what resources you want to commit, what targets you want to achieve, and by when.

RESPONDING TO SUBSTITUTION THREATS

As in developing the core technology strategy of the business, the steps you take to counter substitution threats should reflect your business objectives and build on your technology strengths. There are four possible routes to follow if a substitution threat emerges: exit, defend, build or buy.

O   *Exit the business* allowing the substitution technology and the competitors who are promoting it to take over. This strategy is not as defeatist as it may seem. If a substitution technology meets customer needs better than yours by a large margin, if technology is a key purchase criterion, and if you are poorly placed to make the switch, then you need to face up to the need to withdraw. Many business commentators have criticised slide rule manufacturers for failing to spot the threat from calculators, but it is difficult to see what they could have done to embrace the new technology as it was so far removed form their existing knowledge base. More positively, companies in precision engineering are always redefining their markets to capture segments where their production technologies have a current competitive advantage. If a business is geared up to produce components made of wood, the investment in equipment and skills needed to produce substitute plastic mouldings may be just too large and too risky. A more sensible strategic decision could well be to focus on other wood components for markets where plastic is less of a threat.

○   *Defend the established technology.* Substitutes do not always win. The incumbent technology starts out with many advantages: it is well known and understood, process and manufacturing equipment are already installed, and the infrastructure is already in place, with suppliers and customers down the value chain working together in stable mutually beneficial relationships. Incumbent technologies may also have untapped development potential. Take the use of magnetic media for computer data storage. Magnetic storage appeared to be maturing fast and stabilising with the $5\frac{1}{4}$" floppy disc. However, the threat of optical and solid state data storage prompted the magnetic media companies to renew their technology development effort, resulting in the $3\frac{1}{2}$" disk followed by increased storage density and the development of ever smaller and higher capacity hard disks. Defence is often possible and can be successful, either through buying time by delaying the onset of the substitute or through killing off the substitute altogether by making market entry too difficult.

○   *Develop the substitute technology* yourself. If the entry barriers are not too great, businesses can invest and develop the substitute technologies themselves. The Swatch watch is a good example of this. Again, the incumbent business starts with many advantages. By understanding market needs well and possessing existing channels to market, the incumbent should be able to tune a substitute technology faster and more closely to market needs than a new entrant. This option is not open, however, if the substitute technology is either patented or otherwise protected, or requires disproportionate capital investment. For example, domestic cooker heating element manufacturers could not have resisted the partial substitution of the elements by glass ceramic hob tops, because the glass ceramic material has unique properties, is heavily patented and requires a capital intensive production process.

○   *Buy the substitute technology.* For many technologies purchase is a logical option. Purchase can take several forms: negotiation of a licence, acquisition of a company or purchase of components or equipment.

If the technology is not strategically critical, purchasing components or equipment is often a viable route. An automotive sub-assembly company can buy in plastic injection moulded parts to replace in-house machining of metal components. The same company could also buy in a new adhesives jointing machine to replace its old spot welding equipment. In both cases, the quality of the technology needs to be good so the sourcing must be properly managed, but the strategic importance of the technologies is not enough to make in-house control essential.

If the technology is more strategically valuable, but is not the primary basis of competition, licensing may be the best route. Licences allow companies to gain access to new key technologies and to compete on an equal basis with competitors. For companies competing primarily on critical success factors at the customer interface, such as applications knowledge, delivery response and after-sales service, licensing of upstream product and process technologies can be very effective. Local packaging machinery companies, for example, supplying bespoke equipment to the local industry will often license aspects of the process technology, such as liquid filling systems, as the most cost-effective way of competing.

For technologies that are fundamental to the success of the business, acquisition of a company is likely to be the most appropriate route. For example, companies producing chlorine disinfection equipment for municipal, swimming pool and industrial water treatment have found that such equipment is threatened by new disinfection technologies such as ozone and ultraviolet (UV) which are simpler and safer. Chlorine technology can be defended because of its residual disinfection capability, but even so ozone and UV treatment technology are likely to capture an increasing share of the market. Internal development is not possible, since the companies have none of the skills required, and licensing will be difficult because of unwilling licensors. The only option left is to acquire.

Which of these four routes is the most appropriate will depend on the strategic importance of the technology under threat, the state and speed of development of the substitute technology, and the state of readiness of the principal competitors. Figure 5.10 (page 100) gives a broad indication how to choose the appropriate route.

REDUCING VULNERABILITY TO TECHNOLOGY CHANGE

As technologies evolve businesses have to evolve too, developing new technologies to replace the technologies used today to give competitive advantage. So far this chapter has considered how companies can anticipate radical technology changes by reviewing their current position and

	Exit	Defend	Develop	Buy
Importance of technology as a differentiator	High	Low	High	High
Technology entry barriers	High	High	Low	Low
Commercial entry barriers	Low	High	High	High

FIGURE 5.10   Alternative Actions Against
Technology Substitution
Source: Arthur D. Little

identifying how substitute technologies might arise. Although many businesses go through this process of determining their vulnerability to technology change, they are still often caught out when it happens. The principal reason is that they leave themselves unnecessarily vulnerable to the threat of substitution and technology change. When the inevitable happens and major technology change does occur, they do not have the business capability to adapt.

To ensure that you are as well placed as possible to survive and prosper from change, you need not just to be aware of the changing technology climate and its likely consequences, but also to avoid over-dependence on a single technology, testing the market with new technologies and planning future products to limit technology exposure. You also need to look at how to maintain the balance between technology and other competitive strengths.

AVOID TECHNOLOGY OVER-DEPENDENCE

Many companies are over-dependent on a single technology. In small companies, this is usually a function of history and lack of resources. High technology start up companies are particularly vulnerable. Starting from academia or as a spin-out from a larger group, the only competitive advantages they have are their unique technology capabilities. As the company grows, the pressure to invest in developing the same technology further is irresistible, particularly when larger competitors are pushing resources in the same direction to try to catch up. Domino Printing Sciences plc is a typical UK example. Building on niche ink-jet printing technologies, the company has grown by reinvesting heavily in developing them. In this case, after a few difficult periods when the management had to bet the company on each new product generation, the strategy appears to have paid off. By 1995, the company has grown to a turnover of over £70 million and managed to stay ahead of both principal competitors and competing technologies. It achieved the stability and scale to broaden its technology base slightly and encompass other industrial printing technologies, so reducing its vulnerability for the future and providing further platforms for growth. Many other start ups are less fortunate. Locked into specialist niches and tied to committing all available resources to developing that niche, they find themselves unable to adapt when an alternative technology becomes available. At this size of company, management can do little, other than keep a watchful eye on alternative technologies and try to spot trends as soon as they begin to develop.

Larger companies often fall victim to the same problem. Once a high technology company has reached the stable stage that Domino Printing reached, complacency can set in and a false sense of invulnerability may lead company managements to believe that they can repeat the success story for ever. At this point, a substitute technology in the hands of an aggressive competitor pushing hard for new business can seize significant market share. The rapid rise and equally rapid decline of many firms in the computer and computer peripherals sector illustrate this well. Each firm uses technology to build business rapidly in one niche. If they do not then move fast to broaden their technology base and secure their position, they lose business to the next new entrant.

To avoid this problem, management needs to be aware that it *is* a problem, and monitor both dependence on a specific technology and the emergence of potential substitutes. Broadening the technology base of the business becomes a business priority, with the objective of gaining exposure to alternative technologies to reduce vulnerability. So, a business manufacturing sintered metal powder components could add an engineering polymer component line. A business manufacturing steel framed bicycles could experiment with plastics, composites and non-ferrous metals as alternative frame materials. Heavy investment is not usually necessary. The objective is to gain understanding and reduce vulnerability, and that may be possible simply by finding a friendly supplier who is already using an alternative technology. When major technology shifts do occur they can be rapid but are not instantaneous. Examples documented by Foster (Ref. 5.11) suggest that if a new technology has a clearly perceived advantage and low switching costs then the shift to it will take as little as three to five years to occur. For example, Foster shows how electronic cash registers increased market share from 10 per cent to over 90 per cent from 1972 to 1976 at the expense of electro-mechanical machines. In slower-moving capital-intensive industries, such as steel-making, where switching costs are high, technology switching is more gradual. Figure 5.11 shows the rate of take-up of continuous steel casting as a percentage of total steel production. In either case, the timescale is long enough for most companies to decide how to

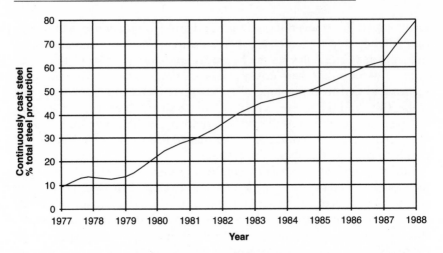

FIGURE 5.11   Rate of Take-Up of Continuous Casting of Steel
Source: Reproduced from the Proceedings of the
Institution of Mechanical Engineers, Part E, *Journal of
Process Mechanical Engineering*, Issue E1, 1989 by
C.E.H. Morris, by permission of the Council of the
Institution of Mechanical Engineers (Ref. 5.12)

respond and then act. As soon as the switching process starts, however, the incumbent is losing market share and so is under pressure. Investment in alternatives at this stage is often politically difficult, which is why it is necessary to anticipate the situation and have a solution already thought through.

TEST THE MARKET

Experimentation with new technologies calls for flexibility and open-mindedness. Since new 'S' curves usually start below the old 'S' curve, new technologies are still imperfect when they are introduced to the market. The skill is in getting technology into the marketplace to gain market knowledge and start moving down the experience curve without exposing the core business to undue risk. There are many ways to do it. Companies can test market products in niche geographic areas where the costs of failure, recall and subsequent damage to reputation can be controlled. For this reason, Hong Kong has been a favourite test market for many Japanese consumer electronics companies as it both has a reputation for embracing innovation and is well separated from core US and European markets. Companies can also apply new technologies in markets that are willing to take on technology risk in the search for performance improvements. Motor sport, defence and personal sports equipment are typical markets. Active suspension systems, for example, were first used in Formula 1 racing cars. A decade later they are only just beginning to find acceptance in high performance sports cars. Similarly, sports equipment is one of the biggest markets for carbon fibre reinforced composite materials, and has been the proving ground for many of the carbon fibre material process technologies, including filament winding and pultrusion.

Less adventurously, companies can test the market for new technologies in niche products in the core business area. Sony uses its professional broadcasting equipment business as a driver for new technology, then cascades it down into consumer electronics. Many of the automotive companies use sports models and niche models to test ideas before including them in the volume ranges, and many industrial OEM suppliers trial new equipment with key customers before launching them commercially.

Test marketing is therefore a simple practical way to reduce the commercial risk attached to new technologies. With technical risk reduced by intelligent focusing of resources, and commercial risk managed by test marketing, businesses can move quickly to adopt new technologies in the core business and gain maximum commercial benefit from them.

CREATE NEW MARKETS

New technologies can also be used to open up new business areas, as long as no one gets too carried away with enthusiasm. This option may at first sight appear attractive but is fraught with difficulty. The risks inherent in introducing a new technology are compounded by the risks inherent in entering a new market (Figure 5.12). An established business with knowledge of the market, secure distribution channels, and customer trust starts with an immense advantage over a new entrant, regardless of how good the new entrant's technology is. Diversification based on new technology is therefore risky. It can be done, provided the risks are understood and managed. Experience in helping companies diversify suggests that two factors are critical: understanding the market and sticking to what you know.

Market understanding can only come from personal experience of the market. Therefore the company must already be in the market in some form, or must recruit experienced people, or should enter into some form of alliance or joint venture.

Sticking to a familiar business model is another way of managing the risk. Stay with the same position on the value chain and compete on the same key success factors. A components company in one industry could

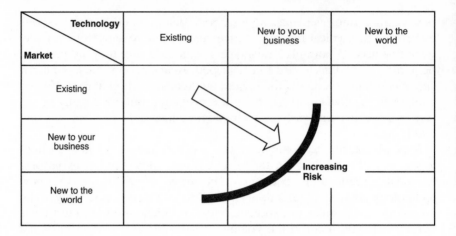

FIGURE 5.12   Technology and Market Risk
Source: Arthur D. Little

become a components company in another. Companies competing mainly on the basis of rapid delivery could diversify into other areas where speed is a principal source of competitive advantage.

Defence electronics companies attempting to use their technology expertise to diversify have been most successful where they have moved into businesses supplying complex systems to large bureaucratic customers. Signalling systems for national railways, broadcast and satellite equipment, and telecommunications switching systems have all been successful diversifications. Personal computers, telephones and automotive electronics have all been failures. The conclusion seems obvious: technology can provide a focus for diversification, but cannot compensate for weaknesses in other aspects of the business.

PLAN FUTURE PRODUCTS

Experimentation with new technologies is a necessary, but not sufficient condition for preventing over-exposure to substitution risk. Companies also need to look at how to reduce dependence on a single technology by better product planning. A product strategy that calls for the regular release of new products into the marketplace provides the opportunity for fast introduction of alternative technologies when the need arises. Structuring the range around a set of modules allows changes to be introduced at the module level. In the automotive industry, for example, companies mix and match bodies, transmissions and engines to give a wide range of products. New technologies can be introduced as alternative modules. If an automotive company wants to introduce its new CVT (constant velocity transmission) system, it can start by marketing it as an option alongside standard manual and automotive gearboxes, positioning itself to build up to volume product as and when the market requires.

This approach is effective except when the product plan becomes so structured that it cannot cope with the unexpected. A module approach leads to module boundaries which are inevitably a function of current technologies. The need for new technologies to cut across these boundaries may pose problems. In optical CD players for example, the laser tracks across the disc, driven by a tracking mechanism controlled by an integrated microprocessor chip (IC). Originally the mechanism and IC were separate. The accuracy of tracking could be improved either by refining the tracking mechanism or by enhancing the IC. In contrast, magnetic computer storage devices concentrate the tracking technology in the software on the IC. The mechanism is designed to be of low accuracy and its position is adjusted continuously by control signals from the IC. This approach could well reduce the overall cost for CD tracking but the current module structure inhibits its development and introduction.

STRENGTHEN NON-TECHNOLOGY FACTORS

The last way to reduce vulnerability to technology change is to raise the entry barriers to new technology, by increasing the importance of non-technology competitive factors such as brand image or distribution channels. A product based on old technology but produced by a well established business with good market access will triumph over a product based on new technology produced by a new entrant with no market position.

Investing in developing non-technology based competitive strengths will therefore strengthen a business's competitive position and reduce its vulnerability. The business will also find it culturally more acceptable to switch technologies when the need arises than a business which is more technology dependent.

No simple guaranteed solutions to the problem of technology change are available. However, having a broad awareness of which new technologies could pose substitution threats, coupled with a sound business strategy aimed at reducing dependence on a single technology, can keep vulnerability manageable.

6

BUYING IN TECHNOLOGY

❖

N O company can afford to develop in-house all the technologies it needs. The cost is too great and the constraints that in-house development capabilities impose on strategy are too severe. So all companies must buy in some of the technologies they require, either as skills and know-how, or embedded in components and products.

Taken to extremes, this view appears obvious. Consumer goods companies do not develop and manufacture their own office paper, forklift trucks or IT systems, preferring instead to focus their resources on developing their core products and associated manufacturing processes. Food processing companies do not make the stainless steel tanks and pressure vessels they use, and consumer electronics companies do not make copper wire. However, the situation is not always so clear cut. Most consumer goods companies get involved in primary product packaging, arguing that it can confer competitive advantage. Other companies move even further from their core business. Some transport companies, for example, get involved in the technology of vehicles they use. TNT, the parcels and newspaper carrier, was instrumental in developing trucks with lower wind resistance. Tiphook, the European freight operating and leasing company, developed special high capacity rail/road containers. In these cases, the technology of the vehicle was considered important enough to the core business to merit in-house attention. Many of the primary materials processing businesses also get involved in the details of process technologies. RTZ, the global mining and resources group, maintains a specialist business developing zinc smelting technology, arguing that this technology is too critical to outsource. The question you need to ask is: where should you draw the line in your own business between in-house development and external sourcing?

This chapter explores the issues that management needs to address in sourcing technology from external suppliers and suggests guidelines for sourcing strategies. The chapter looks first at why you should consider outsourcing, when outsourcing technology makes sense, and what sorts of technology should be outsourced. It then explores how external sourcing should be managed, and discusses the pros and cons of a range of options, from close-knit alliances to arm's length contracts. Finally, it considers issues related to outsourcing longer term research, one of the prime candidates for collaboration to save costs and accelerate progress.

WHY BUY IN TECHNOLOGY?

Why do businesses rely on others for technology development? The main reason is that no one business can afford to develop all the technologies it needs. The results of a study into the impact of lubrication technology development on the design of gears, bearings and similar components show why. Gear coupling design, for example, is based on the results of over 47 research projects, and the current design approach used for plain oil lubricated journal bearings is based on over 70 technology developments (Ref. 6.1). It would be nonsense for any one business to try to do all this work in-house. Instead, those engaged in research, development and design take in information from published research papers and other sources so that they can build on work done elsewhere. Success relies on adequate information collection and interpretation. This is normal research practice, but does not go far enough. You may learn a lot by looking at what others have done, but because you cannot control what research is done elsewhere or what results are published, you are unlikely to learn everything you want to.

Outsourcing is the next logical step, particularly when you move into technology and product areas that extend beyond your current core capabilities. Figure 6.1 illustrates the options that are normally considered by businesses making explicit decisions to buy in technology development in selected areas of need.

There are several reasons why outsourcing makes sense (Ref. 6.2):

○   It can save time, if technology is already well developed elsewhere.

○   It can save money, and reduce the commitment of critical internal resources. In so doing, it may also reduce management's nervousness about new technology.

○   The risks may be reduced, as the technology supplier may be able to manage risks better, or have the capabilities to reduce them.

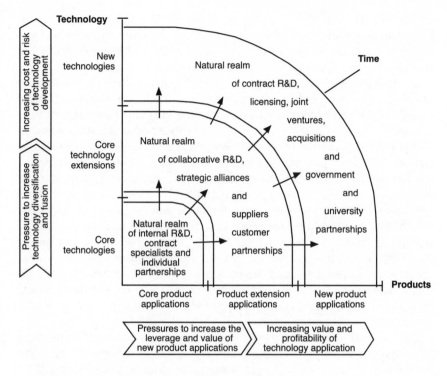

FIGURE 6.1   Technology Sourcing Options
Source: Arthur D. Little

O   The results may be better, because the supplier of the technology
       may have the specialist skills or experience to develop the full
       potential of the technology.
O   It may be the only option, if the technology is well protected by
       patents owned by others.

This last reason is often less substantial than the others. If a technology is
important enough to its success, the business will usually be able to find a
way around whatever patent protection may exist. Canon is a good
example of this. It set out with a clear intent to become a major player in
plain paper copiers, despite Xerox's stranglehold on the market and
comprehensive patent protection. Over many years, Canon built a market
position via thermal copiers while simultaneously investing heavily in
R&D to circumvent Xerox's patents one by one. Canon is now a leading
plain paper copier company, and Xerox now has to tread carefully to
avoid falling foul of Canon's patents. Patent protection rarely buys

invulnerability – it usually just buys time. So if a business chooses to license in or acquire technology from a patented source, the reason is less because it cannot develop the technology itself, and more because the cost of so doing is not justified by the strategic rewards.

In strategic decision making, all these reasons for not wanting to develop technology in-house reduce to two. The first is that the strategic benefit of the technology does not justify the cost and management time needed to develop it. If others can do it cheaper and better than you can, and you have better uses for your investment resources, then you should buy in. For example, for a primary aluminium producer operating a smelter pot line, accuracy in temperature measurement is important in ensuring that the smelter operates efficiently. However, it is not so important in terms of the competitive benefit it gives as to justify investment in developing more accurate temperature measurement technology. It makes more sense to buy in from a specialist instrument company. In contrast, a nuclear reactor operator may well decide that accurate temperature measurement is a key technology that justifies in-house development, as the consequence of inadequate technology would be severe, and the availability of appropriate technology may be inadequate.

The second reason that you might want to outsource technology development is simply that you can't afford to do it yourself. All companies have finite resources, and some technology development will be beyond their means even if the benefits appear to justify the costs. Far better to share the costs with someone else, or to buy technology that someone else has already paid for.

All other justifications for outsourcing technology development are subsets of these two. For example, many managers argue that they need to maintain strategic and operational flexibility, and do not want to be locked in to a single in-house technology. In essence, they are arguing that the strategic benefits of in-house development do not justify the potential costs of inflexibility. Managers in product assembly businesses also often argue that technology development is best left to their component suppliers, as it is they who have the critical mass of development resources and the market demand to justify such development. Again this argument reduces to one of cost benefit. An assembly business does not compete primarily on component technology and in most cases cannot justify the expense of in-house component technology development.

These various arguments and justifications for sourcing decisions can be brought together to indicate general guidelines as to why you should buy in technology. These guidelines go beyond the core / non-core principles laid out in Figure 6.1. The danger with basing outsourcing decisions solely on the degree of relatedness to the current business is that you can end up

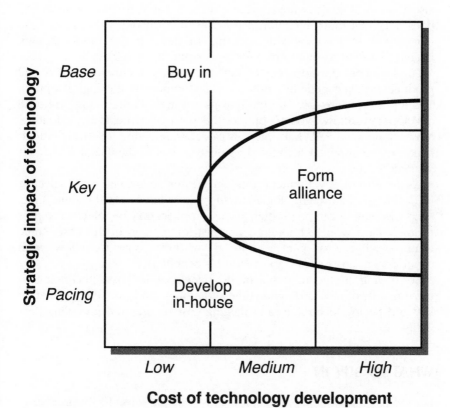

Cost of technology development

FIGURE 6.2   Technology Sourcing Decisions
Source: Arthur D. Little

outsourcing all future core areas. You don't want to – and can't afford to – develop them all in-house as we have discussed earlier, but equally you shouldn't outsource everything. The cost benefit argument is the one which should dominate. Figure 6.2 shows the influence of technology strategic impact (using the base, key, pacing categorisation developed in Chapter 3) and development cost on technology sourcing decisions.

For a base technology with low cost of development and low strategic impact, buying in, either by licensing the technology or acquiring it as technology embedded in a component or subassembly, is the logical choice. Bubble packaging for industrial components is an example. From the engineering component manufacturer's viewpoint, the cost of acquiring a plastic blow moulding machine and developing the technology to produce the bubble packs is relatively low. However, the strategic value is also low. Packaging is not a critical success factor for the product and does not merit much attention. Far better then to source the packs from outside, or to pay someone external to develop the mould design, keeping internal resources free for higher priority activities.

For low cost development of key and pacing technologies that will produce strategic benefits, in-house development is the logical option. The input costs are low and the returns are high. Furthermore, in-house development allows you to protect the strategic benefits by patenting. Most commercial R&D falls into this category, spending relatively little to make an incremental technology gain that has a significant knock on strategic value.

As the cost of development rises, businesses need to be more selective in deciding which technologies to support in-house. At the same time, simply buying in can be problematic as suppliers may be reluctant to pass on their hard won technology gains just for money. In this case, some form of alliance or joint venture is the best route to follow, with development costs shared to everyone's benefit.

So buying in technology can be beneficial for base technologies, providing flexibility, and saving time and money, and can be beneficial for key and pacing technologies facilitating cost sharing and providing flexibility.

WHAT TO BUY IN

For the reasons outlined above, it makes strategic sense for businesses to buy in some of the technologies they use. With this principle established, you need to choose what to buy in. In particular, you need to decide how many of the base technologies, which will have little strategic impact, you can outsource and for what proportion of key and pacing technologies the high development costs and risks outweigh the high strategic impact.

In selecting which technologies to buy in, the starting point should be that *all* technologies can be bought in. You can then look at the exceptions where there are strong arguments for in-house development. This is the opposite approach to that taken by most managers who start with the supposition that all technologies should be developed in-house unless there are compelling reasons for outsourcing. If you accept that outsourcing is to be encouraged, there are three criteria which can be used to provide a guide for action:

O   Does the technology have a high impact on product performance and hence competitive positioning? If the answer is yes, outsourcing may make you vulnerable even if the technology is base.

The heating element technology in a domestic fan heater, for example, is fundamental to the product's saleability. Although it is a base technology, outsourcing could be risky, unless you as a fan heater manufacturer can establish a secure relationship with your supplier or elect to compete on a different basis entirely, such as positioning the product as a fashion item, concentrating your efforts on changing the product's size, shape and colour.

O   Does the technology influence a high proportion of the product cost? If it does, it is important to remember that outsourcing implies relinquishing control over much of the cost base, again increasing your vulnerability. The involvement of transport companies in vehicle design, described at the start of this chapter can be viewed as an attempt to bring more of their cost base under their control.

O   Are sources of technology are limited, either because there are very few sources, or because switching between sources is difficult? Outsourcing electronic circuitry design is not a problem in this respect, whereas outsourcing superconducting magnet design may well be. If you buy in a critical technology from a sole supplier, you should be aware that you are offering up a hostage to fortune.

Answering yes to any one of these questions is unlikely to be justification in itself for deciding against outsourcing. However, if the answer is yes to two or three, one should probably be thinking about in-house development.

Most companies tend to err on the side of keeping as much technology development in-house as possible. Nervous about relying on others for technologies that are fundamental to their products, and conscious that sourcing decisions tend to be irreversible, because of the costs and delays inherent in rebuilding technology capabilities, managers are reluctant to outsource anything. The practical difficulties of outsourcing technology add to their concern:

O   What is a piece of technology worth?
O   How do you buy development effort, when the costs, timing and output are uncertain because they depend on the developers' creativity?
O   How do you ensure that the technologies which are developed will provide commercial benefit to your business?

Faced with such questions, it is not surprising that many managers take what appears to be the safe option and continue with in-house development. However, in the long run, developing everything in-house is *not* the safe option; ultimately it will dilute resources and lead to irreversible loss of competitiveness. Ad hoc outsourcing, making decisions on each technology independently, can also be ruinous in the long term. It runs counter to the basic strategic principle of focusing resources to give core competences in a limited number of areas.

The diesel engine manufacturer that outsources fuel injection technology for one product range, automated manufacturing technology for another, turbocharger design for a third and so on will soon find that it no longer has any real technology competences of its own. Outsourcing technology gives many benefits but decision makers must have a clear idea of what they are willing to outsource and what they plan to keep in-house. What they need is a structured approach to provide the rationale for outsourcing decisions and ensure that they form a coherent plan.

There are three key stages. First, you need to identify which technologies *can* be outsourced, using the screening criteria described previously. You need to look at these technologies as a whole, and check to make sure that you are not proposing to go too far, outsourcing so much that you undermine in-house capability. You also need to keep in mind both the direct reasons for retaining in-house capability (for example, to generate competitive advantage) and the indirect reasons (such as marketing advantage, manufacturing and applications know-how or credibility for international standards negotiations).

Second, based on this knowledge, you can develop an initial hypothesis on *what* to buy in and what to keep in-house. It is probably best to start from the presumption that all base technology development should be outsourced and that many key and pacing technologies of low strategic benefit should be outsourced. If in doubt, you should assume that outsourcing is preferable to in-house development unless proved otherwise. That way, you overcome the natural tendency to keep everything in-house.

Third, you need an integrated plan which optimises the benefits of buying in by matching the approach followed to the nature and maturity of the technology.

MANAGING TECHNOLOGY OUTSOURCING

Managing technology outsourcing is a multi-faceted process. For each technology, you first need to choose which outsourcing approach to follow, from purchase or license through to alliances and collaborative development. A paper making company is likely to rely on machinery suppliers and textile belt suppliers who have much more experience and skill in the critical process technologies used in paper making than the paper makers themselves. A mechanical clutch manufacturer may use a contract technology firm to supply electronic control systems for much the same reason, as well as to save time and money and reduce the risk of failure. In contrast, breweries that want to produce canned draught beer will have to consider licensing one of the proprietary widgets for making canned beer frothy, since there are only a few available technologies and each is well protected by patents.

You then need to check the proposed outsourcing options for consistency. Clearly the technologies that you plan to outsource should not include critical elements of your core competences, but you should also check that they do not underpin or support your core competences. You should then ensure that the actions you propose form a consistent portfolio. For example, it would probably make sense to use a single contract development organisation for a group of outsourced development studies, rather than spread them among several organisations. You also need to review licensing and purchasing decisions to maximise synergy and minimise conflicts. In reviewing the overall portfolio, you can look at the scope for strategic leverage. Many licensing and sourcing agreements can be used as levers to build more complex strategic partnerships and relationships. This topic is covered in detail in the next section of this chapter and in the next chapter. Even if you are not planning to build such partnerships in the short term, it makes sense to try to align sourcing decisions to support whatever partnerships you might want to create in the future.

Lastly, you need to revisit and review the portfolio regularly in the light of new information on markets, competitors and technologies as the relative strategic importance of technologies will change with time. The relationship between IBM and Microsoft is a salutary lesson. IBM, seeing itself as a computer hardware company, and viewing personal computers as a niche market peripheral to its mainframe business, was quite relaxed about outsourcing operating system development to Microsoft. In hindsight, this was a poor business decision. The growth of personal computers, combined with the shift in embedded value from hardware to software allowed Microsoft to surge ahead while IBM languished until it also moved into software with the acquisition of Lotus and others.

Outsourcing decisions must be made at corporate level as they are critical to future survival. If you do outsource, you run the risk of getting it badly wrong, like IBM. But, if you do not, you will spread resources too thinly and run the risk of decline. Action is better than inaction in this situation, and all you can do is ensure that you understand and manage the risks involved.

Of the various facets of the outsourcing decision, selection of the most appropriate outsourcing route is the one which merits most attention. As mentioned earlier, a range of outsourcing options is available, each implying a different level of external dependence and different value to the business. Ranked by increasing involvement and interdependence, the four main options are:

O   Contract technology development
O   Purchase/licence of technology
O   Risk sharing supplier development of technology
O   Alliances and joint ventures.

CONTRACT TECHNOLOGY DEVELOPMENT

This requires least management as the interdependence is low. Business managers say what they need and the contract development business delivers to a time and cost target. The deliverable is aimed at a specific client need and can take one of many forms:

O   A feasibility study report
O   Experimental results
O   A proof of principle demonstrator
O   A pre-production prototype
O   A piece of process machinery.

The contract should state the timescales, effort expected and deliverables. Although this should all be straightforward, complications can arise.

First, definition of objectives is critical. If you want a new sensor with several attributes (for example, size, weight, sensitivity, resolution, repeatability, temperature tolerance), you should recognise at the outset that you may not get everything you want. Technology development is inherently uncertain, and placing an external contract doesn't necessarily increase the probability of success. You need to ensure however, that compromises are made where they least matter. This means that the contractor must understand not only *what* your requirements are but *why* you want them.

To make sure of this, you need to spend time early in the process explaining in some detail not only your technical requirements but the business needs that the technology is intended to address. It is also necessary to think through at the start what you plan to do with the technology once it has been developed. If the contractor is developing a new sensor, you should make sure it can be made on your production plant. If you want to be able to develop the technology further, you need to ensure that the type of technology adopted has adequate room for subsequent improvement. Once work is underway, involvement should be more intermittent. This is a delicate balancing act. Too little involvement, and the project can deviate from your requirements. Too much, and you can stifle the contractor's creativity by imposing your own techno-logical preconceptions.

It is essential to agree at the start on who owns the intellectual property. Normally you, the client, can expect to own whatever intellectual property is developed on your behalf, although you need to allow some flexibility in interpretation. You probably selected this contractor in the first place because he has expertise developed while working for others. Ultimately, the question is one of trust and business ethics. The contractor who works well with you rather than for you is more likely to deliver real technology value to your business.

PURCHASING OR LICENSING TECHNOLOGY

Purchasing and licensing are fairly clear-cut processes. It is a case of looking at what's available, deciding whether or not to buy, and then negotiating on price. What you see should be what you get. In practice, though, most successful technology sales or licence arrangements require interaction and trust. Technology can rarely be readily packaged. Rather it is a combination of drawings, documents, experience and know-how. As for contract development, success depends on whether or not suppliers or licensors really understand why you want the technology, so that they can tailor their offering. Computer companies supplying engineering design technology in the form of packaged software are careful to supply not only the software but a whole support network of training, telephone hot lines and user clubs. The reason is simple. The rules for using computer aided design software to maximum benefit are not only too complex to write down, but are constantly evolving.

Aluminium companies supplying smelter technology licences to devel-oping countries go one step further, seconding teams of engineers and designers for years at a time to ensure that licences are properly under-stood and the embedded know-how implemented correctly.

Even more than for contract development, the interdependence between licensor and licensee make it very difficult to draw the line on deciding whether or not you have received what you paid for. Linking payment to results, that is products or processes in commercial use, rather than the technology itself is the rule rather than the exception, although there are as many variations in payment structure as there are deals. Expert advice is needed here.

The interdependence also makes it difficult to decide when the agree-ment is at an end. The Rover Group still uses the V8 engine design it purchased from Buick in the 1960s. However, the detail of the design has changed considerably and 30 years of Rover engineering development has improved the engine dramatically. Today's engine may have the same configuration as the Buick engine but it is now a Rover engine, not a Buick engine. This situation, which is not uncommon, raises interesting questions. Can Rover now license the engine technology to a competitor of Buick / General Motors, or even to Buick itself? Can General Motors relicense the design to one of Rover's competitors? Indeed, what are the technologies and designs under discussion; is the technology embedded in the basic original design or is it embedded in the countless modifications made by Rover? This debate is difficult to resolve, as it is not usually clear whether it is the designer or the adapter who has made the bigger contribution to the technology or product's success. Technology sales and licence agreements need to cover these issues comprehensively, setting both time limits and clear definitions on what the sellers and purchasers can continue to do with the technology once the time limits have expired.

RISK SHARING TECHNOLOGY DEVELOPMENT

Risk sharing with suppliers is the next option. Relying on component, product or production machinery suppliers for technology can yield huge benefits but compounds problems of intellectual property ownership and competitive behaviour. The Chrysler Liberty advanced vehicle programme illustrates both the benefits and the problems (Ref. 6.3). Liberty is the umbrella programme that Chrysler is using to develop technologies that will be used in their production vehicles over the next decade. The close involvement of suppliers and their contribution to the technology is impressive: some 600 engineers from suppliers are working on this programme, compared with only 70 from Chrysler itself. The benefits are obvious. Close working both reduces development times dramatically and improves product performance by facilitating better performance matching of components and sub-assemblies. However, who 'owns' any one technology is no longer clear, as all the parties are actively involved in its development. For this not to matter, the whole basis of the relationship between supplier and customer must be changed. Suppliers can no longer be selected because they meet a given part specification most cheaply. Instead, long term relationships are needed, in which the supplier works with the customer business to develop the optimum solution, secure in the knowledge that the technology investment will be rewarded.

This approach calls for a shift from the traditional approach to procurement that most large products companies follow with an emphasis on arm's length relationship, governed by price and with regular competitive rebidding. The change to the principle of long term relationships is one that businesses find hard to adopt quickly. For most technology-based product businesses, though, it is clearly the way in which businesses will increasingly have to behave, as the number of technologies used in a business increases and the complexity and cost of development of each technology escalate.

ALLIANCES AND JOINT VENTURES

Closer alliances and ventures are the next logical step in this trend. Several types of alliance are possible, ranging from the ad hoc partnership formed to tackle a specific problem, through complex alliances and joint ventures to complete acquisitions.

Ad hoc alliances are normally used to develop a technology that is critical to two or more businesses. Toshiba, IBM and Siemens formed such an alliance to develop the 1 Megabyte DRAM chip (Ref. 6.4). The principal goals of this alliance were to save time and money and to share skills and manufacturing equipment. The problem these three companies all faced was the speed and cost of innovation in Dynamic Random Access Memory chips (DRAMs). New generations of DRAM are developed every three years with commercial lifecycles which are only four years (Figure 6.3).

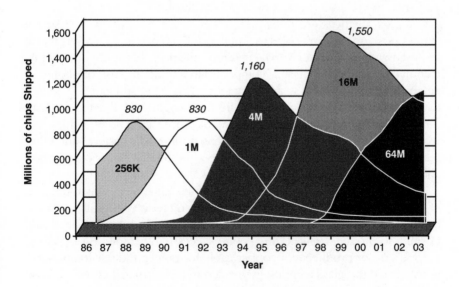

FIGURE 6.3   Past and Forecast Lifecycles of DRAM Generations
Source: Instat, Siemens (Ref. 6.4)

With each successive generation costing more to develop and requiring new capital investment, alliances were the only route forward. To put this in perspective, Siemens found that the new production plant cost for the next generation product was roughly equal to their annual DRAM sales. It was not surprising therefore that Siemens sought an alliance with others. The challenges of managing such an alliance between competitors and across strong national cultures are discussed later in this chapter.

In this, as in many other similar alliances, the strength of the participating companies helped them to set de facto worldwide standards, by providing them with the scale to impose their approach on the rest of the industry. Participating companies, particularly those whose other businesses overlap, need to be careful to partition the alliance off from the rest of the business. In this example, Toshiba, Siemens and IBM may be close allies in memory chip development but they are fierce competitors in other arenas.

The complex alliance is used to help two businesses operating in different sectors pool their resources and generate synergy. The alliance between Apple and Sony is representative. Apple, with strong computer hardware and software competences, lacked the miniaturisation technologies to make small notebook computers. Sony, with strong miniaturisation and manufacturing technologies, lacked hardware and software skills. Together, the two businesses are a powerful force.

Complex alliances are often used to enable a business with a strong market position to gain access to a pacing technology in which it is weak, as discussed in Chapter 3. The various alliances between automobile manufacturers and the plastics companies to explore the use of plastics in automotive body panels is an illustration. This type of alliance is longer term and more wide ranging than the ad hoc alliance. It often leads to further collaborations, as in the case of Apple and Sony, which are working on optical computer data devices, multi-media systems and other relevant technology areas. It can also be a prelude to closer cooperation and ultimately merger.

The joint venture is a variant of the complex alliance in which the area of cooperation is well enough defined and long term enough to merit the creation of a separate legal entity. The joint venture between BICC and Corning to produce optical fibre is one successful example. BICC, one of Europe's major producers of copper cable for power and telecommunications, lacked the glass technology needed to make optical fibres. Corning had the glass fibre technology, but lacked an understanding of the telecommunications industry. Together, the two created Optical Fibres Ltd., which became Europe's biggest producer of optical glass fibre.

Finally, acquisition is the most certain way of securing a technology and preventing others from acquiring it. Unfortunately, acquisition brings its own problems and the post-acquisition integration of two companies can be slow and difficult. Because of these problems, technology is rarely a good enough reason on its own to justify acquisition. Northern Telecom of Canada acquired STC primarily to get a foothold in Europe, not for STC's undoubted technical expertise. The technology has been valuable, but the time and trouble to extract and exploit it have been such that it would not have been enough justification on its own for the acquisition. The only time technology is a good enough reason to justify acquisition is when the target is a small focused group that can be readily absorbed. North West Water's acquisition of ICI's small ceramic membrane filter group is such a case.

Moving through this spectrum of alliances from ad hoc alliances to acquisitions, risks rise, flexibility decreases, and management complexity first rises and then falls (Figure 6.4). The greatest scope lies in the middle group, where shifting patterns of supplier relationships and ad hoc and focused alliances may cause considerable management problems but offer immense commercial potential.

Regardless of the nature or complexity of the alliance, each bilateral relationship must both fulfil the needs of each party and provide combined business benefits. Such relationships will work only in a win-win combination, in which each partner benefits from what the other can offer. In a supplier partnership, the supplier offers technology and guaranteed supply of parts in exchange for a secure order stream. In an ad hoc or complex alliance, businesses trade technology and product know-how for market understanding and access. In an acquisition, the acquiror offers security, stability and money in exchange for technology and technologists.

The trend towards alliances and increasing interdependence, driven largely by the need to pool resources for effective technology development and commercialisation, is creating a manufacturing economy in which any one company is part of a complex network involving numerous relationships with suppliers, customers, contract developers, licensors and licensees. If all works well, such networks of alliances can yield immense benefits. However, networks are very fragile. They rely on a series of interdependencies all staying in balance. The collapse of any one partnership or alliance, as a result of changes in market needs and competitive position, can change the needs of the partners from their other partnerships and lead to a domino effect with disintegration of relationships throughout the network.

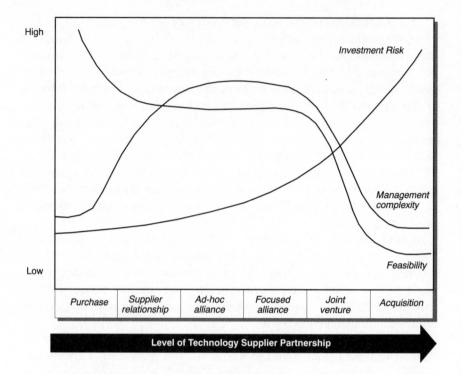

| Purchase | Supplier relationship | Ad-hoc alliance | Focused alliance | Joint venture | Acquisition |

Level of Technology Supplier Partnership

FIGURE 6.4   Alliance Trade-Offs
Source: Arthur D. Little

Because of this fragility, businesses must take steps to maximise the chances of success. These management and strategic issues are too important to leave to the procurement department or the acquisitions team. Instead, top management must take the time and invest the resources needed to decide:

O   Which technologies to outsource, from whom, and why.
O   What form of alliances are most appropriate.
O   Where the alliance boundaries lie in terms of scope and time.
O   What exit options and fall-back positions are allowable to the partners.

Only when such decisions have been made and clearly communicated to all those involved will you be able to manage the external sourcing of technology effectively.

LONGER TERM COLLABORATION

So far, this chapter has concentrated on the use of external sources to supply well defined technology needs, be they base technologies of low strategic impact or key and pacing technologies for which in-house development would be too costly or time consuming. However, a third category of technology development is frequently outsourced: long term, emerging technology development, where the costs of each technology are often quite low, but the choice of technologies to back is vast, their relative merits are unclear, and the timescale long. Such developments often seem to require disproportionate management time and attention.

In this situation, outsourcing can appear to make a lot of sense. If you have 30 long term interesting technologies, the argument goes, set up 30 university projects and have one internal academic liaison manager to oversee and coordinate them. If you are asked to contribute £50,000 to a government-sponsored research club investigating a technology of peripheral interest but uncertain benefit, why not contribute? If you have a chance to benefit from EC R&D funding, why not take it, even if the technology is not strategically critical? Many of Europe's leading companies follow this approach. Perhaps not surprisingly, the outcome is a great deal of published research, some patents, the occasional breakthrough, and an enormous waste of time and money.

Sadly, when companies realise that they have wasted their efforts, their response is often to swing to the other extreme, stopping all long term activity and focusing on short term development. This is an understandable response, but short-sighted.

Outsourcing longer term research and development into emerging technologies *can* be enormously beneficial, both directly and indirectly, if managed with care.

Direct benefits include:

O   Sharper focus by those scientists and engineers working on the emerging technologies, with a better chance of real results

O   Access to complementary technology skills and specialist facilities owned by others, so reducing learning time and so increasing the likelihood of real results

O   Exposure to related technology activities in other arenas (competitors, universities, other industry sectors), again increasing the chance of real results

O   Reduced costs through sharing and, if appropriate, direct government or EC support

O   Greater influence over standards discussions through increased knowledge and increased credibility.

Indirect benefits can include:

O   Preferential access to a pool of good quality potential recruits in universities
O   More credibility with suppliers, customers and potential recruits
O   Increased government lobbying power
O   Increased exposure of in-house development staff to technology challenges from outside.

Taken together, these benefits are worth going after, and can be achieved without too much difficulty. All it takes is recognition from top management that the output from outsourced technology effort will be directly proportional to the amount of management time invested in it.

Consider the simplest example of a university research student, partly or wholly sponsored by a business: the research student and his or her university supervisor both have clear objectives. They are both looking for a steady stream of published papers together with a student who passes.

These objectives have nothing to do with the needs of the business. The only way to ensure that business needs are met is to make them explicit at the start and then apply pressure throughout to ensure that they are not ignored. As the controller of the finances, the business is well placed to apply such pressure, and needs to make sure that it uses this position. You need to be clear from the outset why you are prepared to fund the research, what you propose to get out of it and how you are going to use it. You need to explain all this to the student and his or her academic supervisor. Then you need to keep the pressure on to make sure it all happens. It is also worth considering how to make your explanation and management pressure more understandable to the student. Take the student out of the university and into your in-house labs for a few weeks or months. Place one of your key researchers with him or her in the university on a short term secondment. Get the student to give a seminar to your research staff. Any or all of these will help both to generate understanding and to build mutual trust and commitment.

More complex long term technology outsourcing structures bring additional complications. Multiple business sponsorship of R&D clubs introduces more confusion to the objectives. In a research club project on ceramic engines, the engine designer sponsor is looking for guidance on engine design, the fuel company sponsor wants to know what additives may be necessary and the ceramic materials company wants a market for the material. Trade-offs will therefore be needed between the objectives of the sponsors, leading to changes in objectives of the project. As for the sponsorship of university research work, the message is clear. If you do not know precisely what your own objectives are, you are unlikely to achieve them.

COLLABORATING WITH COMPETITORS

The most extreme approach to long term technology outsourcing is to collaborate with direct competitors in the same industry. At first sight, this would seem a lunatic thing to do. However, a growing number of corporations are setting up collaborative research ventures and finding them beneficial. There are three main drivers for technology collaboration with competitors:

O   Sharing can cut development cost and risk. Pechiney develop aluminium smelting technology and then sell it worldwide to other smelters. It is a win-win situation. Very few companies can afford to develop this technology on their own, so it makes sense for most to buy in the technology. Even Pechiney can only afford to continue the technology development by sharing the cost with others via its licence arrangements. Furthermore, the size of the installed base gives a broader technology feedback than Pechiney could hope to generate on its own. The net result is faster, lower risk technology development at reduced cost.

O   Sharing can allow one group of competitors to create new industry standards and so distance themselves from the rest of the pack. In theory, this could constitute illegal anti-trust cartel behaviour. In practice it is rarely the only reason for collaboration and rarely explicit enough to cause problems. Much of the current collaboration on microelectronics, digital television, multimedia and telecommunications falls into this category.

O   Collaboration can be the most cost-effective way of addressing non-competitive technology issues, allowing an industry to compete more effectively against alternative industries. The joint work undertaken by battery manufacturers looking at new recycling processes is an example of this, as is collaboration between the world's railway operators on new technologies to improve reliability and cut operating costs.

The difficulty of collaborating with direct competitors is in ensuring that such arrangements are beneficial to all partners. This problem occurs whether the collaboration is a simple outsourcing arrangement or a fully-fledged joint venture. This is the classic 'prisoner's dilemma', named after a classic game theory problem involving the plea bargaining of two prisoners sharing a cell. If they can trust each other, they both win. If they can't, one may win and the other lose. Translated to technology collaboration, we find a similar effect. If you collaborate whole-heartedly, but your competitor seeks to exploit the situation, then you lose and he wins. If

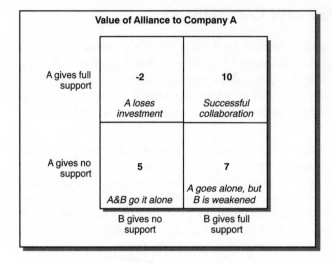

FIGURE 6.5   The 'Prisoner's Dilemma'
Source: Arthur D. Little

you exploit a gullible competitor, the situation is reversed. If neither of you trusts the other, you both lose. However, if you can both trust and commit to the arrangement, you both win handsomely (see Figure 6.5).

How then can you generate this atmosphere of trust and so improve the chances of success? Speculative long term research into new technologies is inherently risky anyway, so you have to work hard to minimise associated commercial and business risks. A wide-ranging report on what makes alliances work published by *Business International* (Ref. 6.5), and a recent survey by Arthur D. Little of collaborative research projects identified five critical actions that successful collaborators took:

○   *Select compatible partners.* You need to employ great care in choosing suppliers and partners. Experience suggests that alliances and collaborations work best when participants share similar aspirations and influence. Look for inherent compatibility, as evidenced by:
    − Size and geographic scope.
    − Complexity (e.g. R&D spend, capital intensity, product range).
    − Cultural similarity (e.g. management styles, accounting policies, ethics).
    − Shared strategic objectives (e.g. offensive / offensive rather than offensive / defensive).

These are all common sense. If you are a giant multinational like Siemens, you will find it easier to work with other giant multi-nationals, rather than with small start ups. Your personnel will share the 'big company' culture with theirs, and everyone will be comfortable with working together on committees, operating with formal documentation, and taking decisions in a politically complex environment. Unfortunately, many technology collaborations do not fit this mould well. The reality is that large corporations often need to link up with small entrepreneurial organisations to tap into their technological expertise, for the reasons outlined earlier. In such a case, inherent compatibility is low. There are disparities in most areas: size, complexity, culture and operating practices. There may even be a difference of strategic objectives. It is therefore not surprising that many such collaborations fail to live up to expectations.

One well-documented example is the alliance between Ana-martic, Tandem and Fujitsu (Ref. 6.6). Anamartic was a small UK-based start up with a novel silicon wafer technology. After some ten years of low level technology development, the company attempted to move on to a more commercial footing in the mid-1980s, first with backing from Tandem Computers and then with backing from Fujitsu. Problems between the partners began to emerge and after some six years of wrangling, Anamartic closed down in 1993. In hindsight, it is easy to see that this alliance was likely to fail. Anamartic was looking to develop their technology and build a business. Tandem wanted a technology it could use in its products, and applied pressure to ensure that Anamartic developed the product Tandem wanted and was managed in line with Tandem's needs. Fujitsu wanted to capture the technology know-how and take it back in-house. With such conflicting objectives, it is no surprise that the alliance ultimately fell apart.

To circumvent such problems, it helps to establish very high level linkages between the partners. If the chief executives and other key board members know each other at a personal level, then the alliance is more likely to survive, even if there are differences of opinion over strategic direction.

○ *Build trust.* All the evidence of past alliances and collaborations points to trust as the single most important factor in achieving success. Trust is critical for two reasons. First, you can never anticipate all the problems that might arise downstream. However, if an atmosphere of trust pervades, partners are more likely to resolve difficulties quickly and without argument. Second, if conflict does arise, trust between the key individuals creates a forum where open discussion is possible, greatly increasing the chances of conflict resolution. Partners should therefore invest effort in getting to know each other and understand each other. This applies at all levels. In the case of Siemens, IBM and Toshiba, all those involved on the project were put through intensive cross-cultural courses to raise their awareness of their partners' cultures. In addition, staff were deliberately mixed up on the different sites and encouraged to socialise. As the project progressed, the partners provided ongoing support and coaching to the teams to continue to foster an atmosphere of cooperation. Partners were explicit about their strategic objectives from the start, and also made the effort to revisit them as the project progressed to see how they were changing.

Trust also comes from anticipating problems early in the process. In particular, successful partnerships all had simple conflict resolution procedures, based on concepts of trust, fair play and reasonableness rather than litigation. Common costing systems were also important, with pre-agreed valuation of staff contributions by salary level and skill, and agreement on the value of unique facilities and test equipment.

○   *Select good collaboration managers.* Key requirements for the success of any R&D project are a strong sponsor and a project champion. Without such clarity of responsibility and accountability at the top, projects are liable to founder when problems arise. In a collaborative project or alliance, there are multiple sponsors, which can lead to conflict unless they are willing to put the project's interests ahead of their own company's interests. In contrast, the project champion must, by definition, be singular, and will inevitably face difficulties when operating with partner company personnel, as here he or she cannot possibly meet the needs of all of the sponsors all of the time. There is no prescriptive solution to this problem. Successful alliances report that their success depended on the skill of the project champion or collaboration manager. This individual has to combine the credibility to transcend company boundaries with a willingness to powershare. There is no substitute for a good individual in this role. Once established, his or her task can be made easier by promoting and supporting cross-company working to dilute the separate partner company cultures, as discussed earlier.

○   *Be pragmatic.* You need to be pragmatic about funding and intellectual property ownership. Again, following the principle of trust and openness, partners need to agree simple and fair funding rules (equal funding is the easiest method) and simple robust rules on intellectual property rights (equal ownership offers the lowest risk of conflict). You also need to look ahead and think how the alliance will dissolve. The objective here, as before, is to keep things simple. Plan possible exit scenarios, deciding who will keep which assets and what subsequent rights the partners have over intellectual property. Pace the commitment so that should the collaboration dissolve suddenly, there won't be any complex unravelling of budgets. Also anticipate the unexpected, such as a hostile takeover of a partner, and decide in advance what action you would take.

O   *Invest in a common culture.* As discussed earlier, anything which promotes trust and common thinking greatly increases the chances of success. The first step is to establish a common language and terminology. This may sound trivial, but is not. Precise definitions of what is meant by terms such as project, department and milestone are invaluable. Confusion here can be a fertile breeding ground for petty disagreement which can grow steadily to open conflict. With common ground-rules in place, the next stage is to educate researchers in working practices and cultures in the different companies and countries. Softer actions such as team-forming and team-building techniques to create a team identity and culture can also be immensely valuable. Finally, promote both vertical and horizontal communication by whatever means possible. In the early stages of collaboration, it is vital to establish rapport with frequent face-to-face meetings and off-site socialising before switching to cheaper and more efficient e-mail and video-conferencing techniques.

PUBLIC SECTOR FUNDING

Government or EC funding is sometimes used to justify shared or outsourced research into new technologies. This introduces yet another dimension, helping to cushion the financial costs but putting constraints on objectives, flexibility and time. EC projects in particular can be slowed down by administrative complexity. You need to remember that the reason for considering outsourcing or collaboration in the first place is the longer term nature of the project, so cost is unlikely to be a major issue. This being so, a good starting point is to accept government or EC funding only on projects you would have undertaken anyway. This runs counter to government and EC objectives, but the opposite – to embark on a project just because finance is available – is misguided. Money is not the scarce resource. Management time and resources for transferring technology into the business are. It is pointless to waste them on technologies that do not matter.

From a government perspective, a business focus on those technology projects that appear to make the most commercial sense would suggest that direct government support of research effort, and particularly support focused on specific technology areas, is a waste of money. In most cases, it probably is. Governments are not in the business of picking winners and leading industry to them. When they have tried, they have been singularly unsuccessful, as evidenced by the UK Alvey programme and System X telecommunication system, and by the problems experienced by MCC, the US micro-electronics consortium (Ref. 6.7). Industry itself is far better placed to pick winners, particularly when left to get on with it without governmental interference. The role of government in supporting technology development should be limited to providing information and communication links, particularly between academia and industry, and facilitating industry investment in outsourced research.

It is not the purpose of this book to debate government industrial and fiscal policy and make recommendations on how government should best support technology development in industry. However, it is clear that government does have a role in encouraging industry to invest in technology development where this will lead to commercial benefit, and that it should use whatever tax and subsidy mechanisms are at its disposal to provide such encouragement.

GENERATING COMMERCIAL RESULTS

The final issue of importance in outsourcing emerging technologies is how to make sure the results can be used in the business. By definition, emerging technologies have no clear product application and their application potential is ill-defined. Consequently, there is a high risk that the doctoral thesis produced at the end of a piece of sponsored university research work will just gather dust on the business R&D director's bookshelf. Even if the research is unsuccessful, the knowledge of this failure can be useful. At this stage in the development of a technology, however, it is as valuable to know what does not work as to know what does.

You can minimise the risk of outsourced R&D into emerging technologies being wasted by taking positive steps to encourage successful transfer into in-house development:

○   Put in place a well defined 'home' for the technology in the form of an in-house development project that builds on the results obtained but is more tightly focused on explicit commercial objectives.

○   Ensure there is a hand-over period, in which the researcher(s) stay in close contact with the R&D staff in the business so that they can communicate everything that was left unsaid in the thesis or reports.

○   Try to minimise the time lag between the outsourced emerging technology project and the subsequent focused development project, to ensure that information is not lost or forgotten and to maintain momentum.

Above all, be prepared to spend the time and management resources needed to ensure that investment is focused on the right things and that you have enough control over it to get the results that you want.

7

SELLING TECHNOLOGY

THE last chapter explored the reasons for buying in technology and discussed what sorts of technology companies might want to buy and what purchasing arrangements are appropriate. This chapter looks at the technology transfer issue from the other side and explores the circumstances in which companies might want to sell technology. It gives guidelines grounded in broad business experience on:

O   Why you should consider selling technology at all
O   What you might consider selling under different circumstances.
O   Who you might sell to and with what objectives in mind
O   How you can organise and manage the selling process
O   How to put a price on technology.

Much of the material in this chapter reflects the findings of an Arthur D. Little survey conducted in 1990 on how companies sell technology. In the survey, senior managers in nine large European companies were asked to explain in detail how they managed the sale and licensing of technology. Their answers were surprisingly consistent, with all the companies having moved over the past decade towards a common approach. More recent experience in this area suggests that the approach has not changed, although it has become an even more important facet of corporate business management.

WHY SELL TECHNOLOGY?

Reasons for wanting to sell technology fall into two broad categories: reactive and proactive.

REACTIVE SELLING

The first and most obvious of the reactive reasons is that you have spare technology that you don't need for your own business. Technologies peripheral to the core business, whether as a result of a refocused strategy or of accidental development, are typical candidates for sale. You may, for example, have followed the approach described in Chapter 4, focusing your R&D programme more narrowly on your strategic priorities. For example, a large aluminium group set its research laboratory to identify new uses for aluminium. By the time they had discovered a promising collection of downstream productions and associated production processes, the group strategy had moved to concentrate on the core smelting business. Still, it seemed a shame to ditch the promising results of the R&D programme, and selling them to someone for whom these could be core technologies seemed the logical answer.

The situation can also arise as a consequence of a more radical shift in business strategy. When their parent groups divested their consumer durables subsidiaries in the mid-1980s, the central research laboratories of both the TI Group and THORN-EMI found themselves looking for new customers for their domestic appliance technology skills. In the case of THORN-EMI, the problem was particularly serious. The group divested virtually all its manufacturing business, focusing instead on music and rental services. The retained central research laboratory was encouraged to capitalise on its technology base by selling its skills and developed technologies to other companies.

Even with a tight and consistent focus, mainstream R&D can still produce unwanted technology. R&D, and particularly longer term research, is by its very nature uncertain in outcome. A project on high strength pulp fibre, with the objective of developing tear-proof paper, led one paper company to a pulp fibre ideal for plastic resin reinforcement. Producing fibre reinforced plastics was not this firm's business, but the technology was too valuable to discard. Selling seemed the obvious answer. Perhaps EMI should have taken this route when it developed its body scanning technology in the 1960s. Arguably, it could have sold the technology to a business better able to manage the commercial aspects of building sales in the medical equipment sector. As it was, the company expanded too far, too fast in a sector that it did not understand (Ref. 7.1), collapsed and was taken over by Thorn.

The second reactive reason for considering selling technology is to hand over a critical technology to someone better able to develop it. Rolls Royce engines provides a good example. Its core business is the design and manufacture of jet engines for aerospace and industrial power generation. The associated technologies include aerodynamics and thermodynamics design technologies, an understanding of combustion, and high temperature materials design and application engineering. Less central to the business, but still important in engine manufacture, are a variety of testing and measurement technologies. In particular, Rolls Royce developed a measurement probe technology for accurate setting up of machine tools, and acoustic emission sensing, for use in remote measurement of vibration patterns. The company then faced a problem. It lacked the skills and interest to develop these technologies further, but retained a wish to benefit from such development. Sale was an obvious way out of the dilemma. Rolls Royce therefore sold these technologies to small specialist instrumentation businesses, remaining as a large customer to provide stability and security. For the probe technology, Rolls Royce did more than just provide stability. It supported Renishaw, the purchaser, in patent actions, allowing it to fight off much larger companies such as GTE in the US that would otherwise have been able to infringe the patents with impunity (Ref. 7.2). The security provided by a friendly giant allowed the small instrumentation businesses to develop their technologies, find new applications, and feed back applications knowledge to develop even better products. Rolls Royce now has access to products far better than it could have developed in-house, and its managers have not had the distraction of trying to nurture a new, peripheral, technology business.

The third reactive reason for selling technology is to reduce commitment to supporting its development, financially or otherwise. In the process industries in particular, the cost of trial or pilot plant can be immense. Selling the results to others can allow a business to off-load some costs without losing all control of the technology. The same is true of specialist facilities. The Perkins diesel engine group has impressive test facilities, including a fully equipped anechoic chamber for measuring engine noise. These facilities, and the expertise to use them, are available via Perkins Technology for commercial use, even by competitors. There are also other routes to obtaining support for development. For example, if a business needs to keep a design team together, but has only enough projects to keep it busy for half the year, it is tempting to rent the team's services out for the other half.

The fourth reactive reason is the realisation that technology is valuable, and that its sale can bring in worthwhile income, particularly if revenues are tied to royalty payments. For an R&D manager strapped for cash, this can look like a tempting option.

The reactive approach arises because companies' management realise they have got something that someone else might want. They then look at how to off-load it to their benefit, and congratulate themselves on their commercial astuteness. From a corporate perspective, however, the picture can look very different. In spite of some success stories, reactive selling is a dangerous approach. Managing the sale of technology is difficult and time-consuming. Post-sale support is costly and time-consuming. Even worse, the damage if things go wrong can be catastrophic, both to finances and, more important, to reputation and industry credibility.

Consider the following example. A large European manufacturer of polymers decided at business unit level that selling process technology would be advantageous. It would generate cash, help in the development of staff by exposing them to the outside world, and raise awareness of competitive activity. So far, so good. The company set out its stall and was soon rewarded with some lucrative contracts to design, build and commission processing plant. The activities were managed by a small department within one of the operating divisions with little corporate control. For a few years, all seemed to be going well, but then the cracks started appearing:

O   Operating company performance deteriorated as key personnel were repeatedly pulled off for temporary assignments to the external contracts.

O   Pre-feasibility studies, carried out without charge and often without formal cost tracking, did not always lead to a successful licence sale, causing significant irrecoverable losses.

O   Services were sold on a fixed-fee basis, but this did not always cover the costs incurred, particularly in less developed countries where the company underestimated the degree of support needed.

Even worse, there was no way to escape. The group's reputation in several emerging key markets was inextricably linked to the company's performance on its contracts there. The group was therefore obliged to complete these contracts at great cost to itself to keep a toe-hold in the market.

In another case, two employees deep in the entrails of the organisation built a £12 million turnover business buying and reselling process equipment as part of the company's process plant technology business. These individuals were very proud of their success in generating turnover and profit, but completely oblivious of the performance guarantees and contractual commitments they were giving.

In a third case, a research laboratory was struggling to persuade the parent group to continue to fund the development of a semiconductor test machine. In frustration, the laboratory manager accepted a request that he design and build a machine for another company. This machine allowed that company to break into the market in which the parent competed, and capture market share from it.

In all these examples, those selling technology either did not consider the possible consequences, or were simply not equipped to manage the technology sale for strategic commercial advantage.

In short, before you start, you need to know not only why you are thinking of selling technology, but how you plan to go about it and what you hope to get out of the sale.

PROACTIVE SELLING

The people who sell technology proactively do so to meet three possible objectives:

O   To make money
O   To support the core business
O   To gain strategic leverage.

These three are the best reasons for selling technology. Not just because it is there, but because you can turn its sale to real commercial advantage.

Selling technology to make money proactively suggests that this activity in itself is one of your core business activities, as is the case for contract design or technology development houses. However, for most products or businesses, selling technology to make money is usually fundamentally incompatible with the product core business. The problem is one of both strategy and scale. On a strategic front, it makes no sense to sell the technologies that underpin the rest of the business. If technological competence is one of prime differentiators of your products or supporting process, you cannot afford to make those competences available to others. You are therefore limited to selling those technologies which are peripheral to the core business. Unfortunately, although peripheral, these still require ongoing investment in development, which cannot normally be justified without the scale of returns that would follow from in-house use. Nonetheless, several companies have tried this approach in recent years, typically by setting up an external business ventures unit or by dedicating a team at the research labs to seek external business. Most have found that the returns do not justify the effort.

The second reason for the proactive sale of technology is to support the core business. As discussed earlier, selling technology can be a useful way of spreading the cost of development or specialist facilities, and ensuring that peripheral technologies receive the attention they need. The sale can help keep a technology 'alive', by generating a wider user base and stimulating development. For the chemicals and other process industries, where in-house use of a technology is intermittent, depending on the frequency of building new plants, selling technology can be particularly helpful. Depending on the technology, its sale or licence can also help generate downstream demand for the core business products. For example, work on the technologies for welding aluminium undertaken by the primary aluminium companies has undoubtedly stimulated downstream demand. Selling technology also has knock-on benefits for the core business. It gives technical staff a broader outlook, exposing them to the practices and views of the customers for the technology. It also enhances the company image, reinforcing the impression that it is a technology leader and facilitating inter-company relationships.

Gaining strategic leverage is the third and most important of all the reasons for selling technology. Whether your objective is entry into new markets or the development of new core businesses, technology capability can be a key card in establishing a joint venture or alliance. Offering your technology is one of the actions you can take to position yourself ahead of the competition and to convince your target partner that you will bring more to the partnership than anyone else can.

MATCHING TECHNOLOGIES TO STRATEGIC OBJECTIVES

Trying to sell the old or peripheral technologies in your store cupboard is unlikely to achieve any of the above objectives. The technologies will not be worth much, selling them will do little to help the core business, and potential partners are unlikely to be impressed. Go too far the other way, however, selling your latest and best technologies, and you may find that you've weakened your core business irretrievably by giving everyone your secrets.

Somewhere between these two extremes is the position to aim for; precisely where depends on what you are trying to do. If you are trying to set up a major strategic alliance, you may need to transfer most of your key and pacing technologies to your strategic partner, accepting that the returns justify the increased strategic vulnerability. If, however, the intention is just to support the core business, you are more likely to limit yourself to selling less strategically critical technologies.

In trying to decide what to sell, you may find it useful to group technologies into three categories:

O   Key and pacing technologies that provide scope for differentiation. These should not be sold off lightly.

O   Base technologies that are essential to be in the business but provide little scope for differentiation. These can be sold off readily, but there is less market demand for them.

O   The design know-how of your engineers, designers and draughtsmen. Their know-how is really a key technology, but it merits separate attention here because you cannot readily parcel it and sell it off.

The matrix in Figure 7.1 shows how to match the type of technology you plan to sell with the strategic objective. You can start from either axis, either deciding what your objective is and testing to see what you should sell, or deciding what you would consider selling and then checking what objective the sale could help you realise. Whenever possible, start with clear objectives for developing the business rather than treating technology sales as a windfall.

Technology	Strategic Objectives		
	Strategic Leverage	Core Business Enhancement	Revenue Generation
Key and Pacing Technologies	✔	✘	✘
Base Technology	✘	✔	✘
Design Know-how	✘	✔	✔

FIGURE 7.1   Matching Technologies to Strategic Objectives
Source: Arthur D. Little

GAINING STRATEGIC LEVERAGE

Looking across the top of the matrix, you can see that, not surprisingly, you can usually gain strategic leverage only from selling key or pacing technologies. To use technology as a strategic lever, you need to offer technology that gives real scope for differentiation. Precisely what you need to offer depends on what you are trying to achieve. If your objective is geographic expansion, you may need to offer both product and manufacturing or process technology to give the local purchaser a real chance of success in its geographic market. An example is the role that GEC played in establishing a transformer production plant in Russia. GEC took full responsibility for designing and installing the production plant and developing the products to be made in it. By keeping a stake in the production joint venture, GEC gained the geographic expansion it was looking for. There was inevitably some back cannibalisation of its European business, but better that this should come from its own venture than from someone else's.

In developing a completely new business, each interested party supplies only part of the jigsaw. BICC and Corning, for example, joined forces to produce optical fibre cables for telecommunications applications, with BICC providing the cables applications technology and marketing knowledge, and Corning providing the glass fibre production technology. Together they were well placed to build a strong business in a new growing market.

Companies can also gain strategic leverage up and down the supply chain. European aluminium companies, finding themselves with too high a cost base to compete effectively in primary aluminium smelting, have sold their smelting technology to South American smelters in exchange for a secure supply of metal to their downstream, high value added extrusion operations. They might have weakened their own smelting operations as a consequence, but it is a strategic choice that ultimately benefits the group as a whole.

In another example, the engineering polymer companies have worked with the automotive companies to produce plastic automotive body panels. It's a win-win arrangement. The polymer companies create downstream demand for their products, while the automotive companies learn a new production technology.

The stakes are high. To meet your strategic objectives, you need to offer technologies that have real value. In consequence, you need to insist on some form of joint venture or alliance to control the use of the technology; licensing is unlikely either to give adequate control or to ensure adequate returns. Only if you lack the resources to participate fully in the partnership with the purchaser does it make sense to sell outright. A good example is Pilkington's exploitation of the float glass process they developed. At the time, they were a relatively small player in the glass industry, lacking the resources to keep control of an alliance. The only option the company had was to sell some licences and reinvest the revenues to build the core business. This option was viable because the glass industry was relatively localised, with little inter-continental trade in finished product. Pilkington therefore knew that licensees in the US and the Far East were unlikely to have much of an impact in its own markets. But the Pilkington approach will not always work. Small high technology companies in electronics components often find themselves in a real dilemma. Unable to fund global expansion internally, and lacking the business credibility to attract adequate commercial funding on the open market, they seek to leverage their technology in an alliance. However, the alliance partner often has the financial resources, market coverage and technology capabilities to commercialise the technology on its own. As a result, the small company may be relegated to the role of the R&D source, soon left behind by the pace of technology development by the larger partner.

To management of a large corporation, this may seem an attractive proposition. However, big corporations can also face the same sort of problem, if their partners have some specific technical market or financial edge over them. To avoid running into this sort of trouble, you should try to find a partner whose strengths and weaknesses complement your own, rather than one who needs something from you but cannot offer anything of strategic value in return. Only an alliance that benefits both partners equally will be successful. For example, consider a typical European heavy electrical engineering firm with the pattern of strengths depicted in Figure 7.2. Looking for geographic expansion in the Far East, this group is able to offer product and manufacturing technology and financial muscle, together with a strong presence in its home market. One option, therefore, would be to link up with a local firm with distribution and sales strength and local applications know-how. A better option might be to

Competence	Relative Strength			Alliance Strategy	
	Strong	Fair	Weak	Offer	Receive
Product technology	⬯			✔	
Manufacturing capability	⬯			✔	
Applications know-how			⬯		✔
Design skills		⬯			
Distribution / sales strength in home market	⬯			✔	
Distribution / sales strength in new market			⬯		✔
Availability of skilled human resources		⬯			
Availability of investment capital	⬯			✔	

FIGURE 7.2   Matching Alliance Competences
Source: Arthur D. Little

find a larger company, such as one of the Japanese multi-nationals, which itself is looking to expand into Europe. Such collaboration can be a dangerous game, but as discussed in the previous chapter, can also be immensely successful.

If you are unhappy about letting key and pacing technologies out of your business, you can explore two other routes to gain strategic leverage. The impact will be less, but may be enough for your needs. First, you can try to sell proprietary base technologies, that is those base technologies in which you have enough know-how and experience to have a decent competitive position. Some Western companies follow this approach in dealing with the newly industrialised countries, with some success. To go this route, you have to be clear about your objectives. Selling base technologies because they meet the purchaser's needs is one thing. Selling them to generate strategic leverage cheaply is another, and carries the risk that the purchaser's management will realise that you are selling them short and will draw appropriate conclusions about the value you are placing on your alliance or relationship with them. Furthermore, selling base technologies may be a false economy just in simple practical terms. You will still need to provide follow-up support after the sale of proprietary base technologies if the purchaser is to realise their strategic impact, and providing such support to yesterday's technologies may be more demanding on resources than providing support for current key and pacing technologies.

An alternative route to gain strategic leverage is to design know-how and consultancy. These services can be the glue that holds a strategic alliance together, but they are unlikely in themselves to drive the creation of an alliance. The provision of such services can disrupt the core business, placing too many demands on the time of senior people.

Whether you gain strategic leverage from the sale, therefore, really depends on the quality and strategic value of the technology you are prepared to offer. In short, the more you are prepared to put in, the more the strategic value is likely to be.

ENHANCING THE CORE BUSINESS

Moving along the matrix in Figure 7.1, the second strategic objective for selling technology is to enhance the core business. The sale of key and pacing technologies is seldom the right route to enhancing the core business, since the resulting loss of competitive advantage is rarely offset by the gains from the sale. The exception is when the key or pacing technologies are not important to the core business, but the resulting benefits from sale are. Johnson Matthey, for example, has developed novel applications technologies for using platinum group metals in a

range of electronics and medical applications. The sale of these technologies generates downstream demand for the core platinum refining
business without having any negative effect. Selling base technologies to
enhance the core business can have several benefits. It broadens the user
base and provides valuable operational feedback, helps to keep the
technology alive and stimulates its ongoing development. On a more
mundane level, selling base technologies can help to keep in-house
technology development staff busy and maintain critical mass. The only
difficulty is likely to be in finding a customer: market demand for base
technologies is limited, and competitors abound.

The sale of custom design and engineering services can also help to
maintain a critical mass of staff and keep technology development alive. It
also assists in the personal development of staff, providing a range of
challenging problems and suggesting new ideas that can be fed back to
the core business. Particularly in process technology businesses, where
major in-house capital expenditure is infrequent, selling design services to
the external world can be very appealing. Several companies have gone
down this route, some even setting up their engineering services arms as
stand-alone profit centres.

Setting engineering up as an independent business puts the spotlight on
performance. The parent negotiates a long term purchasing agreement
with the new business and buys only what it needs. The business stands
or falls on its competitive strength.

There are three routes to setting engineering up as an independent
business:

O   Keep it within the parent company.
O   Enter into a joint venture with a partner with compatible skills.
O   Sell to a stronger supplier.

Porsche's Engineering Services division is independent within the parent
company. It takes in research and engineering projects for other car
manufacturers; management, at the time of writing, now plans to turn the
division into a profit centre and to open a design centre in China.
Courtaulds reorganised its central engineering department into Courtaulds
Engineering Limited (CEL), an independent business that services both
Courtaulds and external customers. Group companies do not have to use
CEL, but to date it has won most of its major projects in competition with
external contractors. Both sides have benefited: group companies have a
more competitive supplier, and CEL is now stronger, gaining the bulk of
its sales from external customers and contributing profits to the group. ICI
reorganised part of ICI Engineering into Eutech Engineering Solutions, an
independent business servicing both ICI and external customers. The
objective is to make Eutech stronger and more competitive. British

Airways has set up its engineering services as a separate profit centre, to reduce costs and expand services to other carriers.

Yorkshire Water took the second route, putting its engineering division into a joint venture with Babcock's international process plant contracting arm to form Babcock Water Engineering Limited, which supplies the water industry in the UK and overseas. Here too, both parties have gained. Yorkshire Water has a more competitive supplier; Babcock an entry to the water industry.

Other companies have sold their engineering divisions. North West Water sold its engineering division to Bechtel, as part of a broader alliance. The new organisation supports North West Water's UK capital programme and international ventures, and competes for external business worldwide. North West Water also believes that, with a clear dividing line between customer and supplier, its core operating utility business will obtain a more competitive service.

Competing externally stimulates performance, provides the potential to learn from outside and allows you to balance the workload through internal peaks and troughs. It works best when internal customers and external customers both need services that demand a critical mass of engineering and technology skills.

Joint ventures and sale are faster routes to independence than keeping engineering services in the parent company. But whichever option you choose, gaining the full benefits takes time. Relationships with the parent or former parent will not change overnight. Conflicts over priorities may arise between the parent and other customers, who may well be competitors. As one manager put it: 'You have to treat the Group like a proper customer, but it takes a long time to shake out old habits'. Old customers will find the loss of preferred status hard to accept and people in the new business will not enjoy competing for business that they once received as of right. The parent will need different skills to manage the new arms-length relationship. The business will have to develop new commercial skills.

The danger, of course, is that this can be a distraction from the core business. If you place hundreds of millions of revenue at risk by failing to upgrade your own oil refinery because your technology group is working for tens of millions on someone else's refinery, you may well question why you are trying to sell outside. However, if you pursue external sales only on the understanding that they can never have first call on your services, you are unlikely to win many orders. Whatever specific approach you adopt must provide a mechanism for reconciling this dilemma.

On balance, external sales of technology and engineering services are usually worthwhile for the market exposure they bring. But it is vital to keep your attention on the core business.

GENERATING REVENUE

The last objective is selling technologies to generate revenues. As we have already discussed, just trying to make money is hardly ever worthwhile. Key and pacing technologies are too valuable to sell just for money, except to customers who compete in totally different markets where there is no risk of competition. And since the sale of base technologies seldom generates enough to cover the true costs of sale and support, the gain there is not worthwhile either. It is only when design know-how is involved that the sale of technology for revenues make sense. Real experience and know-how greatly reduce the risk associated with taking up any new technology. Consequently, people involved in technology development, design or applications engineering within a business can usually command a premium for their services outside because of their track record in supporting their own business's success. 'Selling' the time of such people can therefore be a profitable sideline, particularly when the sale has knock-on benefits to the core business.

MANAGING THE SALE OF TECHNOLOGY

Selling technology is a complex activity, not to be undertaken lightly. Defining what you are trying to sell is often the first hurdle. The next is ensuring that you get the returns you want without giving away too much of your core business's competitive advantage. At the same time, you face the ever present risk of diverting too much management attention away from the core business. Our survey showed that all the companies who had put in place some corporate policy on technology sales were following similar basic guidelines on strategy and organisation and on the management of implementation to overcome these difficulties.

STRATEGIC GUIDELINES

Most applied three key rules to the strategy of selling technology:

O   Don't sell technologies that are not fully proven. Using a customer as a test bed for a new technology can have serious consequences both financially and in terms of market and commercial credibility. What is more, customers are unlikely to make good test beds, since they will interfere and modify technologies in unexpected ways. Consider the example of Lotus Cars in the 1970s, who supplied an unproven engine design to Jensen Healey for their new sports car. Initial problems with the engine were so great that the reputation of Jensen Healey was significantly undermined, contributing to the company's early demise. Lotus itself also suffered, both financially and in reputation. Experimenting on customers like this will often cause harm to both buyer and seller.

O   Don't develop technologies just for commercial sale. Quite simply, it's not worth it. Organisations that do contract R&D for a living operate with extremely tight project control and still make modest returns: few manufacturing companies, for whom selling technologies is just an interesting sideline, will be able to operate as efficiently and make money. And a technology is only of value if it meets a market need. An upstream materials supplier, for example, is not well placed to develop technologies for use by downstream customers unless it understands their markets as well as they do themselves. If you do not need the technology yourself, you are unlikely to come up with something that meets someone else's need, and you are unlikely to be well placed to develop it as the need evolves.

O   Don't try to broaden the scope of the sale by getting enmeshed in equipment manufacture or procurement. It may look like easy money, but the risks are too great. One engineering company, selling manufacturing plants around the world to support its core components business, found that it had incurred potential liabilities on two contracts in excess of its market capitalisation. Junior staff members in the technology group had taken it upon themselves to act as procurement agents and were accepting performance guarantees without securing cover from their suppliers. Luckily, the position was retrievable, but at a high cost in management time. The message is clear: stay in businesses you know and understand.

Some companies have organisational guidelines that follow on from these principles. In many cases, every sale of technology has to be approved at senior level to ensure consistency with corporate objectives, since even minor sales can have a knock-on effect. Often a member of the group main board is nominated as the decision point. Most companies also administer technology sales centrally, rather than devolving the activity to the division or business unit.

With any technology sale there is a risk of conflict with other parts of the group. If you choose to sell your aluminium smelting technology to secure metal supplies for your downstream operations, you are likely to upset your own smelting business. If you provide design services to assist a competitor to build capital plant, you are likely to antagonise your own plant managers. Conflict may be unavoidable, but keeping the decision making at the top at least ensures that someone considers both sides of the argument.

Intuitively, one would expect companies to veto sales to competitors. In practice, they do not. Selling technology to competitors need not be a problem provided you are aware of what you are doing and have agreed explicitly that you are selling the technology to meet the agreed strategic objectives, as described earlier in this chapter. If you follow these guidelines, the benefits of the sale should always outweigh the costs.

IMPLEMENTATION GUIDELINES

At the implementation stage, following a technology sale, the seller needs to encourage good customer relations and generate adequate information feedback without being sucked into providing excessive support and help. Many businesses balance payment structures and risks to achieve this compromise:

O   Payment for technology know-how is often in two parts. The first part is a combination of fixed fee and ongoing royalty payment, dependent on the product or process technology sold. The second part is a per diem fee for additional technical support and consultancy services.

O   Seller and buyer establish a user club to maximise the exchange of technology information, set objectives and provide the resources needed for further technology development.

O   To keep the risks low, contracts are structured to transfer liability to the contractors, and care is taken to select and work with reputable contractors.

  To minimise the risks further, you can restrict yourself to politically stable countries and supply only those customers who have demonstrated that they have the skills and resources to operate the technology. More pragmatically, you can inflate the fees to provide a contingency to cover training and support services.

The sale or transfer of technology is fraught with difficulty. As a combination of tangibles and intangibles, of drawings and computer programmes, and of know-how, experience and credibility, technology cannot be packaged and air-freighted. A sale is therefore really only complete when the purchaser has built up the experience and expertise to operate the new technology and benefit commercially from it. The guidelines presented here are intended to help companies to recognise the problems inherent in selling technology, and to tackle them successfully.

VALUING TECHNOLOGY ASSETS

If you are planning to sell or license technology, or indeed to buy it, you need a sense of how much it is worth. Whether or not you attempt to get full value from the purchaser depends on why you are selling the technology, as discussed in the previous sections. Nonetheless, unless you appreciate the real value, you run a high risk of taking a false position in negotiations. How then do you value technology assets?

In principle, you can value technology either on what it costs to provide or on what value it gives to the customer. For an intangible asset, such as technology, valuing on the costs of provision will nearly always lead to under-valuation. Most of the costs incurred in technology development are sunk costs that will already have been offset against other income. The actual costs incurred in selling technology are usually therefore limited to the incremental costs of marketing, documentation and support. Since these incremental costs are typically a small percentage of what a technology is worth to a customer, charging on this basis is unlikely to generate an adequate return.

You need to value the technology therefore on the basis of the benefits it will give, rather than just on the costs of provision. There are four main ways to value on the basis of benefit. None is perfect. Which to use depends both on what can sensibly be estimated and on why the customer wants to buy the technology. The four approaches are:

○   Supplier replication cost
○   Customer replication cost
○   Future value
○   Time dependent future value.

These four approaches and their advantages and disadvantages are summarised in Figure 7.3.

SUPPLIER REPLICATION COST

The supplier replication cost approach assumes that the value of the technology to the customer is equal to the full cost to the supplier of developing the technology. This will be the case if there are several suppliers of technology. Such technologies are usually base technologies, but can also include key technologies at the component or sub-assembly level. For example, a customer looking for a new type of sensor will be able to get quotations from several contract R&D companies, all of whom will quote on the basis of what it will cost them to develop the technology, plus a profit margin. If you are supplying a sensor you have already

Valuation Approach	When Appropriate	Advantages	Disadvantages
Supplier replication cost	Base technologies Peripheral key technologies (e.g. components)	Simple to assess	Doesn't add value for supplier expertise Doesn't include risk premium
Customer replication cost	Base and key technologies	Relatively simple to assess Includes costs of risk-taking and value of in-house expertise	Doesn't attribute value to knowledge that technology is proven
Future value	All technologies and particularly when customer takes risk on the technology	Values the 'comfort' factor of proven technology	Difficult to estimate
Time dependent future value	All technologies when time is critical factor	Helps supplier recover a time premium	Very difficult to estimate Risk of over pricing

FIGURE 7.3   Alternative Valuation Approaches
Source: Arthur D. Little

developed for yourself, the maximum you will be able to charge will also equal the development cost plus profit margin. This valuation approach has the advantage of simplicity; knowing the cost of development of the technology, the supplier should be able to give a reasonably accurate figure quite quickly. The disadvantage is that it attributes no value to the fact that, with the technology in place, the supplier can deliver technology to the customer with less risk. For some commodity technology developments, like the sensors described above, the risks are well known and so minimising risk does not equate to increasing value. For other technologies, however, such as chemical and metallurgical process technologies, risk becomes more important, and the lack of it should attract value. The simplest way to estimate the value of risk is to calculate the customer replication cost.

CUSTOMER REPLICATION COST

Customer replication cost is what it would cost the customer to develop the technology. The figure is likely to be higher than the supplier replication cost because the customer will need to build up experience and will inevitably follow a sub-optimal development process. In short, the customer will have to devote effort on the presumption that some development avenues will turn into blind alleys. Calculating the customer replication cost accurately will be difficult, since the inevitable risk will generate uncertainty. Nonetheless, as for any real development project, it should be possible to budget for the effort likely to be needed.

With this approach, the supplier receives some recompense for having taken the initial risks. The approach is therefore appropriate not only for base technologies, but also for key technologies that carry higher development risks. This valuation approach presents a problem, however, in that it still compensates only for the costs of risk-taking, not for the value to the customer of knowing that a technology is proven. For technologies whose application involves high capital investment, or which carry a high consequential cost, knowing that the technology will work from the outset can be very valuable. An automotive company planning to introduce a key component, for example, will pay a premium for the comfort of knowing that the component will work, reducing the risk that the product will fail. In such circumstances, the future value valuation approach is appropriate.

FUTURE VALUE

Basing valuation on the value of the technology to the *customer* provides scope for attributing value to risk factors. However, estimating this value presents problems. A glass producing company like Pilkington or St Gobain, planning to enter the glass-ceramic sheet market, will willingly pay a premium to Schott, the German glass and ceramics firm, for access to technology know-how, rather than develop it from scratch. Glass-ceramic production is notoriously difficult, and the capital investment is large. Although Pilkington is undoubtedly capable of developing the technology and putting it into production, access to Schott's world-leading experience and know-how would dramatically reduce the risks.

To place a value on the premium the company would be willing to pay, you need to develop optimistic and pessimistic scenarios for in-house technology development and take a view on how far access to proven technology will shift the scenarios. Developing and comparing net present values is complex and of questionable accuracy. At best it will provide a rough baseline for negotiations, but no more precise approach is available.

TIME DEPENDENT FUTURE VALUE

The previous two approaches assess the effect of time on value in general terms as an element of the risk factor. The last of the possible valuation approaches introduces the time dimension explicitly. On occasion, time is the overriding factor, as, for example, for the water authority that needs a sludge treatment technology by a set date to comply with EC anti-pollution laws. Legislation is at one end of the spectrum of time dependency, where the supplier of the technology can charge a very high premium for a distress purchase. The authority has no option but to spend whatever is needed. More common are businesses that need technologies to fend off competitive threats, launch new products or enter new markets. In all cases, the window of opportunity may be narrow and businesses will pay a premium to move quickly. The decision to act is, however, voluntary and businesses will not pay premiums that are so great as to make the project unprofitable. Where they draw the line, and what premium they are willing to pay, depends on the importance of the project to the business and on how many suppliers there are.

These approaches are all related to the value of the technology to the customer rather than the cost to the supplier. The differences in approach reflect the differences in perceived customer value. For some, the value is equal to the costs of developing the technology. For others, the value is increased by other factors, for example, if the technology is unique, has proved successful or is not available elsewhere.

The approach you adopt depends on the relative importance of these factors to your company. Usually it is best to try most, if not all, the different approaches and then agree on the one you want to apply, taking account of the strategic environment within which you are making the buying or selling decision. It is important to recognise that, as for any other technology investment, the value of the investment by the customer should also take account of the impact on future products and future business as well as the immediate short term benefit.

The approaches described above are intended to provide a guide to obtaining an initial value for use as a baseline negotiating position. Since technology is inherently an intangible asset, it is inevitable that the final price will be agreed more by negotiation rather than predetermined analysis.

8

STRUCTURING TECHNOLOGY ACTIVITIES

S
O far, this book has concentrated on the strategic aspects of managing technology: identifying strategically important technologies, tracking long term trends, and placing technology buying and selling decisions in a strategic context. However, deciding what to do is only the start. Organising the business to get the results you want is at least as important. So the following chapters address the management of technology activities: *how* to achieve the *what*.

O   This chapter discusses how to organise corporate and business unit activities.

O   Chapter 9 then explores ways of integrating technology with other aspects of the business, examining, in particular, the need to make sure that technologists and engineers work more closely with other business functions.

O   Chapter 10 looks at the problem of measurement of technology and innovation, and outlines possible solutions.

O   Chapter 11 tackles the difficult question of justifying technology investment to shareholders, reconciling the need for long term strategic technology competence with the pressure for short term performance.

Countless management books cover organisational and managerial theories in depth. These four chapters, however, concentrate on issues concerned specifically with managing technology and innovation, which is less straightforward than managing other functional disciplines and so merits separate consideration. *Third Generation R&D*, a previous book by Arthur D. Little (Ref. 8.1), explores some of the topics discussed here in more depth, focusing more on the research aspects of technology management.

This chapter addresses the three critical elements of organisational structure that corporate management should address:

○   Management roles and responsibilities, particularly at the corporate level

○   The structure of technology development activities, particularly those that cross business units or divisions

○   Funding and related monitoring processes.

Deciding how to organise technology, and its linkages to the rest of the business, to maximise corporate innovation is a complex task, requiring analysis, multi-functional input and management judgement.

Small- and medium-sized enterprises need little formal structure for technology activities. The chief executive can take responsibility for all technology issues, balancing business needs with resource availability. In slightly larger companies, the board of directors can play the same role, agreeing in informal discussion on the actions required, and delegating detailed decisions and actions to the technical director. However, as companies grow, the informal approach breaks down. Most businesses with more than 100 employees, more than one big subsidiary, or a turnover of more than £10 million need a more formal structure. In the largest global businesses, like Unilever, Siemens or Ford, formal structures and control mechanisms become indispensable.

This chapter is aimed at the larger corporations requiring complex formal structures. For smaller companies, the principles remain the same, but elements of the structure and process should be collapsed and merged.

The first part of this chapter looks at managerial roles. Many businesses have created the role of chief technology officer (CTO), to ensure that technology and innovation receive top management attention. To decide whether your company needs a CTO, and what he or she should do, you need to explore the roles that CTOs play, and how these roles fit with semi-autonomous business units in large corporations.

The chapter goes on to cover the merits and disadvantages of different approaches to structuring technology functions, and in particular addresses how to decide between the critical mass of a corporate function and the responsiveness of decentralisation. Guidelines are suggested for each link in the chain from long term strategic research to operational technical support.

Internationalisation is the next issue discussed. As many corporations are discovering, international technology management can yield many synergies, but brings problems of language, distance, cultural difference and politics.

The last question is one of funding, deciding if corporate R&D funding has a role, and identify how best to ensure that those responsible for funding decisions are made accountable for the outputs.

MANAGEMENT ROLES

In most functional hierarchies, the management of technology is the responsibility of a functional technical director. Technology is rarely recognised as a business activity in its own right; instead the technical director is responsible for the R&D group, the product development group, and the manufacturing engineering group. Procurement is sometimes included where procurement decisions have a strong technology element. QA, environmental management, and standards compliance may also be allocated to the technical director, ostensibly for the same reason, but often because there is nowhere else to put them. This traditional approach has the advantage of giving all technology related activities to the same functional head, but it does have three major drawbacks.

First, as in all such structures, inefficiency is built in to business processes that cross the functional divide. Development projects become like batons in a relay race, with each department doing its bit before passing the project on. This practice runs counter to the current emphasis on multi-functional team working and simultaneous engineering. Consequently, most firms are moving towards a matrix management model, managing cross-functional business activities, such as product development, as processes. Product managers, therefore, often take full cradle to grave responsibility for the design, development and production of specific product ranges. The functional director then takes responsibility only for recruitment, pay and resource allocation, as well as becoming the arbiter on functional decisions. In consequence, the functional head of technology may become little more than a figurehead, reactive rather than setting strategic direction.

The second drawback is that stressing the functional aspects of the job takes the spotlight off technology strategy. The job is defined as managing the R&D and product development departments rather than as managing the use of technology in the business, with all the wider strategic and sourcing issues that implies.

The third, and perhaps most serious, drawback is that functional structures imply functional responsibilities. Consequently, marketing, manufacturing and sales directors will all see technology as outside their interest and influence. Pigeon-holing functions breeds inefficiency and exacerbates the effects of the lack of a strategic technology overview.

In small companies, these drawbacks can be overcome. Close, informal collaboration between senior managers can ensure that technology has high priority on the management agenda. For example, in a volume engineering components business with a turnover of £120 million, the operational board manages the application of technology by discussing technical issues at the end of every fortnightly meeting. The board – the chief executive and the finance, operations, manufacturing and technical directors – discuss new product requirements, R&D and manufacturing capital investment and agree informally on decisions and trade-offs. In larger companies, and particularly in multi-business unit or multi-divisional corporations, the drawbacks of a functional approach to tech-nology management increase, with the risk of inappropriate resource allocation, lack of strategic direction, and inefficient product development processes. More formalised communication and authority are essential.

The best solutions to these problems are based on the 'chief officer' model. Many diversified corporations now have a board that comprises a chief executive officer, a chief operations officer and a chief financial officer or financial controller. The operations officer is the de facto managing director, responsible for running the corporation day to day: divisional and SBU managing directors, reporting to him or her, are responsible for delivering profit and cash to target budgets. The CEO takes the strategic role, planning growth and / or divestment. The financial controller's role is self-evident. Other functional senior managers report to the appropriate chief officer. This structure concentrates attention on the business essentials: strategy, operations and finance, rather than on specific functions, making it more likely that board members will spend time on business issues rather than on functional squabbles.

However, functional issues may not then receive enough attention. In particular, the main board may neglect functional issues that cut across group businesses, since the chief operations officer will be pressing the operating units to run as autonomous businesses. To avoid this problem, some corporations introduce a CTO, to elevate the importance of techno-logy and innovation and increase inter-business technology and product development support.

Since technology is no more critical to a business than marketing or manufacturing, you could argue that firms should also create chief marketing officers and chief manufacturing officers. The effect would then be to return to a board representing the traditional functional hierarchy. But the reasoning does not stand up. Technology and innovation are the lifeblood of a manufacturing company. Corporations gain immense syner-gies from rolling critical technology competences out to their subsidiaries.

For evidence, look at Sony and the product innovation it has driven across its subsidiaries, building on its competence in miniaturisation. Honda's high-speed internal combustion engines and Rolls Royce's turbine blade technologies are other examples. Multi-divisional companies dependent on technology core competences undoubtedly benefit from introducing a CTO. In contrast, other functions rarely number among the core competences of the business. Marketing is business specific, and within an agreed overall strategy, best dealt with locally. Marketing synergies between businesses, and opportunities for sharing marketing development, can be exploited as they occur. Manufacturing, similarly, is usually business specific; in most businesses, opportunities for synergies can be dealt with ad hoc. There are exceptions, of course. Mature, process-intensive industries such as steel, base chemicals and paper may well consider their manufacturing skills their core competence. For them the role of chief manufacturing officer will be key.

If technology underpins the core competences of your business, however, as argued in Chapter 2, the board needs to be heavily involved in technology decisions. For that reason, you will need a CTO, or at the very least, acceptance by the board that someone at board level will play the CTO role.

THE ROLE OF THE CHIEF TECHNOLOGY OFFICER

What should the role of CTO comprise? A survey of 25 CTOs in the US by Adler and Ferdows (Ref. 8.2) identified five principal activities:

O   Coordinating the technology efforts of business units
O   Representing technology at top management level
O   Supervising new technology developments
O   Assessing the technological aspects of strategic initiatives
O   Managing linkages to the external technology environment.

To these roles, some firms add the hands-on management of corporate R&D laboratories and of technology-based new businesses.

Most of the roles listed above are, understandably, reactive since in many diversified corporations, local autonomy in the business units or divisions is sacrosanct and local managers will fight hard to keep the freedom to manage without corporate interference. However, without corporate checks and balances, local autonomy can be dangerous. Three examples make the point. Consider:

O   The small subsidiary of a large electronics group that sold a critical piece of manufacturing technology to the main competitor of the group's largest subsidiary

O   The middle-sized UK mechanical engineering group that spread its R&D funding across ten universities via separate subsidiaries instead of coordinating and focusing resources to increase the likelihood of success

O   The two divisions of a laser products business that pursued diametrically opposite research directions – neither had adequate resources and between them they lost technology leadership to a competitor.

To prevent such inefficiencies and errors, and to implement some of the ideas outlined in earlier chapters, the CTO must take a more active role, setting the strategic direction and persuading the local managers to follow it.

Building on Adler's list, the five activities for the CTO can be adapted and then extended to give seven key roles:

O   Determining technology strategy
O   Creating R&D plans
O   Coordinating strategies across and between divisions and business units
O   Taking responsibility as functional head for the SBU technology development managers
O   Controlling sales and licensing of technology
O   Providing technology advice to the board
O   Supporting new technology-based businesses.

DETERMINING TECHNOLOGY STRATEGY

The responsibility for creating a technology strategy for the business must rest with the CTO as chief scientist. The main task is to coordinate the technology strategies of the divisions or SBUs and their requirements for research and underlying technology development. The output will be a written strategy for the next two to ten years covering:

O   Principal technologies
O   Enabling technologies that need to be developed as a priority
O   Core product or component modules that need development
O   Priorities for action and allocation of responsibilities.

The CTO will need to develop the strategy in discussion with research group leaders and business managers, and communicate it throughout the corporation. As this task is likely to prove time-consuming, having a technology planning manager report to the CTO may be desirable. That person's task will be to supervise and control the efforts of a group of technology planning officers. In smaller companies, a single technology manager, or an informal group of other functional managers, may be able to undertake the work, without drowning in bureaucracy. If the company has tens of thousands of employees in sites around the world, a technology planning group may be the only sensible route forward. The challenge is then to keep the group small and focused, and to stop it becoming an irrelevant staff function.

CREATING R&D PLANS

With the strategy clear, the CTO has a clear role in planning and coordinating the research and development activities needed to deliver it:

O   Deciding which inter-disciplinary research topics are worth pursuing
O   Specifying boundaries and objectives for long term research
O   Specifying which work should fall to divisional R&D and which to corporate research
O   Coordinating divisional requirements to gain commonality and eliminate duplication
O   Controlling and coordinating divisional research funding
O   Ensuring that the R&D portfolio balances risk and return over specified periods
O   Deciding on funding of research outside the company – e.g. through universities and contract R&D laboratories
O   Planning and implementing corporate ventures to acquire access to new technologies and products.

To achieve these objectives, the CTO needs considerable power. A little can be formally vested in the role, but he or she will need to persuade people in autonomous subsidiaries what to do, rather than order them to do it. The role is one requiring credibility in the boardroom and the laboratory, and strong skills in influencing others. There is, however, one way to strengthen the CTO's role, and that is to modify the mechanisms by which innovation is funded, as suggested at the end of this chapter.

COORDINATING STRATEGIES

For obvious reasons, business and technology strategies need to be coordinated across the corporation:

O   To ensure that there are no gaps between business unit and divisional boundaries
O   To ensure that technology decisions made in developing a product in one business area (e.g. a commercial optical storage device) do not present barriers to the development of related products elsewhere (e.g. a domestic computer data drive)

O   To manage the distribution of the output from a piece of research to the business areas that need it.

In essence, the purpose of this role is to exploit operational and strategic technology synergies within the company. Operationally, know-how synergies may develop from shared applications or manufacturing experience. These operational benefits can only arise informally, since formal networks often fail to meet erratic but frequent information needs. The CTO's role here is to encourage cooperation, taking an active role only when necessary. Strategic technology synergies are the direct responsibility of the CTO and include benefits of scale from shared use of resources, and benefits of scope from greater understanding of application issues.

To help realise the synergies, the CTO needs to perform a balancing act. Coordination may well maximise technology synergy, but it can increase the time it takes to develop products, or result in technologies that meet everyone's requirements in part and no one's in full. Maintaining the balance is particularly important in multi-national companies, where the drive for standardised products may lead to neglect of local market requirements. For example, developing a new low emissions burner technology to German environmental standards and selling it worldwide may seem sensible, but different regulations may mean that the product is over-specified, and possibly over-priced, in some markets. The balance is also important in vertically integrated companies in which components companies supply both in-house and out. Reconciling market and technology needs here is problematic, especially if the corporate financial structure encourages autonomy rather than close working relationships. Standardisation and coordination are fine objectives. Compromise will always be necessary, however, to allow business units to grow their businesses in the way they want.

ACTING AS FUNCTIONAL HEAD

Part of the CTO's role as chief scientist is to be head of the technology function. The functional role gives the CTO the authority to supervise and coordinate the corporation's technology activities. Usually the CTO will have a dotted line responsibility for all technology development so that he or she can monitor progress in the subsidiaries, liaising with local operating management on decisions. The functional role is also important in maintaining technical standards across the corporation, and coordinating technical training and development of staff. Again, the skill is to get the balance right. Centralising may save costs and ensure that the corporation collects the maximum amount of information, but all the information will be at a distance from those who need it. Strong cross-linkages, both formal and informal, are needed to ensure that the right people receive the information they need. We discuss way of providing these links in the next chapter.

CONTROLLING SALES AND LICENSING

Technology sales have a direct impact on competitive position as discussed in Chapter 7. Only the corporate board will have a broad enough grasp of strategic issues to decide which technologies have strategic value and which do not. The CTO is therefore the logical point of responsibility and accountability for technology sales and licensing.

PROVIDING TECHNOLOGY ADVICE

The boards of larger corporations often need a centralised point of contact for technology knowledge and expertise to provide advice and guide decision-making. This central group should be able to:

O   Advise on sources of technology
O   Provide technology forecasts
O   Monitor external threats and opportunities
O   Keep in touch with competitors' activities.

The group does not have to lie directly under the control of the CTO, but if it is to do the job properly, he or she must have unrestricted access to it. The CTO can then communicate knowledge both to the board and down to the businesses.

SUPPORTING NEW BUSINESSES

In large diversified firms, corporate management often maintains control of business units by applying the same financial and non-financial performance measures to each. Even with hundreds of subsidiaries, corporate managers can then monitor progress and identify problems quickly. An unfortunate consequence of this approach is that it tends to imply that mature businesses perform better than emerging businesses as they score more highly on short term financial measures. The emerging business may have long term potential, but what shows up is the short term costs. For companies such as Hanson, whose policy is to manage mature cash generating businesses tightly, this method of control is a reasonable line to take. Critics of other conglomerates, such as GEC, argue that such strict financial control can kill emerging technology businesses before they have a chance to become profitable, and so stunt organic growth.

For many corporations, this is a real concern. Without investment in innovation and corporate renewal, including the development of new technologies, products and services, businesses will ultimately decline.

One solution is for the CTO to take responsibility for providing a protected environment for new businesses – a 'nursery ground' – as discussed in the next part of this chapter. The CTO can provide hands-on executive management, linking the commercial and technical aspects of the business, and adapting the financial controls to the needs of the developing businesses.

ORGANISATIONAL STRUCTURE

In a product manufacturing business, technology moves along an R&D chain from strategic research to product support. Not all product manufacture and support needs strategic research, and not all strategic research results in new products, but all the links of the chain are likely to exist in most large companies in some form. For all but a handful of corporations, fundamental or long term research is too esoteric to merit in-house effort, and is best left to universities. The chain therefore has five main link parameters, as shown in Figure 8.1.

Parameter	Strategic Research	Technology Projects	Product Development	Product Manufacture	Technical Support
Objective	Knowledge	Proof of Idea	Product	Sales	Production
Time scales	Long	Medium	Short	Immediate	Short
Business Unit Relevance	Low	Medium	High	Very high	High
Certainty of outcome	Low	Medium	High	Very high	High

FIGURE 8.1   The R&D Chain
Source: Arthur D. Little

The activity undertaken within each link has different objectives, timescales and, by implication, risks and returns. However, the boundaries between the links are often blurred and indistinct. Research begins in an unstructured way, crystallising gradually into structured work and then into a firm project, gaining support from business units as its commercial relevance becomes apparent. Exploratory work on the emulsification behaviour of edible oils, for example, might lead to a structured examination of the spreadability of dairy spreads at different temperatures and then to a technology project on achieving a spreadable dairy spread with a specific set of consumer properties.

Despite the somewhat arbitrary boundaries between the links in the chain, the activities within each link are different and should be managed differently. What then is the best way to organise the activities at each stage? Where should managerial responsibility lie, and where, physically, should the activities take place?

Figure 8.2 shows a range of organisational options from full centralisation to full decentralisation. Most companies use a blend of these structures, depending on the technology synergies to be gained between divisions and business units, the timeframe of the R&D, and the need for

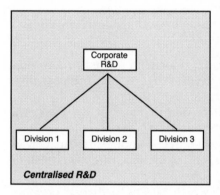

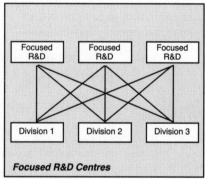

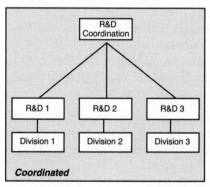

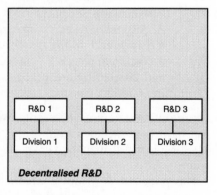

FIGURE 8.2   R&D Organisational Options
Source: Arthur D. Little

market responsiveness. Since these three factors vary together along the chain, the choice of structure often depends on the activities concerned. The structures appropriate for each of the five key activities in the R&D chain are discussed below.

STRATEGIC RESEARCH

Strategic research is research intended to reinforce the technology competence of the business and support strategic direction. It is not product specific, nor even undertaken with any particular product in mind: examples are the development of fluid flow modelling techniques by a heat exchanger business, the analysis of organic molecular structures and the development of fuzzy logic algorithms. By implication, most if not all such research should take place under corporate managerial control. *Where* it is undertaken will depend on many factors, including the need for a critical mass of skills, the commonality or diversity of business unit technologies, and the availability of key people.

The range of organisational structures and associated management and operational approaches includes:

O   A stand-alone corporate research laboratory, funded by a corporate overhead charge or by direct charge to the business divisions

O   A corporate facility attached to one or more of the divisional laboratories

O   Centres of excellence – decentralised corporate research, with groups of corporate researchers co-located with divisional or business unit development groups

O   A joint venture long term research facility, with one or more customers or suppliers

O   A corporate research management group, subcontracting long term research to the divisional laboratories

O   A corporate research management group, subcontracting work to and purchasing technologies from external organisations, including contract research organisations and universities.

These options are not necessarily exclusive. Some companies, for example, have twin facilities, with an applied research site beside an existing laboratory, and a small, university-based, fundamental theoretical research unit.

The principal decision is whether to decentralise. In the past, many large companies ran centralised corporate research laboratories set in rural splendour, to provide an attractive environment for creative thinking. This approach guarantees a critical mass of specialist skills, working towards one goal. The disadvantage is that most rural laboratories are a long way from the businesses and their needs, and their environment and culture decouple them from strategic thinking. As a consequence, creativity may be high but commercial applicability is likely to be low.

Decentralisation, with strategic research carried out in the divisional or business unit development groups, ensures closer linkage to the businesses, but risks loss of focus and of critical mass. It has two further disadvantages. First, the strategic researchers will be in a small minority within the development group, under strong peer pressure to work on short term projects with measurable results. Second, isolation from other researchers is likely to hinder creativity, discouraging blue sky ideas. Despite the disadvantages, most European companies, tired of seeing little or no return on their investment in corporate research, have taken R&D closer to the market. Interestingly, some of the larger Japanese companies, including Toshiba, are moving in the opposite direction, setting up small, focused corporate research centres close to universities, well away from the day-to-day business. They believe that critical mass and focus more than compensate for the disadvantages of the ivory tower. As yet, there is no convincing evidence to support their view.

In any event, improvements in information and communications technology are making the critical mass and creativity arguments less relevant. Five specialists working in five sites around Europe can network informally almost as well as five specialists on a single site, provided that they know each other well and are not blinkered by local company prejudice. Nowadays, the arguments are about how to measure the researchers' performance, not where to put them. Decentralised but coordinated strategic research, with enough corporate muscle to resist local pressure to switch to short term activities, appears to be the most promising model.

TECHNOLOGY PROJECTS

Technology projects are essentially proof-of-concept type activities, intended to provide a robust foundation for a commercial business. In an ideal world, business units should drive these projects in their search for activities to regenerate their business. However, short term financial pressures make many business units reluctant to invest in longer term, higher risk R&D. One solution is to introduce a nursery ground for projects that:

O   Lie outside the scope of existing business units
O   Need more resources and management attention for longer than any one unit can provide
O   Have applications across several business units.

Ideally, the role of the nursery ground should be to facilitate the early development of new products, provide a critical mass of technology skills, champion development projects until a business unit adopts them, and pioneer technologies beyond the scope of the business units. To do these things, the nursery ground needs both to provide a development laboratory and to supply the necessary functions to develop new products and businesses.

Its precise role will depend on the degree to which business units are willing to be involve in advanced product development:

O   *Willing and able to assist:* The nursery ground is responsible for product development to the working prototype stage, and then transfers the project to the business unit.

O   *Willing to assist, but only as spare capacity:* The nursery ground is responsible for product development, product engineering and first series production and marketing and only then transfers the product to the business unit.

O   *No involvement:* The nursery ground takes full product and business development responsibility.

The nursery ground can stand alone, usually as a development laboratory at divisional or corporate level and often under the management of the CTO. The Advanced Development Centre of Philips Consumer Electronics Division is an example. As for strategic research, the arguments for a separate centre are based on the trade-off between critical mass and closeness to market. The outcome is a little different, however, since technology projects are intended to lead to viable business activities. The ivory tower approach can hinder the transfer of projects into the businesses. Researchers may be reluctant to hand over projects because they want to keep busy on familiar work, or because they fear that business units will change the scope of the project, stop it, or take credit for its success. For their part, people in the business units may be unwilling to take on the project because of their short term focus. They may lack the resources for major new product development, or have other priorities. Even if the two groups agree to the transfer, the change of project manager can lead to discontinuity. Researchers may be reluctant to stay involved, seeing downstream activities as less interesting than their own. Other barriers to close joint working on project transfers are perceived differences in labour cost rates, lack of a transfer pricing mechanism for know-how, and different computer design tools. The result may be long delays during the transfer process, while barriers are overcome and compromises negotiated.

If you are faced by these problems, there are two steps you can take to overcome them. First choose high level project managers, and give them visible top management support. This sends a very clear message that projects are important, that you want them to succeed, and that if there is any dispute, the balance of power is clearly tilted towards the project managers. Second, you can make business unit product managers accountable for allocating priorities and projects and managing the process of aligning projects with changing market needs. This creates the necessary business and marketing pull on the project, and forces the business units to take an active interest.

PRODUCT DEVELOPMENT

The objective of the product development link in the R&D chain is to deliver a manufacturable product to a well specified design brief by a given deadline. There is little debate here about how to organise the activities. The need for close collaboration with marketing dictates that product development must be under the managerial control of the operating businesses, either in the business units or in the divisions. Current best practice is to identify a dedicated team leader, who reports to business unit or divisional management and controls a multi-functional team. The team leader's job is to agree on the product specification with the internal customer for the product, usually the product marketing group, and then to ensure the product is delivered to specification, cost and time. The team leader then retains some responsibility through the product launch and for the first few months of production, so that early production teething troubles can be resolved quickly and without internal argument. To ensure the product development process remains on track, it is usually divided into a series of well defined stages, separated by key milestone review points or gates. Selected divisional managers, often joined by the CTO, act as the gate keepers, reviewing progress and allowing continuation to the next stage. *Product Juggernauts* (Ref. 8.3) and other published material by Arthur D. Little provide more detailed descriptions of the organisation and management of product development (Refs. 8.4 and 8.5).

The development of key components, used in the products of more than one business unit, is often organised differently. Examples of such components include transmissions for heavy trucks, electric motors for domestic appliances and concentrates for food and drink. Centralising the development of key components at a single point in the corporation prevents duplication of effort, increases competitor awareness and improves longer term planning. Indeed, moving the development and manufacturing of key components into stand-alone businesses and allowing the businesses to sell to both external and internal markets is a way of realising scale economies and encouraging competitiveness. Many companies adopt this approach. For example, JCB, the UK based earth moving equipment company, has set up JCB Transmissions, which sells axles, differentials, and gearboxes both to JCB Excavators and to other construction equipment companies such as Komatsu and Caterpillar. Although this stand-alone approach works well, it can create tensions:

O   If its prime role is to serve the business units, the components company will not be able to compete effectively in the open market. The business units will always take priority, receiving preferential treatment in product development. In the extreme, the components business will be forced to devote valuable resources to developing products which are not saleable on the open market. Even if products do have open market potential, the business units may want to limit the sale of state-of-the-art products to OEM customers, to prevent potential weakening of their competitive position.

O   If its main role is as a corporate repository for key technologies, the components company may not be able to make enough profit to satisfy corporate financial targets. Long term development is rarely compatible with short term profit focus. In such cases, it must be clear that the objective is to develop and secure strategic technologies. Non-strategic technologies, even those embedded in some key components, should therefore not be included in the component company, but should be either outsourced or left in the business units.

Moreover, creating a component company can lead to technology push on the business units, while the strategy of the business units is likely to be based on market pull. The right approach to key components will depend on the trade-off between the competitive impact of the component technologies and the commercial value of selling components to external markets. As discussed in the previous chapter, current key and pacing technologies need to be kept in-house by and large, with external sales carefully controlled. Base technologies or previous generation key technologies can be sold to external markets.

PRODUCT MANUFACTURE

In most cases the business units responsible for the products should be responsible for manufacturing, to tie production to market needs. Within this framework, several variations are possible. For example, as discussed above, key components may be manufactured by a stand-alone business unit that sells to other business units on an arm's length trading basis.

Also, in multi-national corporations, businesses often split development and production from marketing and sales, managing the first two as a dedicated business unit and the others geographically. These variations do not affect the argument that production should be linked to the business unit responsible for the market.

TECHNICAL SUPPORT

The location of technical support for manufacture is contentious. In many companies, a central engineering services group performs the role. However, this arrangement is under question, since organisational barriers between central engineering services and their customers can make team working difficult. Consequently, fixed assets costs are not optimised, and lead times are too long. With ever increasing cost pressures, having a large central engineering service group can be an unacceptably expensive way of ensuring security of supply, confidentiality, and organisational learning. Understandably, many companies are seeking other solutions.

One option is to centralise the small groups that provide specialist services needed by different parts of the business that do not belong obviously to any one part. Companies that have to run vast process and infrastructure projects may need to organise project managers and owners' representatives centrally to build experience. In DSM, the Dutch chemicals company, for example, the central engineering division builds know-how in core engineering and supports procurement with contractor selection and management. BP retains a small central shared resource under the control of the company's operating divisions, to provide the services that all the divisions need. These include project management, since BP has to manage the risks on large oil, gas and chemicals projects, often as a member of a consortium. Similarly, other companies centralise safety-related engineering activities to ensure independence from the businesses they audit.

A second option is to disperse the central engineering group across the business units. This works best in companies where the divisions or business units have different requirements and little need to share specialist skills. Decentralisation has always worked well for plant engineering and maintenance functions, where a close working knowledge of the plant is more important than critical mass. Managers favour dispersion because it puts engineering firmly within the control of the business and facilitates the transfer of expertise to the business. Henkel, one of the larger German chemical producers, set up a small engineering department within each division, supported by a business process oriented, central engineering department with project management and specialist engineering skills. Companies in other industries have done the same. Jaguar, for example, found that moving to decentralised engineering services stimulated local innovation and improved ways of working. Other variations on decentralisation also work well. Some companies, for example, have set up centres of excellence, under the control of the business unit that makes best use of their skills, but tasked with serving the whole company.

A third option is to separate the central engineering group from the business units and create an independent business serving both internal and external customers. The new engineering organisation then stands or falls on the competitiveness of the services it provides. In most cases, the business may still be owned by the parent (although it need not be), but competes for business outside as well as in. As discussed in the previous chapter, Courtaulds' central engineering department is now Courtaulds Engineering Limited (CEL), an independent business that serves both Courtaulds and external customers. Group companies do not have to use CEL, but it wins most of the big projects in competition with external contractors. Group companies have a more competitive supplier, and now that CEL gains the bulk of its sales from external customers, it can contribute profits to the group. Lucas and ICI are two other examples of companies which have taken this approach.

Competing externally stimulates performance. It also enables the service provider to learn from the market, and to manage peaks in demand by balancing the workload. Contributing additional profits to the group is a secondary objective in most cases. This form of decentralisation works best when internal customers have similar needs to external customers, and when a critical mass of engineering skills is needed to provide the services. It also works when engineering resources are surplus to internal customer needs, or when external business can help fill the gaps between peaks in demand from internal customers. However, it can take a long time to reap the potential benefits of creating an independent engineering services company. CEL, one of the most successful examples of this form of organisation, was set up about 30 years ago.

Furthermore, changing to a more arm's length commercial relationship with internal customers can create tensions. For example, the independent engineering business has to ensure that the internal customer will pay compensation for changes in project scope. Before, as an internal department, it may have been more flexible. Conflicts may also arise over priorities between the internal customers and external ones, who may well be competitors. As one manager said: 'You have to treat the Group like any other customer, but it takes a long time to shake out old habits'. Internal customers often find their loss of preferred status difficult to accept. They will have to appoint representatives to manage the new arm's length relationship with their engineering services suppliers, as their interests will differ from those of the supplier. Likewise, the new engineering business will not enjoy competing for internal work. It will also have to develop new commercial skills to serve the external market. Longer term, if the engineering services business establishes itself as an external consultant for contracting work, its profitability, its need for capital and its risk profile may conflict with those of the parent. If so, engineering services may have to be floated off as a separate company.

A fourth option for enhancing the central engineering group is to create a joint venture. This not only offers a faster route for setting engineering up as an independent business, but also makes it clear to the internal customers that the relationship must now be on a formal, contractual basis. Several companies have taken this route, creating independent engineering subsidiaries by forming joint ventures with partners that have complementary skills. Yorkshire Water, for example, merged its engineering division with Babcock's international process plant contracting arm to form Babcock Water Engineering Limited (BWEL). United Utilities went one step further, selling its North West Water Engineering business to Bechtel as part of an alliance to develop international business. Complete sale rather than joint venture does not resolve the conflict issue, but it does make it explicit. United Utilities knows that Bechtel will be looking to profit from its supply of design and build services, and Bechtel knows that United Utilities could use another supplier if dissatisfied. The relationship will work only if there is trust on both sides. Otherwise, United Utilities will need to rebuild its in-house function to make it an informal specifier and purchaser, which defeats the objective of selling in the first place.

In deciding how to manage your central engineering and technical support functions, choose the option that best meets your specific needs, assessing the advantages and disadvantages of each option in the context of your business. There is no one formula for success.

THE TREND TOWARDS DEVOLUTION

Overall, the trend is towards devolving technology development activities to business units or divisions. For many short term product development and technical support activities, devolution is a logical step: the only decision to make is on how much corporate managerial control or coordination is compatible with operational autonomy. However, devolution of longer term research and technology development can be problematic. These activities can have an impact on the business as a whole, both because they offer the potential to add value across the business and because they are often high cost and need specialist resources. These activities need greater corporate involvement; in the extreme, they may need to be managed in a corporately funded central research laboratory. Central research laboratories are anathema to the chief executives of most modern corporations, who believe that lower corporate overheads and more business unit autonomy lead to a more flexible, profitable business. However, the goal of the chief executive is not just to generate profits but to create a sustainable business. These twin objectives require a broader corporate responsibility for technology. As Figure 8.3 suggests, your views on the strategic importance of technology to the business and on the technology strategy you need will dictate how you organise the management of technology.

THE INTERNATIONAL DIMENSION

The degree to which you need to adapt your organisation to address the international dimension will depend on your strategic objectives. For example, focusing on cost reduction will put the emphasis on eliminating duplication of development resources, and achieving manufacturing economies of scale by designing internationally standardised products. An automotive component supplier, operating in a mature industry, is minimising its development and manufacturing costs by designing common products. As one of its divisional R&D managers said, 'A good engineering design is the same the world over'. Where there are differences between markets, you can increase manufacturing efficiency by developing standard product platforms, adaptable to local customer needs. If, however, the goal is product performance leadership, then you will need an organisation that encourages a free exchange of ideas, skills and information between development and technology centres; you will also need to consolidate development efforts in critical technologies that may require significant investments. Once you have clarified your objectives for an international development organisation, you need to decide what changes you will have to make to the structure you already have.

MATCHING STRUCTURE TO STRATEGY

Possible structures vary by degree of geographic centralisation and by level of technology interaction across sites (Figure 8.4).

○   A national product centre develops most or all of the company's product range required in its local market.

○   A focused product centre concentrates on only one product type and develops the variations that may be required to cover the whole international market.

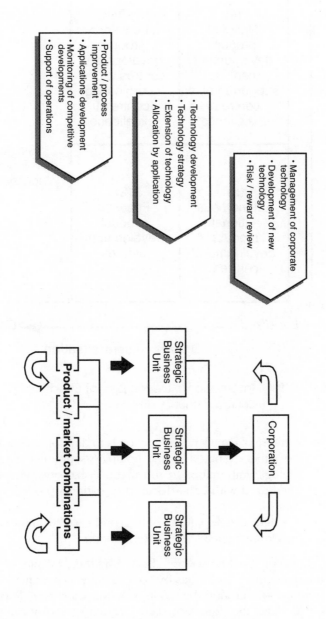

FIGURE 8.3   Responsibilities for Technology Management
Source: Arthur D. Little

Within the figure:

- Product / process improvement
- Applications development
- Monitoring of competitive developments
- Support of operations

- Technology development
- Technology strategy
- Extension of technology
- Allocation by application

- Management of corporate technology
- Development of new technology
- Risk / reward review

Product / market combinations

Strategic Business Unit
Strategic Business Unit
Strategic Business Unit

Corporation

173

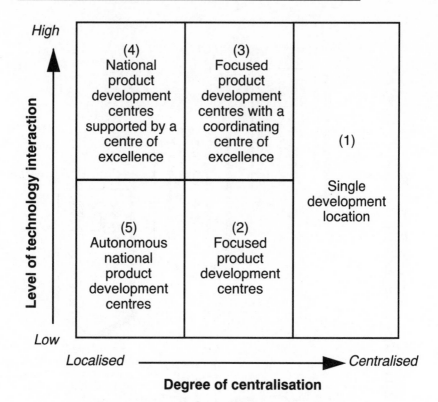

FIGURE 8.4   International Development Structures
Source: Arthur D. Little

O   A centre of excellence's function is to develop technologies which are either common to the company's product range or are of strategic importance to the international organisation. They are often used with either focused or national product development centres.

O   A single development centre conducts the entire international development activities in one location.

Your choice of structure will be affected by the dynamics of the markets you are operating in as well as by your strategy. If your market is more or less homogenous around the world, you will want a single centre. If one market provides the dominant share of your company's revenues, your choice will be the same. At the other extreme, if your national markets are highly differentiated you will want to maintain national product centres, possibly with a supporting global or regional centre of excellence to

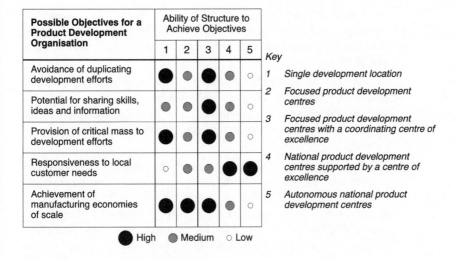

Possible Objectives for a Product Development Organisation	Ability of Structure to Achieve Objectives				
	1	2	3	4	5
Avoidance of duplicating development efforts	High	Medium	High	Medium	Low
Potential for sharing skills, ideas and information	Medium	Medium	High	Medium	Low
Provision of critical mass to development efforts	High	Medium	High	Medium	Low
Responsiveness to local customer needs	Low	Medium	Medium	High	High
Achievement of manufacturing economies of scale	High	High	High	Medium	Low

Key

1   Single development location

2   Focused product development centres

3   Focused product development centres with a coordinating centre of excellence

4   National product development centres supported by a centre of excellence

5   Autonomous national product development centres

● High   ◉ Medium   ○ Low

FIGURE 8.5   Competitive Advantage of International Development Structures
Source: Arthur D. Little

conduct longer term products in common technology areas; one leading supplier of packaging to the consumer goods industry prefers to develop products locally to cater for big differences in customer requirements in each of its national markets. In contrast, most industrial product companies find that the competitiveness of their industries and the technical complexity of their products lead managers to opt for a matrix structure of product and technology-led centres.

The various development structures can be assessed against a range of criteria based on possible development objectives (Figure 8.5). The conclusion is that a number of product-focused centres with a coordinating centre of excellence offers the greatest potential for meeting a broad range of development objectives.

Ultimately, you need to decide what advantages you are looking to create or emphasise within your development organisation, and choose your structure accordingly.

COPING WITH INTERNATIONAL BARRIERS

As many corporations are finding, locating businesses in different countries complicates the management of technology development:

O   *Language barriers* cause irritation and delay. They affect all
     functions of the business, not just technology. To remove these
     barriers, you need to develop close working and mutual trust,
     which takes time.

O   *Remoteness and time zone disruption* present stronger barriers.
     Taken together with language differences, they make coordinat-
     ing long distance activities difficult. The problem can be reduced
     by more communication, more travel, and more informal net-
     working.

O   *Cultural differences* can be a barrier to technology development,
     particularly in groups built by acquisition. One company's
     attempts to create pan-European centres of excellence, for exam-
     ple, were frustrated by the local business practice of calling on the
     local resource for all its needs. To the locals, the logic was clear:
     dealing with people they knew, they could ignore formal organ-
     isational structure and procedures. To overcome the problem, the
     company initiated job swaps, informal networking, shared train-
     ing, and tighter control over what could be done where; even so
     it was years before the pan-European approach began to yield
     dividends.

O   *Political pressures* may also be important. Governments are keen
     to keep high value adding activities, such as R&D, close to
     production units and resist moves towards, for example, central-
     ising strategic research in a single site. Nationally and within the
     EC, public sector support for R&D carries an in-built geographic
     bias.

These complications can be serious and should be addressed by investment in both the hard and soft aspects of creating a common culture.
Further discussion on this topic lies outside the scope of this book. The
key point, however, is that globalisation does not change any of the
principles of corporate technology management, only the modus oper-
andi.

FUNDING TECHNOLOGY DEVELOPMENT

All technology development has to be paid for, one way or another. At the
extreme, everything is funded by the group, and the businesses claim
whatever support they need. As a consequence, they may ask for more
than they need (since the service is free) and what they get may not be
tailored to their requirements (since R&D people do not see the businesses as real customers). At the other extreme, technology development

is paid for contract by contract. Only the most enlightened business unit managers will pay for something that they see no immediate need for.

As so often in business, a compromise is needed. To clarify the possibilities, Arthur D. Little funded a London Business School project in 1992 to examine the approach that 29 UK-based companies took to technology funding (Ref. 8.6). The project findings provide the basis for the suggestions in this section.

As discussed earlier, technology development activities fall into five main categories: strategic research, technology projects, product development, product manufacture and technology support. Funding mechanisms can be grouped into four categories:

O   Corporate funding, either by a levy imposed on each business or as a corporate overhead
O   Divisional budgets agreed annually, with details of what work is to be done agreed later
O   Internal contracts to an agreed annual level, defining the cost of each piece of work
O   External contracts, with no pre-set budgets and each contract negotiated on a commercial basis.

Perhaps not surprisingly, the research into funding showed a loose correlation between the technology development categories described earlier and the different funding mechanisms: strategic research tended to be funded by the corporation, support work by contract, other research by the divisions. However, as Figure 8.6 shows, this loose correlation disguises considerable individual variation. Furthermore, the project found little correlation between the funder and the part of the organisation responsible for setting technology development objectives. In particular, corporate or divisional budget funded work was often driven by the business units or the researchers rather than by senior managers. This may be no bad thing: the corporate managers may know less about what is needed than the lab managers do. However, in some cases, R&D lab managers may be operating with insufficient direction. The fact that, at the time of our survey, two thirds of the companies were tightening their funding approach suggests that they were concerned about control. If the pendulum swings too far towards contract technology development, longer term strategy may not get the attention it deserves. Indeed, managers in four of the companies surveyed saw a need to inject some sort of corporate strategic research budget into the R&D function to balance the operational focus of the business units. The overall need is to use the funding mechanisms to create a balance of long and short term

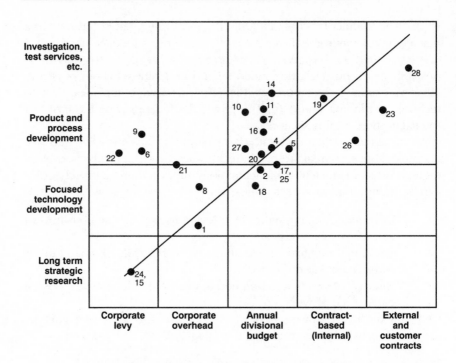

FIGURE 8.6   Classification Versus Funding
Source: Arthur D. Little

activities, matched to the strategic objectives of the businesses and of the corporation.

How to do it? By matching the type of technology development with the type of funding, as shown in Figure 8.7. Simplistically, strategic research should be funded at corporate level, technology and product development by divisions or business units, and support activities by contract. In each case, checks and balances are necessary.

O   Corporate funding suits longer term strategic research that, as yet, has little or no immediate relevance to operations. For such work, the funding mechanism should:
     – Ensure that objectives are consistent with business strategic goals
     – Provide stability to encourage development of skills
     – Allow creative freedom.
     Corporate management and the CTO, or equivalent, should agree on the corporate budget and its overall objectives. It is also desirable to ensure that some slack is built in to the budget to

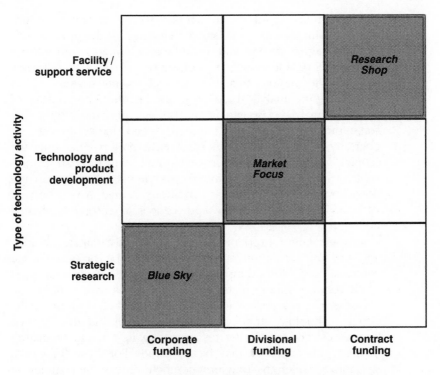

FIGURE 8.7   Objectives Versus Funding
Source: Arthur D. Little

allow the CTO and the research managers to pursue speculative ideas and back hunches. To provide some stability, constraints should be put on year-on-year budgetary variation: for example, next year's budget should be within ± 10 per cent of this year's.

O   Divisions or business units should fund technology or product development projects that have an objective relevant to the operational businesses. Getting this arrangement right is difficult: not only must the budget be stable and have overall direction, but projects must have tighter control and management. Clearly, the operational businesses need the freedom to stop and start projects as business conditions change. However, from the R&D perspective, such freedom causes resource planning problems and reduces the ability to build core competences.

A bottom-up / top-down annual plan solves the problem. Once a year, business units or divisional managers list the projects they need and agree on cost and resource requirements with technology development managers. Corporate managers then review total cost, technology focus and fit with overall strategic objectives, using the analytical tools discussed earlier. The portfolio of projects can be revised to fit the budget, preferably by killing some projects rather than reducing spend across projects. At quarterly meetings, managers track each project, amending the scope if necessary. A year-on-year normalising mechanism prevents business managers from ramping the overall budget up and down too quickly as business conditions change. A year-on-year variation of no more than 10 per cent is a reasonable starting point.

In some large corporations, managers insist that technology and product development projects should be on stand-alone contracts. GEC, for example, has run its R&D centres as quasi profit centre business units. The advantage is tight control; the disadvantage is a risk of loss of stability and strategic integrity. Group technology strategy plays a less significant role in such businesses. For conglomerates operating in a range of mature markets, this approach may be legitimate. For those for whom technology underpins long term competitiveness, the commercial contract approach can mean disaster.

O　Contract funding is an acceptable approach for technology support, testing and trouble-shooting services. These typically involve small, rapid projects set up to resolve specific problems where the objectives, time, cost, and output are usually explicit. There are two caveats to applying contract funding. First is the question of agreeing on the charge rate. When the service is provided in-house, people will debate how much it is worth and whether in-house charges should be higher or lower than on the open market. Often the debate shifts to whether these services should be provided in-house at all. The answer is clear: if a service needs to be in-house, its cost should be at least the market rate. If not, it should be outsourced. Criteria for keeping services in-house include:
– Unique expertise
– Confidentiality
– Experience of the assets being supported.

O　They may also include speed and flexibility of response, trust and familiarity, but these should not be the sole reasons for keeping a service in-house as they are not parameters which deliver sustainable competitive advantage.

The second caveat concerns the service's availability, and who pays for it. If British Rail Research keeps a team of experts on mechanical signalling technology to provide the occasional assistance that may be required, should RailTrack pay only when it calls upon these services? Clearly not. In such a case retainer or guaranteed payment is normally required to cover the marginal costs of the team, even if their services are not needed. In other cases, the issue is less clear cut. Consider, for example, the non-destructive testing engineers in a nuclear power authority. Their specialist skill is rarely required in-house, and could be sold externally, although in-house needs would always have to take precedence. Here again, some form of 'take-or-pay' retainer is in order.

The final point on funding is the need for measurement and control. There is a danger that perceptions about funding colour people's actions. People often think of allocated money as 'free', and therefore not subject to normal supply and demand; some hold this belief because they think it ought to be true, given the inherent uncertainty in technology development and a perception that development cannot be measured in conventional ways. It can. Technology development staff, including those engaged in long term strategic research, can allocate their time to projects and fill in timecards like everyone else. Matching time to targets may be difficult day to day, but the time and cost to reach monthly or quarterly milestones can be forecast and measured.

All of the funding mechanisms discussed have a legitimate role to play in the modern corporation. The role of senior management is to select the right mechanisms for the activities to be funded, to ensure that the funding allocation process works, and to put in place measurement procedures that monitor how funding is used and what output is produced.

9

MAKING IT HAPPEN

'WE need to be more innovative. We know we've done all the right things with strategy and structure, but somehow we are failing to make it happen.'

Everyone in the organisation knows what the business is trying to achieve and what he or she should be doing. But, despite this, the development pipeline just doesn't deliver the stream of new products and processes it should, even when development staff are working as hard as they can. What is going wrong?

If you try to find out where the problem lies, everyone has their own ideas. They certainly know who to blame:

- ○ 'It is all Marketing's fault. They are incapable of looking more than three months ahead, so they never tell us what they want until it's too late.'
- ○ 'We know that we're supposed to do more longer term work, but my budget's been cut and I'm measured on success this year not next.'
- ○ 'The Tokyo lab may well have the expertise we need, but we've never worked with them before and we wouldn't know how to start.'
- ○ 'Make any mistakes around here and you get fired, so why bother with high risk innovation?'

What these familiar responses highlight is the yawning gap that can exist between management's strategy on the one hand and the company's culture and informal operating practices on the other.

Even with the right strategy, organisational structure, funding mechanisms and management processes, you cannot guarantee success in technology development. Performance depends on individuals taking risks, backing their hunches and being creative. Furthermore, although adopting the approaches outlined in this book may help you focus resources on the project with the greatest commercial impact, you may as a consequence reduce the developers' creative freedom. The line between pushing for results and nurturing creative behaviour is a fine one. Too much structure and too many management constraints may well lead to fast development, but at the cost of second-rate products and manufacturing processes. However, with too little guidance from management, brilliant ideas may never progress beyond the laboratory. Experience with companies in many industries and many countries highlights three factors critical to successful development:

O   Creating an innovative climate in which reward systems, management style and cultural factors promote innovative behaviour and persuade innovative individuals to join, and stay with, the company

O   Encouraging team working, so that development staff pool their skills and resources across disciplines and national boundaries to deliver results that exploit corporate synergies

O   Breaking down the barriers between technologists and non-technologists.

This chapter explores each of these themes in turn. Some of the ideas proposed are for implementation at business unit level, others at corporate. In view of the powerful influence on behaviour of employees' perceptions of corporate norms, all initiatives must be championed at corporate level.

CREATING THE CLIMATE

The aim is clear. A group of technology developers working hard, pooling knowledge and making creative leaps to deliver a stream of innovations. You probably know some organisations that work like this, but you will also know many that don't, even though there is little obvious difference between the successes and failures. One example illustrates the point. A global instrumentation business created a corporate research laboratory on a science park next to a prestigious university. To encourage information pooling and create a university research atmosphere, the building, designed by a famous modernist architect, had glass walled offices with numerous coffee lounges. The intention was simple. Researchers would come to work, sit around drinking coffee and discussing their technical problems, then retreat to their offices and work hard into the night – just like university post-graduate research students. The first part of the plan worked well. The engineers and researchers did indeed sit around drinking coffee, being creative and thinking great thoughts. Unfortunately, they then went home at 5 p.m., returning to repeat the process next day. Creativity was undoubtedly very high, but creative output was low. Part of the problem was the recruitment policy. The labs were full of bright, creative thinkers: all idea-generators with no doers or finishers. Consequently, nothing got done.

In another corporate research laboratory, the chief scientist said, 'My people work on whatever they want. How can I say what will work and what will not, or which areas have the greatest commercial potential?' The outcome was predictable. The laboratory was world renowned for its capabilities, making breakthroughs that added greatly to mankind's technical knowledge. Meanwhile, the parent corporation gradually lost ground to all its major competitors, becoming a me-too market follower.

Unfettered creativity has no place in the commercial organisation. The objective for corporate management must be to ensure commercially valuable creative output, not just creativity.

The first step to achieve high output is to create a climate in which innovation can thrive. Surveys by Arthur D. Little of the innovative climate in numerous companies worldwide suggest that five factors are important. In decreasing order of importance, they are:

O   The reward system
O   Communication
O   Management culture
O   Internal perceptions on the value of innovation
O   External contact.

Best practice for addressing each factor is described below, but you should be aware that these examples may not be necessary or even appropriate for your own company. Despite countless academic studies, no one knows precisely what makes a combination of factors work in one organisation but not in another, although some commentators have proposed rules (Ref. 9.1). The critical factor is the set of values held by the employees, which in turn are linked to the organisation's historical values and cultural norms. The best way forward, therefore, is to ask your employees where they think the biggest barriers to innovation lie and to focus on those first.

THE REWARD SYSTEM

Most innovators are creative and self-motivated individuals. Innovation is in the main a messy, iterative, frustrating process, which can take years or even decades to deliver. Anyone who has been actively involved in the innovation process will recognise the picture in Figure 9.1. The team starts full of enthusiasm and a false sense of optimism. Gradually, reality sets in and motivation drops, as setbacks occur, timescales stretch, and other business issues take priority. Finally, the results begin to come through and success occurs. Reward systems need therefore to encourage innovators to stick with the process despite the obvious setbacks. The implication is that something more than just money is needed. Other rewards such as recognition and autonomy may be equally valuable.

Nonetheless, money *is* important. Innovators may well be motivated by higher things, but they need to live. Equally important, money is a tacit recognition of value. Paying your sales and marketing team twice what you pay researchers sends clear signals to the employees and the external world about how much you value your innovators. US companies have led the way in setting up more complex financial reward systems for innovators, using stock options, bonuses, royalty payments and payments contingent on product profitability. European companies take a higher moral line or are just unimaginative, depending on your point of view.

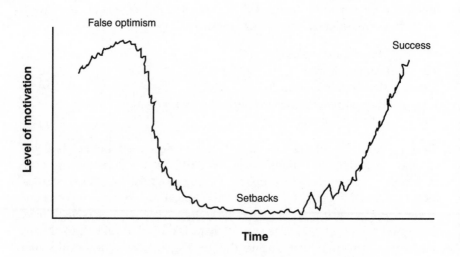

FIGURE 9.1   Level of Motivation During Development
Source: Arthur D. Little

Recognition is important, again because it conveys a perception of worth. Demonstrating your support is always worthwhile, whether by letter, telephone or personal visit. Think back to the time you spent lower down the organisation and the motivation you gained from the occasional senior management acknowledgement of your existence. Tom Peters (Ref. 9.2) elaborates on this theme with authority. There is no doubt that employees work better if they believe their efforts are valued by the corporation. But be careful not to debase the currency – pats on the back that are so frequent that they have lost credibility become at best an irritation and at worst an insult.

Peer recognition is also a significant factor for many innovators. Invitations to give seminars, permission to attend and speak at conferences and similar rewards are often valued highly. Public exposure can however present a problem, if researchers discuss their work too enthusiastically, gaining respect at the expense of commercial secrecy. When patents are at stake, or prior public disclosure can invalidate patent claims, publicity can be dangerous. Because of this problem, many corporations adopt the simple policy of restricting all publication. This is a mistake. It demotivates development staff and stops them networking with counterparts in competing companies, academia, and related industries. A more fruitful approach is to encourage openness and publication, while putting checks and balances in place to screen material and ensure information is not divulged too soon.

Some awards combine top management and peer recognition. Hewlett Packard, for example, instigated the Golden Banana award, a visible symbol of top management's recognition of outstanding work. In Philips Research in Eindhoven, researchers used to be paid a dollar for every patent they were granted. Starting out as a legal necessity for transferring patent rights from the employee to the company, the dollar bill became a ritual award, with employees priding themselves on the number of dollar bills displayed on the walls of their offices.

Increasing autonomy is another reward mechanism, which can be linked to a pin-ball machine reward: 'If you've done well once, we'll give you the chance to do well again, only this time we'll give you a bit more freedom as we trust you more.' This is a win-win reward. The company wins, because its best innovators are encouraged to innovate more. The innovator wins, because the more successful he or she is, the more freedom he or she has to pursue areas of interest. Moreover, with the right management, the net effect is to provide a visible career ladder with successful innovators receiving ever greater challenges and status.

COMMUNICATION

Senior managers in successful innovative companies make a big effort to stay close to their employees. Open communication channels, vertical and horizontal, are essential in motivating people and uncovering ideas at all levels. The most obvious way to improve communications is to adopt an 'open door' policy – advocated by many but practised by few. The success of the policy hinges on top management's ability to set an example by its open and informal management style.

Newsletters can be surprisingly successful. Managers in an engineering firm with some 1,000 employees found that a fortnightly two-page news-sheet on the state of the business that featured technology and innovation dramatically improved the innovation climate. Editorial control was kept out of top management hands, and the news-sheet included a scurrilous gossip column that cut through corporate-speak to the real issues. Launching such a newsletter takes confidence and keeping it going takes persistence, but the rewards can be well worth the effort.

Managers can be encouraged to by-pass the hierarchy to meet their subordinates several levels below. In some companies, managers do this systematically as part of their performance evaluation process; others do it by creating task forces composed of managers from different levels; still others hold special events off site, such as technical conferences and forums. One US telephone company incorporates this hierarchy by-pass into its management process through informal but well-understood policies to stimulate management interaction. For example, on business trips or office visits, senior managers are expected to drop in on field staff, and junior staff members are invited to company functions, such as dinners, on a rota.

Employee attitude surveys can provide management with invaluable information on changes in company morale, attitudes and culture, particularly in times of managerial or strategic change. However, to be accepted by employees and useful to management, the surveys need to be conducted by professional, external organisations that guarantee confidentiality and objectivity. In addition, the results must be both widely disseminated and acted upon. Asking employees what they think, and then leaving them in limbo can be very demotivating.

Employee discussion groups are common in Japan and, increasingly, elsewhere in the world. For example, at one US high-tech conglomerate, 20 per cent of employees are randomly selected to participate each year. They meet, in the presence of the CEO or senior managers and with the director of personnel acting as moderator, to voice concerns and make suggestions for change. The TQM Quality Circle approach, more commonly used in operational aspects of business, has a similar effect. Quality

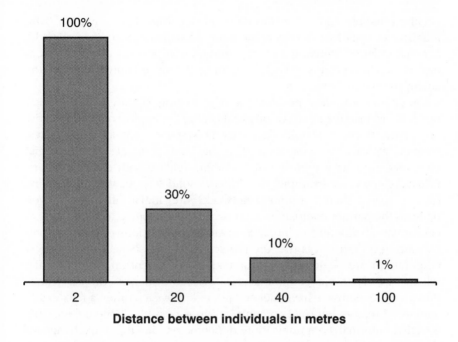

FIGURE 9.2   Level of Informal Technical Communication
Source: Adapted from Allen and Fusfeld
(Ref. 9.3)

Circles are just as valuable in the research and technical environment as to the operational one.

You can also take steps to improve horizontal communications. Such communication is informal, and informal contact depends on physical proximity. So, one option is to arrange for chemists, metallurgists and quantum physicists to sit next to each other rather than in their own enclaves. We will all share problems with the person at the next desk, but are often reluctant to walk down the corridor or into another building without good reason. Figure 9.2, based on research in the 1970s, shows how rapidly horizontal communication drops off as physical separation increases. If informal communication between two people sitting at adjacent desks is assumed to be 100 per cent perfect, then moving them to adjacent offices cuts communication by a factor of three. By the time you are down the corridor, on a different floor or in a different building, informal communication has dropped to negligible levels. Partly in an effort to combat this effect, BMW made its new corporate R&D facility a circular building, and collocated different departments to minimise communication distances between the staff. Management believes that the benefits in lateral thinking and cross-fertilisation of ideas that come from mixing function groups in such a building almost certainly outweigh any administrative inconvenience.

The communication problem is now easing slightly, as computer networks reduce the need for physical proximity. Explosive growth in the use of electronic mail and data sharing systems such as Lotus Notes, coupled with the growing interest in the Internet suggest that informal electronic communication is fast becoming reality. With eight suppliers, British Telecom, for example, developed a solid state answering machine (Ref. 9.4) on a shared computer network. After initial difficulties, developers in the partner companies soon became accustomed to working with colleagues in different companies at different locations. Open communication at all times was the key to success. Some of the world's largest corporations are beginning to undertake development on a global scale, relying on electronic communication to link dispersed project teams. Provided the members have met and got to know each other, a reasonable amount of remote informal communication is possible. Nonetheless, truly effective informal communication depends on the rapid exchange of unstructured ideas. For all but the most computer literate, problems with using keyboards and VDUs, coupled with a lack of interactive body language, make electronic communication far from perfect. For most organisations, physical proximity will remain a key element for successful innovation for the foreseeable future.

Informal networking can have a big impact on innovative output. Training courses, social clubs, amateur dramatics and sport have long been recognised as effective ways of stimulating informal networking and strengthening the climate for innovation. Some of these devices may seem banal, and below the threshold of corporate interest. However, cultural attitudes are set at the top. If the board dismisses informal communication mechanisms as trivial, so will the employees. If the board takes them seriously, so will the rest of the company.

MANAGEMENT CULTURE

The management view of innovation is critical to the innovation climate. Innovators may be well motivated and informed, but they will be very cautious about backing a hunch if the last person who tried and failed ended up in the corporate equivalent of a salt mine. Innovators need to feel that the company is 100 per cent behind them and will provide them with a supportive environment. Their perception of management culture comes from three things: what they perceive management's vision to be, the tolerance of failure, and the time horizon.

The impression the innovator gets from corporate management of how important technology and innovation are to the group comes from what corporate management says and writes, and from what it is seen to actually do. The way the company promotes itself is undoubtedly important. Companies such as 3M, Canon, and Pilkington go to great lengths to promote themselves as innovative companies. For example, Canon's foray into surround sound loudspeakers may or may not be commercially successful, but there is little doubt that it has helped to engender a perception of innovation. However, promotion alone is not enough. Although a glance through the annual reports of most large organisations will find phrases relating to the importance of innovation and innovative products, most organisations are not particularly innovative. Hollow words from the chairman, praising R&D and describing the innovative talents of the company, are often matched by lack-lustre products and a management driven by short term financial pressures. Strengthening the perceptions of management vision is difficult. There are no quick fixes. Instead, the top management must genuinely believe that innovation really is worthwhile, be prepared to say so and be prepared to back its words with action, even if the action goes against the pressure for short term financial performance.

One way in which managers can demonstrate that they believe in innovation is in their tolerance of failure. By definition, many innovative development projects will fail. Failure is therefore a natural consequence of being innovative, rather than an indication of incompetence. To create a good climate for innovation, you need to be positive about failure and not penalise those who fail. One of the advanced development groups at Philips Electronics takes this approach to its logical conclusion. The percentage of projects that fail is recorded, with a target of at least 50 per cent. As the group manager explained, if the failure rate is any lower, the group cannot be doing a proper job in identifying and developing radical new products. A high tolerance of failure is not, however, synonymous with tolerance of poor performance. The tolerated failure is a technical one, arising because the scale of innovation was beyond the team's scope or resources. Acceptable failures happen despite effective project management and skill resource utilisation, not because of poor management and inadequate processes and capabilities. Clearly, steps must be taken to ensure that this assumption is valid.

The time horizon is another factor that top management can use to influence the flow of R&D. Despite quarterly financial reporting and the pressures for short term performance, management who are prepared to stick it out, unwavering in their support for longer term development, will see both tangible results in the improved performance of their business and, less tangibly but equally important, more innovative behaviour in the employees. Most innovations take a long time to pay off. A study in the US in the late 1970s found that, on average, the cashflow in major corporate ventures was negative for about 12 years, and return on investment for seven. At the time, these periods were about twice as long as most chief executives were willing to wait for positive results. More recently, this issue has been explored as part of the intense debate in the UK about whether short term pressure from institutional shareholders hinder innovation. Again, the evidence shows a loose correlation between R&D investment and improved company performance some five to ten years later (Ref. 9.5).

Risk also correlates with time. A risk-averse management will tend to concentrate on short term incremental improvements where the paybacks are small but guaranteed. For fast-follower organisations, where technology supports rather than drives the business, this bias may be acceptable. A fast-food chain, for example, might look for incremental improvements in order collection technologies or food chill technologies, but is unlikely to try completely new methods of processing or cooking food. In contrast, product based businesses, whether in household toiletries or industrial pumps, must introduce radical innovations to grow. Incremental short term innovation will result in a succession of 'me too' products that will, at best, sustain the company's market position, without providing underlying organic growth. The need for radical product innovations applies as much to branded goods as to non-branded goods. As the power of the brand has been eroded in recent years, its residual value is that it increases the consumer's propensity to try a new product. Only by delivering a steady stream of innovative products over the long term can you build new business on the brand while sustaining brand equity. It may seem counter-intuitive, but branded goods companies need to be more innovative and take more new product risk than non-branded goods companies, in order to sustain the value of the brands.

Adopting a medium to long term time horizon is fundamental to innovation and growth. A word of caution, though. Extending the time horizon does not imply relaxing pressure on R&D. You need to maintain as great a sense of urgency on long term projects as on short term ones, particularly in the early stages where the scope for wasting time in blind alleys is greatest.

You cannot mandate for innovation. If you deliver an edict that from now on this company is going to be innovative, take risks, adopt a long term view and invest in the future, people won't believe it. As in all cultural adjustments, a drip, drip approach works much better than a flash flood. You should not underestimate the importance of both consistency and persistency. Cultural climates are fragile, as everyone knows from their own experience in the workplace. The attitudes of the board, chief executive or key senior managers dominate the way the workforce behaves. Nice words about innovation and long term research need to be backed up by action, evidence of purpose, and a consistent message year after year.

INTERNAL PERCEPTIONS ON THE VALUE OF INNOVATION

In many organisations, particularly financial holding groups, employees see technology as a support function like all the other functions. For a few mature products businesses, this view may be appropriate. However, as discussed earlier in the book, for the vast majority of product businesses, technology and innovation are of fundamental importance. The perception remains, nonetheless, that technology is the province of R&D, and that R&D is the domain of a group of specialist personnel. Technologists have to take much of the blame for this, as they have traditionally positioned themselves as the guardians of science, with a double negative effect. First, no one else in the organisation understands or can get close to R&D and second, the technologists do not communicate with other groups. To overcome these problems, raise the corporate perception of the value of technology and reinforce the innovation climate, senior management needs to take proactive steps.

First, they need to ensure high calibre representation at senior management and board level, as discussed earlier. The CTO or equivalent should be on the same level as other board directors, and ideally should have the knowledge to participate in discussions on all aspects of the business, not just technology. Second, management should communicate the value of technology in a consistent way; this point is discussed in Chapter 11. A company that promotes technology in annual reports and other communications will gain a reputation for its high regard for technology, attract innovative people, raise the standing of current staff and strengthen the climate for innovation. Innovative products will reinforce the company's image with customers, shareholders and employees, continuing the virtuous circle. Thirdly, the act of measuring the value of technology innovation, as discussed in the next chapter, in itself raises its importance in people's minds.

EXTERNAL CONTACTS

To create an innovative climate, you need to break out of the Not Invented Here (NIH) syndrome. Nearly all businesses do too much in-house technology development, squandering resources. Even worse, in-house efforts are usually sub-optimal as they are based on the collective skills of a limited number of workers, many of whom carry the historical baggage of past efforts. To break out of this myopic mindset, you need to capitalise on the potential value of external linkages. Support your local technical management's efforts to encourage staff to go to conferences. Increase exposure to the outside world in other ways, encouraging attendance at exhibitions and exposure to the technical press. Use the universities. A sponsored PhD research project is both a low cost way to get basic research and an excellent vehicle for introducing university views on technologies into the company environment. Use suppliers and customers to trigger new ideas. A household products company with its own packaging R&D is deluding itself if it believes that it can differentiate itself from the offerings of the big packaging suppliers such as CMB, Crown Cork and PLM. They have more resources, more experience, and more exposure through their customers to a wider range of product needs. Tapping into these resources by collaborators is a far more certain way of innovating than in-house development.

Finally, make full use of the talents within the group. Corporations such as GEC are beginning to realise that mixing individuals from businesses across the group can produce innovative ideas, taking established technologies from one business unit to give an innovative edge in another.

ENCOURAGING TEAM WORKING

Technology and product development no longer depend on an individual genius with a blockbuster idea. Indeed, whether one person ever did create a commercially successful product is doubtful. An individual may come up with the big idea, but it takes a team to turn it into competitive product.

The first step towards team working is to get technologists working well together. Few technologists are natural team players. Most rely on their expertise to meet their objectives and see sharing work with their peers, as opposed to leading their subordinates, as an admission of failure. However, most successful technological innovations result from team working, for four main reasons:

O   Teams give a mix of personal traits.
O   Breakthroughs come from lateral connections.
O   Advances often depend on changes to disciplinary boundaries.
O   Scarce support resources need to be concentrated in one area, but used by several.

Team working combines people's personal traits to produce a unit that is both innovative and pragmatic, exploring uncharted areas, but delivering results to time and cost. Much has been written about team member profiles (Ref. 9.6) and the need to link idea generators with shapers and detail finishers. Suffice to say here that profiling team members almost always gives insights into how the team members will behave and what mix of members will prove effective.

Many breakthroughs result from the lateral connections that people make in informal discussions. Different backgrounds, expertise and psychological profiles provide fertile ground. The story of the discovery of the structure of DNA (Ref. 9.7) makes the point, showing that it was the mix of people rather than their individual talents that led to the solution.

In the industrial world where many disciplines combine in even the simplest product, advances often depend on changes to disciplinary boundaries. A consumer goods company wrestling with a storage stability problem may find the solution in looking at the product and its packaging as a whole, rather than as separate technologies. The need for cross-disciplinary working is greatest in electronics where there is a continual question over whether the solution lies in hardware or software. Optical data storage, for example, requires accurate tracking of the pick-up head across the disc. It can be done mechanically, with precision-made components, or via software, with continuous tracking adjustment fed back to the pick-up head. Unless mechanical and electronic designers and software engineers work well together, the chance of finding the right compromise is remote.

Finally, team working concentrates scarce technical resources in one place while freeing them to work on several projects. A good computer modelling group working on structural and thermal analysis should be able to turn its hand to fluid flow modelling, a more cost-effective solution than adding a new flow modelling group, provided others accept this group's involvement.

Team working is therefore a prerequisite for success. It depends on both an effective team leader and supportive team dynamics. First, the team needs a leader whom everyone respects and who can keep the team working to a common goal. Then, as described by Belbin (Ref. 9.6), teams must be able to generate ideas and develop and finish projects.

CREATING THE RIGHT ENVIRONMENT

A successful team also needs the right working environment, and providing that environment for them can entail a significant cultural shift.

Specifically, you need to remove the barriers of mistrust and incomprehension, and align individual motivation with team objectives. Four actions are worth considering:

○   *Swap people around.* Although moving people from one discipline to another may be difficult; moving them from group to group within the same function is feasible. This type of move not only strengthens relationships, but can provide a catalyst for new ideas. In larger corporations, swapping people between business units, laboratories and countries can have an even greater benefit. Transfers should be frequent enough to prevent any one group from becoming too comfortable and cosy, but not so frequent that continuity is disrupted and quality of development is put at risk. The practicalities will depend on company structure and on the intensity of the technology thrust. As a guide, a group of ten researchers, with two or three transferees and one or two transfers each year, is a viable model for medium technology businesses such as electronics, instrumentation, automotive components and consumer goods. If this seems too radical or too expensive, consider shorter secondments. Once the benefits become clear, you will soon want to move towards longer term transfers.

○   *Reward the team.* If you want team behaviour, then you must reward team behaviour. Unfortunately, this prescription is easier to write than to fulfil. After all, promotion, one of the clearest corporate signals of reward and recognition, is individual, not team-based. You therefore need to offer team-based rewards at two levels. First, recognise the success of the team as a team by a one-off financial reward, a non-financial prize or simply peer recognition. Managers need to find creative ways to make the team feel special. For example, in Philips Consumer Electronics, members of the original CD project team all treasure the special CD desk ornaments they were given. A small machinery company that called its new project the Tiger project gave all team members Tiger stickers and put them in a Tiger room. Soon, people in the company felt that the Tiger team was the elite and as a consequence, team members were highly motivated. Second, you need to look at and reward the behaviour of individual team members, recognising explicitly their part in the team. Individuals need to know that their progression depends more on the success of the team in which they participate than on their ability to stand out from the team. Get this right, and team working will flourish.

Get it wrong, and team members will vie for personal recognition to the detriment of the team.

Many organisations explicitly address the need to encourage team behaviour by adopting an appraisal or promotion selection process with two elements, one linked to individual performance and one to team performance. In theory, success in both elements should be a prerequisite for advancement. In practice, the personal element often dominates, despite the good intentions of those who defined the process and those who use it. Persevere, however, and you can make this type of appraisal process work. Adopt a rigorous approach to the process, or change the people responsible for the evaluation – for example, make marketing and technical heads jointly responsible for all promotions in their departments. And don't be surprised if the results are not what you expect. The really good team players are not necessarily those who leap to mind when promotion is considered.

O   *Change the 'rules of the game'.* Peter Scott-Morgan of Arthur D. Little writes extensively about the 'rules of the game', the unwritten rules that influence behaviour in a corporate environment (Ref. 9.8). Looking around your own organisation, you will soon unearth examples. A familiar one is the 'you need to move around a lot to get on' rule. Many multi-national organisations look for breadth of experience in those they promote. Ambitious executives soon realise that the unwritten rule is 'Change jobs as often as possible, preferably to an area you know nothing about. In five years, you won't have contributed much to the organisation, but you will have learnt a lot and, more importantly, you will have been noticed'. Consider a representative example. A competent research biochemist working for a US pharmaceuticals company had jobs in pensions, strategy, auditing, sales and computer services within a seven-year period, and then left when it became clear that further promotion would depend on one-year stints around the globe incompatible with family life. With this pattern, driven by the unwritten rules, effective team working seems unattainable. But you can change the unwritten rules to encourage the behaviour you want. For example, you can promote key team players faster than you promote forceful individuals who get results. The first time you do it, employees will think it's an aberration. The second and third times they will start to show interest. By the fourth and fifth times, they will be formulating a new unwritten rule that team working is important. It is, of course, not quite that simple. Change the unwritten rules and you run the risk of triggering new unanticipated rules, which create unwanted side-effects. Furthermore, the unwritten rules might influence behaviour, but they don't control behaviour, and so there are limits to how far you can rely on them to achieve your objectives.

O   *Match physical and organisational structure.* In the 1960s and 1970s, the Tube Investments Group had a corporate R&D laboratory in Cambridge, UK. It was a think-tank laboratory, very much first generation in Arthur D. Little's terminology (Ref. 9.9). The way it was run limited commercial input to research projects, and the physical layout hindered attempts at cross-functional team working. The laboratory was in a former stately home outside Cambridge; the group's manufacturing sites, at the time predominantly in the UK, were a hundred or more miles away in the Midlands and the North. Communication between the two was infrequent. When communication did take place, it was uneasy. The researchers in the laboratories wore tee-shirts and jeans, and worked irregular hours. Partly as a consequence, many visitors had difficulty in accepting that the laboratory was as effective at technology development as it was. Within the laboratory, functions were separated into a physics wing, a metallurgy wing and an engineering building. Problems were usually defined as lying within one of these disciplines, rarely in a combination. Not surprisingly, team working was rare. By contrast, the Advanced Development Centre at Philips Consumer Electronics, and the Product Development Group at BMW are both organised into multi-functional groups, each focused on a product area, and both located close to the manufacturing and commercial parts of their business.

MANAGING DISPERSED TEAMS

Additional problems can arise in multi-site and multi-national organisations, as mentioned in Chapter 8. The first problem is physical distance. As soon as travelling time makes informal meetings impractical, team working itself becomes impractical unless steps are taken to force communication. The most obvious step is to increase formal communication by, for example, weekly progress meetings. In many firms, these meetings fail to live up to expectations, becoming little more than presentation sessions, where each 'side' presents its findings and then listens critically to the others. An alternative and usually more successful approach is to hold fewer formal meetings, but make each a combined business and social event. The social part of the meeting provides the forum build trust between the participants, facilitating subsequent informal communication.

For larger projects, you need to invest more heavily in glue to keep the team together. Team names, team clothing and team newsletters can unite the team by separating it from the rest of the company. Dedicated resources and facilities do even more to help build a cohesive group with a clear identity of its own.

The second big problem in multi-national operations is language. Most international groups use English as either the sole language or one of the accepted global languages, so that everyone can communicate, at least at a basic level. The danger is the assumption, usually by the British and Americans, that all the team members are as fluent as they. They are not, and even if they were, they would interpret words differently. 'Exploitation', for example, is an acceptable word in the UK, where its meaning in terms of seizing and developing an opportunity is well defined. In Norwegian English, however, exploitation carries overtones of corruption and money grabbing, usually at the expense of others. Suggesting to a Norwegian state-owned company that it should 'exploit' the opportunity offered by a local firm is tantamount to advocating rape and pillage. Choice of words can therefore have a disproportionate impact on the effectiveness of communication. The other language problem is that you tend to speak in direct terms when not speaking in your mother tongue. A native English speaker might say, 'It's a nice idea, John, but I'm not sure I agree with you completely on the way you've structured the drive components'. A non-native speaker, thinking the same inner thoughts, is likely to be much more blunt and to the point: 'The drive components are wrong and the design will not work'. This, understandably, can be a major barrier to international team working.

The solution is, much as before, to break down barriers of distrust. You should not be deluded into thinking that this is a trivial exercise. An engineering group with companies in the UK, Germany, US, Brazil and Australia had to set up a full-time team supported by consultants for six months, located away from all the primary manufacturing and trading locations. With a multi-national team practically living together, there was ample time in the evenings to iron out misunderstandings over a beer. There was also immense pressure to deliver results, so that everyone was motivated to resolve misunderstandings and to work well together. As a consequence, team members become loyal first and foremost to the team, and set aside years of inter-company distrust. The results were spectacular, with a complete new product range that cost less to make, sold more widely and doubled of company profits.

In multi-business unit corporations, the challenge is to ensure that team members function as a team despite the bias towards business unit accountability. Working across business units, the team needs to place the objectives of the corporation ahead of those of an individual unit. For major projects, the balance of power can be tipped by interference by the chief executive or chief technology officer. Less visible technology work needs a protective structure that allows the technologist to work on cross-business unit activities without antagonising the business unit manager. Free market transfer pricing is unlikely to work, and some other form of cross-funding mechanism is needed. A cost-based time allowance is the most common, and although less than perfect, is usually acceptable to all parties.

MANAGING THE TEAM DOWN THE DEVELOPMENT PROCESS

With an effective team working environment in place, you need to ensure that you manage the team dynamics as the development progresses.

Multi-functional development teams make use of technical staff to a greater or lesser extent as development proceeds. The early stages require creative input both from technical functions (e.g. R&D) and from non-technical functions (e.g. marketing). As development proceeds, the technical input becomes more pragmatic, with a shift away from research towards development and then production engineering (Figure 9.3). In large projects, the shift is managed by changing the technical personnel on the project team. The teams assembled to develop new aircraft, for example, are virtually companies in their own right, with hundreds of dedicated staff, plus specialists recruited and divested over the many years. For small projects, the picture is a little different. Team members are likely to stay the same, but their roles change as the project progresses. For example, the recent development of a modal analyser by an electronic instruments company was carried out by a dedicated five-person team; two design engineers, one marketeer, one manufacturing engineer and a project manager who was a production manager. Together, the team took the product from concept to production in 15 months, changing roles and activities as the project progressed.

Teams work best with dedicated human and physical resources. This dedication gives the team independence and flexibility, and strengthens team spirit. If dedication of a whole team is not possible, then at the very least you need a team leader who is the project champion, together with a constant pool from which to draw specialist resources. It must be the same hydraulics specialist who is used on the five one-week stints over the two-year project, rather than whoever the hydraulic group can spare on each occasion.

Whether or not the project team composition changes, it make sense to follow two guidelines. First, since teams work best if they have some

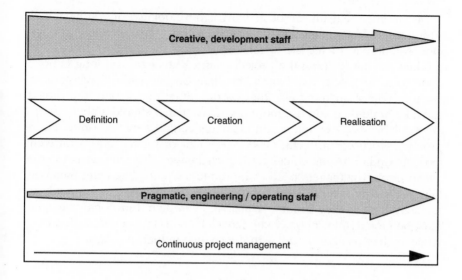

FIGURE 9.3   The Effective Product Development Team
Source: Arthur D. Little

continuity, keep staff changes a minimum. By all means, replace a research engineer with a design engineer, if the project warrants it, but do not replace one design engineer with another as the project progresses. Similarly, having one project manager from start to finish is more likely to succeed than having a succession of project managers. Many small and medium-sized businesses now make the project manager responsible not only for product development, but also for the first year or so of volume production. As mentioned earlier, larger corporations should adopt some variation of this simple, but highly effective practice. It cuts through the interface problems and reduces teething troubles as the product moves from development to design to manufacture.

To drive the team, you need a strong product champion who will motivate team members and push development through. The most likely candidate is the project manager, but a senior manager or board member can play the role if necessary. The internal customer should also be clearly identified. Probably the CEO or the marketing director, the internal customer should act as the focal point for the development, reviewing the project, challenging the choices of the product champion, and constantly reminding the team what the customer wants.

Disbanding the team can be as hard as developing it. If you have built strong team spirit and loyalty, the team members will be reluctant to leave. One solution is to let the whole team carry the product through to production. But keeping the project team together for too long is not a good idea. At worst, the project can drag on because the whole team cannot think of anything else they would rather do. At best, the project can take more time and use more resources than it should. Other options are available. For example, team members could be moved on to a new project, refocused on technical development or rotated into a different job. Disbanding teams efficiently is a challenge. The solution is to plan ahead. Project managers need to be ruthless in shedding team members they no longer require, and functional managers need to be ready to reassign them as they become available. Even then, functional managers must be prepared for people who have left teams to lose motivation for a while as they come to terms with the change in their position.

BREAKING DOWN THE BARRIERS

The greatest challenge in using multi-functional teams for technology development is the difficulty of forging links between the technical people and the rest of the business in order to get the best out of both. The local manager has to fulfil two main roles here. First, to get the technical staff interested and motivated enough to adopt a commercial outlook. Second, to ensure that technical staff in the teams deliver value. Corporate support, yet again, is key.

To add value to the business, research, technology development and product development engineers and scientists have to be commercially aware. Only then will they be able to focus their efforts on what matters, adding innovation where customers see the benefits, rather than adding sophistication that customers are unaware of. And unless technical people are commercially aware, they will be unable to communicate with the other members of a development team, and the benefits of their innovations will be undersold.

The need for commercial awareness may seem obvious, but in most companies it is not. Technical staff are primarily interested in, and motivated by, technical matters. Regrettably, many engineers and scientists still do not believe that activities not directly connected with technology and product development are any of their business. Figure 9.4 shows the results of a survey of development engineers in a large, well-respected electronics company. As you can see, the engineers were happy to participate in prototype development and even in product specification. Otherwise, they did not want to be involved. Even worse, they did not

	Perceived Level of Involvement			
	None	Awareness	Contribution	Participation
Commercial assessment	▓▓▓▓▓▓			
Product specification	▓▓▓▓▓▓▓▓▓▓			
Prototype development	▓▓▓▓▓▓▓▓▓▓▓▓▓▓▓			
Market planning	▓▓▓▓▓			
Pilot production	▓▓▓▓▓			
Mass production				

FIGURE 9.4 The Involvement of Development Engineers in the Product Development Process
Source: Arthur D. Little

want to know what was happening when the product reached mass production, the point at which the product begins to generate useful commercial returns. The technical director was unconcerned by this. As he explained, 'We need to limit commercial awareness to avoid constraining their vision of possible products'.

He was wrong. Commercial awareness does not constrain creativity. Instead, it enables engineers to focus their creative energy where it adds value.

How can the manager stimulate commercial awareness? By giving the development staff as much exposure as possible to the customer and the commercial functions. Some examples illustrate this well.

The Calculator Division of Hewlett-Packard devotes a lot of effort to exposing new junior research engineers to customers, either by placing them in the customer service department or seconding them to retail outlets. The engineers soon learn that the sophistication of the processor IC inside the calculator is not the most important attribute in the customer's eyes. Customers are more concerned about the sticky push buttons and complicated instruction manuals. The electronics engineers become aware that appearance and feel, documentation and reliability are all more important in selling calculators than electronics design. Matsushita – the Japanese consumer electronics giant – has all its latest prototypes on display in an exhibition room in Tokyo. Visitors are invited to explore the new products, watched on hidden video cameras by research and product development engineers. Again the engineers learn quickly that in a consumer electronics product, appearance and ease of use are more important that electronics. Sony goes one step further, displaying pre-production prototypes in its main Tokyo retail showroom, and monitoring customer responses. Glaxo generates commercial awareness internally. A dedicated technology transfer team is responsible for taking technology from the research laboratory into production, explaining to the commercial functions how the technology fits into the business and to the technical functions how it needs to be adapted for commercial success.

Other ways of generating commercial awareness among technical staff include:

O   Putting developers in charge of analysing defective product returns
O   Sending R&D staff out on sales calls
O   Including technical staff in business plan development
O   Letting the technical staff run the staff shop
O   Showing development engineers a video of customers talking about the products.

The choice of technique is almost irrelevant, as long as you know that your engineers are beginning to think and talk about the commercial implications of their work.

Once that process is under way, the next challenge you face is to get technical staff to communicate with the marketing and sales people. The need is clear. For example, a company producing an innovative piece of test equipment for use in a food processing plant found it was gradually losing market share. The reason was that the technical staff held the power within the company. Their focus, not surprisingly, was on the technology inside the product. On successive product generations, they introduced more and more refinements to enhance the product's perform-ance. The marketing people knew that this was not what the market wanted. Customers did not want increased technical performance, as the product was not the rate limiting element of the processing plant. Instead, they were more interested in appearance, ease of use and maintainability. However, within the company, any attempts by marketing to explain the evolution of customer needs to the development department were rebuffed. The technical staff did not believe what they were told. Feeling threatened, they saw the marketing explanations as an attempt to under-mine their power base.

You might ask how people can behave so irrationally. The answer is that rational communication between technical and non-technical people is difficult to establish. For a start, even with the best will in the world, neither understands the other. The technical person talks in specialist terminology – e.g. flux density, vector feed, RS232 interface, or worse, in incomprehensible jargon – e.g. expansion bus, firmware, ladder logic. Marketing people are just as bad, talking about penetration rates, USPs, SKUs, and product positioning. Then, there is often a history of poor communication. People are suspicious of one another. Why does she suddenly want to talk to me? What is she after? They also lack time and motivation. In most companies, people are still assessed and rewarded on short term performance in their own function. Why, then, should they spend time building long term relationships with other functions? The benefits just do not appear to be worth the effort.

You can take several steps to tackle these problems. Better formal communication channels, using meetings or explanatory seminars, often help. Better informal communications, fostered by social events and sports contests are also valuable. Other actions, as already described for reinforcing linkages between technical groups, are equally valid here. Individual job rotation, changes in the reward/incentive structure to cover cross-functional communication, and cross-functional training are all examples. However, strengthening technical non-technical relationships is more difficult than strengthening relationships. You face a continuous battle to change entrenched attitudes and create a more trusting atmosphere. To make it work, you need to:

○ *Demonstrate management commitment* so that everyone understands that the company is serious in its intent to involve the technical staff more closely in the business.

○ *Utilise current work skills.* Be careful, in job rotation and multifunction team working, to keep people working in areas that use or build on their skills. Putting people in environments where they feel like fish out of water can compound the problems of distrust and motivation rather than solve them.

○ *Take incremental steps.* Training engineers in advanced marketing or financial techniques such as discounted cashflow modelling is unlikely to be appropriate. Explaining basic commercial concepts, such as the importance of time to market, in terms of market share and commercial returns, is more likely to have an effect.

In support of these management actions, you need to set performance measures that will that motivate staff to work together. These are discussed in the next chapter.

10

MEASUREMENT AND BENCHMARKING

❖

YOU cannot improve what you cannot measure. Nor, unless you can be explicit about what you are doing and quantify its impact, can you learn from comparisons with others. To put the strategic ideas in this book into practice, you need to measure the impact of your actions and to benchmark against others. These are the two themes of this chapter.

MEASURING THE HARD TO MEASURE

First, measurement. Most capital investments can be assessed quantitatively. If you speed up a canning production line by 20 per cent as a consequence of new investment, you can see the effect immediately in increased production, and you can readily assess whether you are going to achieve the return on investment you are looking for. You know the cost and you can measure the outcome, so you can form an objective view on the worth of the investment.

In contrast, if you improve the innovative climate in the corporation, or strengthen multi-functional, multi-subsidiary working, the impact on the business is likely to be far greater than most other investments, but a lot less visible. Indeed, in the short term and at local level, the results may look worse. Your top metallurgist may be more productive now that he spends four hours thinking than when he spent all his time in meetings, but the improvement won't show to begin with. Similarly, if your Italian packaging expert and your US filling line specialist spend more time working together on a multi-national project team, the immediate result will be a project that takes longer, uses more resources, is difficult to administer and costs a lot in air fares. In the short term, such cooperation may appear unproductive. In the long run, however, you will have a better product, with broader international application, based on shared new core technologies and providing the foundation for a new generation of profitable, standardised products. In a typical case, an investment of £1 million, managed by a six-nation project team, developed a new product range that delivered additional profits building to over £5 million per year. Even here, though, who is to say if that was the technology, and the way the development team was managed, rather than better production, marketing or sales that brought the gain? Attributing the credit for successful new products is particularly difficult in consumer goods businesses, where the short term effects of brand positioning can swamp the impact of any technology improvement, even though, in the longer term, the brand's very existence depends on a steady stream of technology based innovation.

Measuring the impact of technology, and of better technology management, on business performance is therefore fraught with difficulty. Nonetheless, it is worth investing the time and effort to put measures in place:

O   To show management that investment in technology is worthwhile

O   To identify weaknesses, decide what targets to set, and monitor the success of performance improvement initiatives

O   To underpin the broader evaluation of technology necessary to determine the technology investment a business requires, and then to help communicate the rationale and justification for the investment to other managers and shareholders. This communication issue is covered in the next chapter.

Although there are no simple, direct quantifiable measures of the value of technology, numerous measures can be used to indicate some aspects of performance: the number of new products launched, the number of patents registered, the number of projects undertaken, their timeliness and budgeting, and the number of published papers. More indirect measures such as the number of job applications, the average length of service or absenteeism levels can also be helpful. Collectively, these measures can give a fairly accurate picture.

CURRENT MEASUREMENT APPROACHES

Over the years, several companies have introduced measurement models that indicate development effectiveness and highlight improvement potential. Three of these approaches are widely used and merit attention:

O   The efficiency/effectiveness/productivity model. The principle here is that by assessing the efficiency of the process, its effectiveness in delivering results, and its productivity in output per unit resource you get a good overall picture of the development process. This model can be very helpful in providing a description of the development process and measures of overall performance. However, process description alone is not enough. Most importantly, it does not tell you whether ineffectiveness is a consequence of choosing the wrong projects, or of poor management of the right projects. There is also a risk of confusing efficiency and productivity. Rapid on-time development and high output per unit resource could be a consequence of either an efficient process or very production staff. In the limit, the biggest impact on performance comes from choosing the right project, not from how it is managed.

O   The model developed by a task force of the Product Development and Management Association focuses on the customers, the project, and the financial returns (Ref. 10.1). Specifically, the model focuses on:
      – Measures of customer acceptance (including sales)
      – Project costs, time and quality, both actual and actual against target
      – Financial returns.
      It also covers the importance of innovation to the firm, measured as percentage of sales from new products. Figure 10.1 shows the parameters measured. Again, this is a good descriptive model, highlighting at corporate level how well the organisation is performing on product development. What it doesn't do is provide clues as to *why* the performance is as it is. Instead, this model treats technology and product development as a black box, focusing only on inputs and outputs.

O   The Hewlett Packard Break-Even Time measure is a third model (Ref. 10.2). As Figure 10.2 shows, time to break even is an aggregate measure that captures cost, timing, sales and profit, and, by implication, the quality and innovativeness of the output. For comparing projects in the same sector, deciding whether to launch Product A or Product B, this measure is excellent. However, since it provides no guidance on the ideal break-even time,

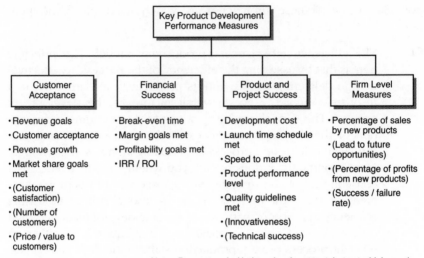

Note: Parameters in ( ) viewed as important, but not widely used

Figure 10.1   Product Development and
Management Association Performance Measures
Source: Adapted from Griffin & Page. Reprinted by
permission of the publisher from the *Journal of Product
Innovation Management*, Vol. 10, Copyright 1993 by
Elsevier Science Inc (Ref. 10.1)

it cannot be used to compare business units or indeed to make absolute judgements. Nor does it give guidance on the effectiveness of technology development, concentrating instead on the output of new products.

None of these approaches goes far enough to be useful at either corporate or local operational level. They do not adequately differentiate between different types of poor performance in development, and they do not identify underlying root causes.

A different approach is needed, separating *macro* measures, that indicate the overall state of the technology development activity within the business, from *micro* measures, that track individual projects or elements of the business process.

Corporate managers need macro measures on their business dashboard to show them at a glance how well the technology development function is working. Local operational managers need micro measures to control individual projects and set improvement targets for project selection and management.

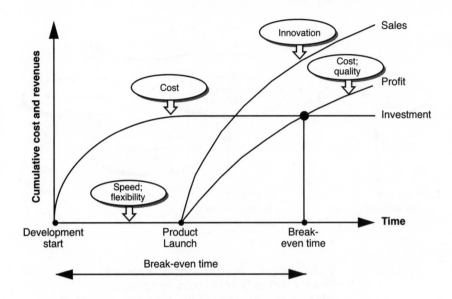

FIGURE 10.2   Hewlett Packard Break–Even Time Measure
Source: Arthur D. Little, adapted from House & Price
(Ref. 10.2)

The macro measures matter more to most readers of this book, and are discussed in detail in the following pages. At the end of the chapter, the role and implementation of micro measures is considered.

MACRO MEASURES

Conventional macro measures place emphases on process and output performance, as shown in Figure 10.3.

The argument is that business success is a function of development output which in turn is a function of development process performance. The approach does not give the full picture. As discussed in Chapter 1, and illustrated in Figure 10.4, for most businesses the impact of better products on a business will be far greater than the impact of cheaper or faster development.

To include this element in the measurement system, we need a measure of creative performance as part of the set shown in Figure 10.5.

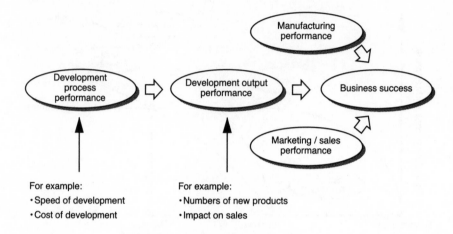

FIGURE 10.3   Conventional Performance Measures
Source: Arthur D. Little, adapted from Loch
et al., with permission of the publisher, *Journal of
Product Innovation Management*, Vol. 13, Copyright
1996 by Elsevier Science Inc (Ref. 10.3)

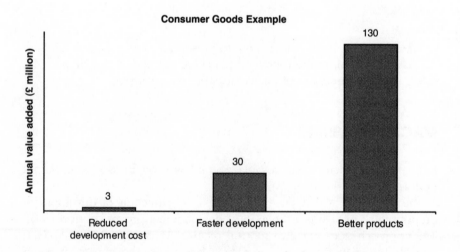

FIGURE 10.4   Impact of Performance Improvement
Source: Arthur D. Little

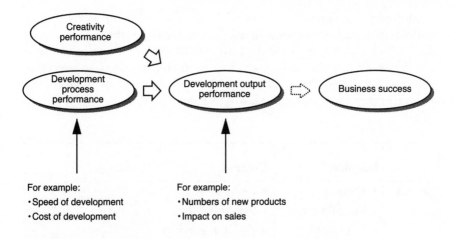

FIGURE 10.5   Technology Development Measures
Source: Arthur D. Little

In short, we need to measure:

O   How creative the organisation is
O   How well it uses that creativity (development process perform-
        ance plus output performance)
O   How the results compare with competitors (business success).

The first two measures provide internal comparisons, showing how well
the business is performing in relation to how well management thinks it
should be performing. For example, measuring creativity by numbers of
patents issued will tell you whether your performance is improving or
deteriorating year on year. It will not tell you how you compare with the
competition, since patent registration is influenced as much by company
policy as by the creativeness of the employees. The third measure is more
objective. For example, measuring the percentage of sales attributable to
new products will give you a clear indication of innovativeness which can
be used to asses your performance against your competitors. Such
comparisons, however, still tend to be descriptive rather than prescriptive.
They may tell you that you differ from the competition, but they rarely
indicate whether that difference is a big issue, what your performance
ought to be, or how you can bridge the gap.

MEASURES OF CREATIVITY

The first internal measure to consider is creativity. You could start by
conducting psychoanalytical tests and team player analysis on all your

technologists to determine who is good at developing ideas and at working in a team to develop them. As yet, however, these tests cannot show which technologists are the best able to create a concept and then turn it into a commercial product. You therefore need to resort to surrogate measures. These can be categorised as direct or indirect, and lagging, current or leading, as shown in Figure 10.6.

	Lagging	Current	Leading
Direct	• Patents • Patents used • Citations • Licence income	• Skills level • Prizes/awards • Opinion surveys • Conference speeches	
Indirect	• Job offers accepted	• Absenteeism • Staff turnover	• Innovation climate assessment

FIGURE 10.6   Measures of Creativity
Source: Arthur D. Little

Direct measures, including the numbers of patents and patents used by the business, citations in the technical literature, and licence income, are all reasonable indicators of how creative the business has been in the past. Measuring current performance is inevitably more subjective, but again the measures available will give a reasonable indication of how creative others perceive your business. The best measure is the skills level, capturing the proportion of developers with academic qualifications, weighted by level of qualification. Of course, this measure actually captures creativity potential rather than creativity; you will therefore need to supplement it with other measures such as numbers of awards and prizes, opinion surveys and invitations to give conference speeches.

Opinion surveys are probably the most useful measure of current creativity, particularly among suppliers and customers whose exposure to competitors will give them a realistic view of your innovative capabilities. Although opinion surveys are by definition qualitative, the data from them can be assessed quantitatively. You can use a structured multiple choice questionnaire, for example, to derive a score for perceived creativity. The questionnaire can then become a benchmarking tool, with repeat surveys to find out whether survey participants detect any improvement.

Indirect measures are less valuable than direct measures. Nonetheless, they provide confirmation of direct measure data, and occasionally offer insights into the underlying causes for the direct data. Typical indirect measures include percentage of job offers accepted, staff turnover and absenteeism. All of these show how your technologists perceive the firm, giving you an indication of morale and, by implication, of the creative climate. For these, and indeed for many of the direct measures, tracking trends may be more useful than making one-off measurements. It is hard to say whether 2 per cent absenteeism is good or bad, but easier to see that an increase from 0.5 per cent to 2 per cent in two years suggests deteriorating morale.

The innovation climate assessment, discussed in the previous chapter, gives a broader measure of creativity. By assessing the factors that influence the climate and its fit with employees' goals, you can gain a view on likely creative performance. You can also use your findings as a benchmark against which to measure future improvement.

Individually, each of the measures discussed is flawed, since all are influenced by factors other than creativity. Take counting citations in the technical literature. On the surface, numbers of citations are a good macro measure, reflecting not just the number of papers published, but their quality and relevance to the industry. But, the number of citations is also a direct consequence of your corporate communications policy. Citations will depend at least in part on whether you encourage your technologists to publish worthwhile technical papers, which will by definition reveal some of your technology advantage. If, instead, you direct your employees to produce articles that are good for public relations but for little else, you can expect few citations, as you will not have published anything worth citing.

Opinion surveys can also be flawed. Responses will be muddied by the respondents' most recent experience with the firm. If one of your products failed at a critical time the day before the survey, you can expect a biased response. We have all enjoyed relieving our frustration by saying what we really think of a company whose products have just let us down.

Indirect human resource measures are also affected by extraneous causal factors, such as the state of the economy and the liquidity of the local job market. Taken together, however, a broad set of measures should give a consistent message on whether creativity is increasing or declining, and on people's satisfaction with the creative working environment.

MEASURES OF THE USE OF CREATIVITY

Creativity of itself has no value unless it is used to commercial effect. You therefore need to look at the second set of measures, relating to the effectiveness of the business at *using* creativity. Some typical measures of effectiveness in using creativity are shown in Figure 10.7. They can be divided into process measures, looking at how well technology development is managed, and output measures looking at the results achieved.

Process Measures	Output Measures
• Milestone hit rate • Budget hit rate • Time to commercialisation	• Number of new products • Percentage of products that go into production • Percentage of sales/profits from new products

FIGURE 10.7   Measures of the Use of Creativity
Source: Arthur D. Little

Process measures are of great value in showing how well the technology development process is structured and managed. The two best measures are budget and milestone hit rates – they tell you whether projects are progressing to time and cost and delivering what they are supposed to deliver at each milestone. In macro measurement, you are not interested in the details of each project. What you *are* interested in is overall performance. For example, if 75 per cent of projects are missing milestones by more than a month, either the development process is not working or the milestones are unrealistic. Either way, you can see where the problems lie, and, having eliminated the problems, what improvements are being made.

Introducing measures that force structure and data collection into the technology development process has hidden benefits. Frequently, managers find not that 75 per cent of projects are missing milestones, but that 75 per cent of projects have no milestones, or worse, cannot be defined as discrete projects at all. The measures clarify and delineate, showing you, often for the first time, where the effort is going. You can then make rational judgements on the technology portfolio, following the guidelines outlined in Chapter 4.

Output measures, although they lag performance rather than lead it, are even more useful in indicating whether top management is getting a bang for its buck. The best measures are the simplest: how many new products are going into production and what percentage of technology projects actually influence the business? People will argue that these measurements are affected, at least in part, by internal and external forces over which technology people have no control. But if the measures show that new products are not appearing, or that those that do are not improving business performance, something is clearly wrong.

Time	Cost	Quality
• Actual time incurred – Project duration – Commissioning • Actual time/ budgeted time • Responsiveness – Lead time to project start – Meeting interim deadlines – Responsiveness to queries	• Actual costs – Design – Equipment and construction – Commissioning • Actual costs/budget • Operating costs • Operating costs/ budget	• Appropriate design • Innovative solutions • Ease of use of product/equipment in service • Overall quality of service provided

FIGURE 10.8   Measures of Internal Customer Satisfaction
Source: Arthur D. Little

Another way to measure output is to assess how happy the internal customers are with the projects undertaken for them. Figure 10.8 shows the parameters an engineering development group used to test whether it was serving its internal customers well. As you can see, they asked respondents to score the time, cost and quality of the deliverable, actual performance versus planned, and service provided on a scale of one to five from very poor to excellent. Aggregating the results gave a single 'Customer Satisfaction Index' score. Inevitably, perhaps, internal customers were more critical than the developers had expected, using the questionnaire to express frustrations with past failings. The index score was depressingly low with a mean score of just over two, implying an unacceptable level of service. Nonetheless, management stuck by its commitment to build the measure into the company's reporting systems and publicise the results widely throughout the business. The survey has been repeated regularly, with consistently rising scores. A new emphasis on customer satisfaction has led to closer working relationships, resulting in work more tightly aligned to customer needs and in greater engineering productivity.

This example highlights the potential knock-on benefits of applying non-financial performance measures to technology and circulating the results widely. With just a few measures (five or six) you can convey consistency of purpose and strengthen inter-functional relationships. This approach raises the visibility of technology development and highlights performance trends. However, it is open to misinterpretation. Consider the following example. One corporate manager, keen both to compare the performance of the various business units in the group, and to raise the overall profile of technology and product development, set five top level dashboard measures:

O   The number of new products launched as a percentage of the current product portfolio
O   The number of new products launched divided by the development investment
O   The percentage of new products launched on time
O   The percentage of new products launched on budget
O   The impact on sales of the new products.

At first sight, this selection of measures appears reasonable. The measures encourage a move towards more new products, coupled with good project management to keep development time and cost under control. One year later, all was going well. The number of new products had gone up, costs were held static, and time and cost delivery performance had improved. Furthermore, as the new products reached the market, sales began to rise.

Two years later, the picture looked less rosy. The number of new products was still increasing, but the sales performance was disappointing. Many of the previous year's products had failed to deliver, and the latest new products were about to repeat the pattern. The company seemed to be drowning in a proliferation of new products that lacked real differentiation and were not sustainable in the market. Worse, the increase in the number of products was overloading both the factory and the sales and marketing organisation, increasing costs and reducing profits.

What had gone wrong? The problem with the measures chosen is that the first two focus on the *number* of new products delivered from given resources. The message to development is clear: go for quick win, focusing on incremental improvements. The third and fourth measures reinforce the theme: concentrate on projects you know you can deliver on time and on budget. In other words, play safe and walk away from big, high risk innovation. The fifth measure should provide a counter-balance to the others. However, as sales are measured over time not immediately, its relative impact is reduced. The first four measures can be assessed quickly and easily – rising sales cannot. The overall consequence is a plethora of mediocre new product extensions.

The principle behind the five measures was right, but the execution was faulty.

To avoid this problem, you need a set of measures of equal weight with similar time horizons that give consistent signals up and down the organisation. As a simple guide, you can assume that the measurement time should be at least three times greater than the time constant of the activity you are measuring. The art of applying performance measures is to break down activities into sub-activities with shorter and similar time constants.

COMPARATIVE MEASURES

Once you have a set of measures to show how creative your organisation appears to be, and whether it is using that creativity, both efficiently and effectively, to deliver commercial results, you need to understand the competitive context. You need a sense of how you stack up against the competition so that you can decide what targets to shoot for. You therefore need corporate level measures to compare your business with others. An Arthur D. Little survey conducted a few years ago (Ref. 10.3), identified on an appropriate set of measures.

O   Output measures:
         – Actual time versus plan (most used European measure)
         – Cost versus budget
         – Initial product quality
         – Product cost
         – Sales volume (most used Japanese measure)
         – Profitability (most used US measure).
O   Development process efficiency measures:
         – Timeliness (most used measure worldwide)
         – Quality
         – Planning quality

- Quality of resources
- Thoroughness of concept design.

These measures provide a useful initial benchmark, but are not sufficient. Three additional measures give a clearer picture of the state of innovation in the firm:

O   New products launched, divided by R&D spend, normalised to reflect relative size of business. If you are launching 10 new products a year to your competitors' 20, but your R&D spend is only 10 per cent of theirs, your development performance will look better (although your strategy may be wrong!)

O   Market share growth divided by R&D spend. This measure indicates how effective your technology development is in supporting longer term business growth compared with your competitors' performance.

O   Average margin levels are also useful, since other things being equal, the more innovative a product, the greater the margins. Rising margins compared to those of competitors indicates innovative leadership.

All measures of this type are open to misinterpretation, and so you need to be careful in their application, and to be clear about what you want to measure and why.

Consider Tellyco, a second-tier global television manufacturer that wants to compare its development performance with that of the three giants: Philips, Sony and Matsushita. First, it needs a view on the dynamics of the industry. The television industry is mature, with new products differentiated primarily by styling and minor innovations, such as easier to use remote controls. In the medium term, wide screen televisions will capture more market share, and in the longer term flat screen displays and projection television will become more important. High definition digital television products are also likely, once arguments over broadcasting standards can be resolved. So, although the industry is mature and stable at the moment, big change could be on the way.

In that context, Tellyco appears to be doing well. It has launched many new products and market share is growing, although margins are light. To find out whether it is managing technology development as well as the competition, Tellyco's management will need to look hard at the various measures, adjusting for the many distorting factors present. Tellyco may have launched more products last year than Sony, but Tellyco's products are mainly incremental and stylistic, whereas Sony's new products incorporate more radical technology development, providing the foundation for the next generation of products. A simple comparison of numbers of new products is therefore not valid.

Problems also arise in measuring technology development spend. Putting on one side the different definitions in different companies, questions remain on what spend comparisons to make and what to infer from them. Spend can be expressed as an absolute value, as a percentage of sales, or as a percentage of costs. If Tellyco is trying to assess the competitive strength of its own creative horsepower, absolute value may be best. If it is more concerned with the efficiency of the development process, in view of the difference in size between it and its competitors, percentage measures may be a better indicator. Market share growth measures may also be misleading, depending more on company history, brand positioning and market channel access than on product and technology. Tellyco's size and immaturity are likely to indicate a better return on technology investment than the competitors will achieve, but the return may underestimate the dominance of the big players.

You need to be clear about which measures you should be using, which competitors you are assessing yourselves against, and what inferences you can draw. You also need to ensure that competitive data are comparable. As pointed out in Chapter 2, R&D spend data can be grossly misleading, with significant national variations in reporting, and distortions arise from discretionary items such as new product tooling and plant upgrading. The only solution is to cross-check available data against your colleagues' knowledge and your own.

MICRO MEASURES

Operational managers apply micro measures within the technology development activity, to track a weakness and indicate progress in remedying it. Typically, they only use a few measures at a time, always linked to an internal customer need. Once an improvement has been made, the relevant measure can be dropped and replaced with another that tackles a different problem.

For example, you may want to encourage one of your regional technology groups to give more support to subsidiary businesses outside its own region. One way to do it is to make 'support given' one of the performance objectives of the regional technology head. The measure could look at the split of the regional work, identifying the percentage of value or the number of projects undertaken outside the region.

The micro measures you chose will depend on the improvement you are looking for. Figure 10.9 gives some easy to understand, results-

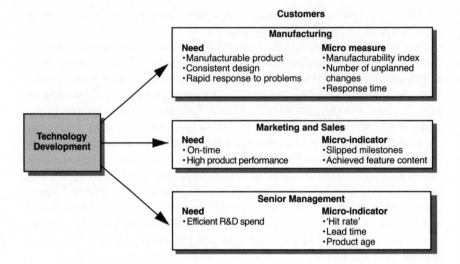

FIGURE 10.9   Micro Measures
Source: Arthur D. Little

focused examples. In all cases, the objective is local measurement, both to drive local improvement and to facilitate cross-business comparison.

Micro measures need corresponding performance targets. Take the regional technology group. If it devotes 80 per cent of its effort to regional work, when you would prefer 60 per cent, make 60 per cent the target. Be aware, though, of possible consequences for the regional work. You may need counter-measures to keep regional work of sufficiently high priority.

More broadly, micro measures divide into two categories. Some have specific targets, linked to business objectives. For example, if the mean length of projects at 15 months is excessive, set a target of 12 months. Base the target on knowledge of benchmarked companies and your gut feeling. You may also want to consider what target you could expect to meet in a perfect world, like the single minute exchange of die holy grail in manufacturing You may never reach your target, and you may not even make it public, but such a target will provide a useful sanity check.

For other measures a half-life target may be best. This type of target is used when the goal is to eliminate wastage and reach perfect performance. If 10 per cent of development time arises from unplanned iterations, set the target at 5 per cent. Once you hit that target, reset to 2.5 per cent, and keep resetting it until deviations from perfection are negligible. You could, of course, start with a zero target. But the danger is that zero targets appear unrealistic to local managers, who will not take them seriously. Half-life targets are a more effective means of getting to where you want to be.

Micro measures are used predominantly to help local management in the drive for continuous improvement. These measures need to be simple and relevant, and need to be communicated widely. Complex performance indices, built up as composites of half a dozen or more individual parameters, rarely work because local managers and workforce can see no direct correlation between what they do and how they score on the index. Simple measures, set up to tackle problems one at a time, are best. For example, if projects are failing to reach milestones on time, you can set up a percentage hit rate measure, and assemble a continuous improvement team to tackle the problem. This objective is clear, the measure is simple and relevant, and you have the resources ready, so results should follow. Once that problem is resolved, you can form a new team to tackle development speed, or the effectiveness of transfer to production, or whatever the next bottleneck is.

These micro measures must be driven by local management to ensure their relevance and acceptance. Corporate management's primary concern should be to ensure that such measures are being used, not what the measures are.

Micro measures can also be linked to reward systems and so used to influence management behaviour. In this way, they can be a valuable means of correcting management action that has arisen in response to the unwritten rules. However, you do need to be cautious: using the same measures both as performance goals and to influence behaviour can send conflicting messages to the workforce and trigger new, undesirable unwritten rules of behaviour.

BENCHMARKING AGAINST BEST PRACTICE

Managing technology development is, as outlined in this book, a complex multi-faceted task. It makes sense therefore to keep learning more about it. The logical place to start is by learning from your own businesses. Pool information from the divisions and business units about which technology management processes and performance measures work best in your cultural environment. Where variations are significant, check whether these are a consequence of variation in strategy or in the nature of the business, or if they point to sub-optimal operation in one or more of the businesses.

Benchmarking is not just a comparative tool; it also stimulates questioning and learning. If you benchmark widely within your own business, sharing objectives and pooling best practice understanding, you can achieve performance improvement, without looking outside, at other companies. This is particularly true for international corporations, where cooperation and co-working can produce synergies sparked off by comparing different national approaches.

With a good foundation of internal benchmarking, you can begin to look outside. Benchmarking against other companies can give you valuable insights into both the structure and the implementation of all your technology development processes, from managing long term research through to product development and launch.

You can benchmark at several different levels. Most organisations start benchmarking by focusing on hard measures of output to identify areas of weakness relative to direct competitors. You can go further, comparing your development processes with those of competitors and similar companies, learning by questioning to yield longer lasting more significant results. Finally, you can spread the net much more widely, looking at how 'world class' companies across a range of industries manage their technology development, and adopting the best elements for your own.

BENCHMARKING DEVELOPMENT PERFORMANCE

This, the most obvious form of benchmarking, is both the hardest to do and the least beneficial. The objective is to quantify how well you manage technology development compared to your competitors. Published data provide the starting point, allowing comparisons on R&D spend as a function of sales and of number of employees. Digging around in the press and with analysts' reports will yield more information on the size of the R&D activity, how it is split between research and product development, and how good the business is at delivering new products. More digging may tell you how many projects are under way and how focused they are. Sometimes, you can find out even more by using consultants to collect data from competitors. The idea is that everyone contributes, on a non-attributable basis, and everyone receives summary data of the main results, with the sponsoring company receiving extra detail, still not attributed.

To broaden the pool of data, you may want to benchmark against companies in other industries with similar characteristics and market dynamics. For example, if you are in steel-making, you can learn from other cyclical, capital-intensive materials processing industries, such as, aluminium smelting, pulp and paper processing and some petro-chemicals.

Benchmarking performance data can give valuable insights into how you stack up against the competition. For example, if you have 400 projects and all your competitors have between 10 and 30 for a similar absolute spend, this is a clear signal that you may be spreading your resources too thinly. If your longer term spend is less than a quarter of your main competitor, the chances are that you are going to lose the technology race. Your people may be good, but they are unlikely to be four times better than the competition. If your total spend is greater than your competitors, but your commercial output is lower, it is likely that something is wrong with the development process.

Furthermore, if you and your competitors show similar performance, but companies in comparable industries perform much better, it may be that all the players in your industry have missed a trick. If you notice the gap before the others do, you stand a chance of seizing a competitive advantage.

Quantitative benchmarking, therefore, can provide useful reference points for improvement. However, it does little else. The data are essentially descriptive and provide little in the way of learning. Data alone cannot help you determine what you need to do to improve your own organisation. Moreover, data may not be strictly comparable. R&D accounting measures vary widely by country and by individual company. Definitions of project also vary widely; if you have 400 projects and your competitor has 30, you may still have a similar degree of focus, but a definition of what constitutes a project. Despite these caveats, quantitative benchmarking is at least a starting point for debate, identifying the key points of variance.

BENCHMARKING DEVELOPMENT PROCESSES

The main benefit of benchmarking comes from getting below the performance measures to understand the development processes competitors follow, *how* they operate and, by implication, what you can learn. Before you can begin this type of benchmarking, you need to map your own technology development processes. Make a checklist of the processes for developing strategy, collecting intelligence, building the competence base, and managing in-house and external development. Determine who is responsible for each process, who is accountable, how the processes work and how they are monitored. For example, if you have a formal technology strategy process of the type discussed in Chapter 4, you will have apportioned management of the process steps to business units and divisional and corporate functions, specified funding and monitoring mechanisms, and determined the frequency of corporate strategy development and review. Check your process map with people in the technology development function and refine it to reflect what really happens rather than what you would like to see happen. This in itself should give you strong pointers for improvement.

With a clear picture of how you operate, you can start to assess how others operate. Collect all the information you can, from published sources and from conversations with suppliers, customers and ex-employees. Be very clear on the ethics before you start. Your objective is not to find out what the competitors are up to, but to learn from how they do things. You don't need to know which competitor is doing what. You do need to know the different ways of managing each process element and the pros and cons of each. The data you collect will inevitably be patchy, but can be reinforced with material from companies that are not direct competitors. Non-competing companies are also more likely to participate in open discussions about process elements, giving a deeper understanding of why processes are managed the way they are.

The advantages of external benchmarking of processes are two-fold. First, the act of documenting a process is valuable in itself, often identifying improvement potential before the benchmarking begins. Second, you can always learn from others, particularly those operating in different cultures under different corporate governance. The one danger is in assuming that what works well in another company will transfer readily to yours. It probably won't. For example, a fast growing entrepreneurial biotechnology firm, worried about competitor intelligence, will not be able to implement the formal competitor tracking programmes that most large pharmaceutical companies use. The problem is partly one of cost and complexity; the biotechnology firm will find it difficult to justify the cost of ten technology intelligence managers. It is also a function of company culture. If you add ten competitor intelligence managers to an entrepreneurial firm, whatever its size, the rest of the staff will see them as an expensive and unnecessary staff resource. Even comparably sized businesses can have very different cultures. Procter & Gamble and Unilever are good examples. One is aggressive and hard-nosed, the other softer, more introspective. Both are very successful and both are full of clever and effective managers. They deliver similar results, but they employ different types of people and work in different ways. As business processes are inextricably linked with management culture, their development process are also significantly different. You therefore need to adapt what you learn from others before it will work in your own organisation.

'WORLD CLASS' BENCHMARKING

The aim of the this type of benchmarking is to learn from the best companies in the world, whatever industry they are in. Such companies will probably include Hewlett Packard in core competence development, Philips in advanced product development, Glaxo in discovery research, 3M in blue skies research management and IBM/Siemens/Toshiba in collaborative work.

With no competitive conflict, managers from other companies are usually happy to discuss their technology management processes in exchange for information on how you manage yours. Such benchmarking can be ad hoc, as part of a wider management club or managed by consultants, depending on the scale of the exercise and the urgency with which you need the results.

If both the company culture and the industry are unfamiliar, the scope for transferring ideas directly diminishes. The benefits of benchmarking are more likely to come in the form of ideas for managing processes differently than in the form of process details for transplanting. However, as a tool for learning, for stimulating questions and internal debate, and for building world class technology management 'world class' benchmarking yields the greatest potential.

11

TECHNOLOGY AND SHAREHOLDER VALUE

❖

G OOD corporate technology management should deliver a steady stream of innovative products and production processes that increase sales and profitability and sustain business growth. In short, it should open and sustain a promising route to commercial success. For most manufacturing businesses, indeed, it is the only secure route to long term success.

The importance of technology management should therefore be self-evident. Too often, however, the board of directors and the company shareholders fail to recognise the true commercial value of investing in technology. Part of the reason is the non-technologist's poor understanding of technology issues, as discussed in Chapter 9, and part is a consequence of a history of broken technology promises and the highly visible failures of technology-based companies. The EMI Scanner, the Rolls Royce RB211 fan blade and, more recently, the commercial failure of digital audio tape are all representative examples.

Underlying these disappointments is inadequate or, as likely, inappropriately constrained funding, resulting from a failure to find an effective way of valuing technology and of assessing and quantifying its impact on shareholder value. This chapter suggests a way out of that vicious circle. It first explores ways to estimate the costs and benefits of technology investment, taking account of the inherent uncertainty in technology development. It then outlines at how corporations should communicate their technology policy internally, between business units and corporate centre and between the chief technology officer and the main board. Finally, it describes how to communicate the right message to shareholders, and in particular how to ensure that shareholders attach the correct value to long term, high risk, high reward developments.

229

ESTIMATING THE COSTS AND BENEFITS

Evaluation tools that will tell you whether an investment is justified are essential if you want to make technology pay. Quantitative valuation is not enough: the results may have only spurious accuracy. You will need to draw on the range of quantitative and qualitative measures outlined earlier in Chapter 4.

The benefits of using these measures go far beyond showing you how well the business is performing in technology. They also provide the data to allow you to manage your technology better:

O   By creating an awareness of project benefits. The tools force clarity on commercial as well as technical issues. Technologists have to be explicit about the objectives, cost, return, timing and risk of a specific project.

O   By enabling the senior management to set priorities objectively, cutting through the emotional attachment that individuals and their departments feel to their pet projects.

O   By facilitating the project manager's tasks, helping him or her define projects more clearly and assess progress against targets and milestones.

O   Most importantly, by helping intra- and inter-company communication. Evaluation facilitates communication between technical and commercial people and gives the board the hard data they need for making decisions and communicating them to investors.

Surprisingly, many companies still do too few formal evaluations. In 1993, an Arthur D. Little survey of more than 550 senior managers worldwide found that 52 per cent had no formal process for evaluating R&D and deciding which projects were worth pursuing (Ref. 11.1). A more detailed survey in the UK the previous year told a similar story (Ref. 11.2). Only 50 per cent of companies routinely used quantitative evaluation of technology development projects. Another 25 per cent relied on qualitative judgement, and the rest on management judgement. No amount of analysis can substitute for management judgement. But to ignore the availability of supporting data is foolhardy.

What should you be evaluating? To justify the benefits of investment in technology, both to colleagues and to shareholders and other investors, corporate managers need answers to three questions:

O   Overall, is the business competent in the technologies it needs?

O   Are individual projects justified, financially and strategically?

O   Will the portfolio deliver the commercial benefits required and with acceptable risk?

By this stage in the book, you should have the techniques needed to answer those questions. What you now need to do is communicate these answers both internally and externally.

SELLING THE IMPORTANCE OF TECHNOLOGY INTERNALLY

All technologists should be able to outline, succinctly and in non-technical language, what they are working on, what the expected outcome is, and how the financial benefits compare against the costs. Managers should then be able to summarise the technology development programme as a whole and outline its costs and benefits in simple terms to senior management, using the portfolio techniques mentioned in Chapter 4. In turn, senior managers should be able to present the overall picture clearly and quickly to the board.

Unfortunately, this is rarely the case. All too often, non-technologists see technology development as something incomprehensible, undertaken by people who are themselves incomprehensible. In that environment, investment in technology is seen as an overhead cost, something that has to be done because all the competitors do it, not because it is fundamental to survival and long term prosperity.

You will be familiar with the situation. At the annual budget planning round, the chief executive will suddenly ask: 'How much are we spending on R&D?' 'About 1.9 per cent, rising to about 2.3 per cent, if you factor in some of the tooling and other costs' will come the reply. 'Well, how much do the competitors spend?' 'A bit more; A spends 2.4 per cent, B 2.8 per cent and C 2.7 per cent.' 'Oh, well then, I suppose we better lift the spend to say 2.5 per cent.' End of discussion. No debate on *what* the money should be spent on. No debate on whether everyone has got it wrong and there is a huge strategic benefit to be gained by spending 5 per cent, or conversely that R&D is unnecessary and could be cut to 0.5 per cent. In short, R&D expenditure is often seen as an overhead and the questions are similar to those one would ask about warehousing costs or packaging costs. The idea that technology has a multiplying effect and can deliver benefits many times its cost often does not register.

To change this situation, technologists, and those who manage them, must become more commercially articulate, and senior technology management must start selling their wares (Ref. 11.3).

To put this need for selling into perspective, you should look at technology as if it was a product like washing powder. Your job is to persuade the consumers (i.e. the other main board directors and the functional managers) that the product is one they should buy. Buying

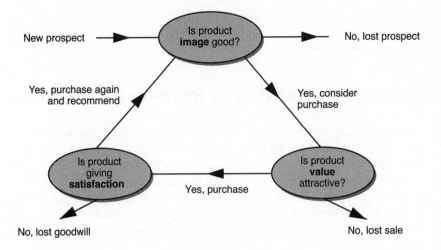

FIGURE 11.1   The Consumer Buying Model
Source: Arthur D. Little, appearing in *Product
Juggernauts* (Ref. 11.4)

behaviour patterns in the fast moving consumer goods industry show
three main buying criteria (Figure 11.1): image, value and satisfaction:

O   The *image* determines whether you are interested in the product
     at all. It is a function of appearance and packaging, brand name
     and past associations.
O   The *value* determines whether this product scores highly enough
     on potential benefit to justify its cost. It is a function of product
     performance claims, external test reports and so on.
O   *Satisfaction* is the consumer's measure of whether the product
     has lived up to expectations. If it has, the image is reinforced, the
     consumer promotes the product's image and value to other
     potential consumers, and a virtuous circle ensues.

Transfer this model to technology management and interesting messages
emerge, for corporate, business unit and other managers.

IMAGE

Technology in most organisations starts with poor past associations and a
second-rate brand name. Technologists promise much, but often fail to
deliver. They are difficult to work with, and they speak a language of their
own. Technology's appearance and packaging are poor. Just think how
many boring, incomprehensible and scruffy technical conference papers
you have sat through in your life. Technologists are often their own worst

enemy. They are dismissive of slick communications and presentation aids, and argue that if the technology is good enough, it should sell itself. It won't. If you cannot change the image you have lost the battle before you have begun. So, look at the checklist in Figure 11.2. Consider investing in building the brand name and changing preconceptions. Change the 'packaging' of technology by stressing the commercial benefits, rather than blinding with science. Pay attention to the detail, using computer generated view-foils with clear graphics rather than hand written pages of equations. It may seem unnecessary, but little details such as these have a disproportionate effect on potential customers. The last time you made a major purchase, such as a car, it is likely that the little things, such as the free cups of coffee and the attentive salesperson, influenced your buying decision at least as much as the performance of the product did. For both technology and cars, you are, after all, buying a promise of future performance on the basis of today's trust. So, if you are selling the value of technology, you need to persuade your internal customers to trust you.

- Train technologists in presentation skills
- Make technology strategy part of the annual strategic plan
- Install a top management business dashboard, with technology meetings
- Value past projects, and publicise the results
- Create newsletters or other publicity about broad technology activities
- Create internal publicity about broad technology activities
- Award prizes for innovation
- Hold technology open days
- Hold technology seminars to publicise developments internally

---

FIGURE 11.2   Image Boosting Actions
Source: Arthur D. Little

VALUE

If the image is right, the consumer (i.e. the board and other senior managers) will start thinking about value. Now, instead of 'let's set the R&D spend at 2.5 per cent this year', the CEO will be asking where the money will be going and what the returns will be. The chapters of this book should be of value here in outlining the answers to these questions, providing the structure needed to produce summaries of the status of technology in the business, the primary areas of focus, and expected future benefits.

It is important to position the value message at a high level. If you are responsible for technology management, your job is to try to persuade the board to invest in a balanced portfolio, not in a collection of discrete projects. Descend to the detail and you will lose all your non-technologist colleagues, as they will not understand and do not see why they should make the effort to try to understand. Quite simply, they don't have time to get to grips with the technical detail. Discussions about technology should stay focused on the portfolio, portraying technology development as a mix of ongoing service and support, incremental development, and technology breakthroughs. The exciting breakthroughs may be what you want to spend the most time on, but your colleagues will equate breakthrough with risk and uncertainty, and CEOs in particular do not like uncertainty. Talking about the portfolio puts the emphasis on maintaining and nurturing the current business, showing the breakthrough work in context as a critical but minor part of the framework.

SATISFACTION

If the image and value are right, the business still needs evidence that investment in technology is helping the bottom line. Evidence can be tangible or intangible. The tangible evidence is a mix of metrics showing the importance of new products and the role technology development has played, together with quantified benefits and costs for past projects. Some metrics were discussed in the previous chapter. Taken together, they can present a compelling picture.

Consider this example. A specialist pumps business within a large engineering group lifted profits from £10 to £19 million per year after investing £0.5 million in technology and product development. The company produced a new product range with fewer variants, that cost less to produce but was better matched to market needs. Not surprisingly, it sold at a higher price and in much greater numbers than the previous range. Furthermore, the product range was matched to international market needs, and so opened up longer term growth potential for the business. The number of parts was also cut dramatically through better design, from over 60,000 for the range to less than 10,000, with knock-on cost savings in administration and raw material inventories. The visible success improved the image of technology development, with the result that both the business unit and the corporation as a whole received future investment proposals more favourably.

Intangible evidence of satisfaction is also important. If relations between functional directors and their staff and the technology development function are cordial, and if the technology function responds efficiently and effectively to the needs of others, satisfaction will be high. Techniques for achieving these goals and building cross-functional relationships were outlined in Chapter 9.

SELLING THE IMPORTANCE OF TECHNOLOGY EXTERNALLY

In active free markets economies, such as the UK and the US, technology often has a bad reputation with shareholders.

Figure 11.3 is illuminating. It shows UK investment growth against the 'tradability' of the sector – a measure of international imports and exports. The conclusion is inescapable: investors favour nationally protected, low risk high yield sectors, such as banking, distribution and telecommunications. They see higher risk internationally competitive manufacturing industries, on the other hand, as less attractive, partly because they are nervous at the prospect of high R&D investment and uncertain outcomes. Most investors have a short term focus, and are unwilling to wait for the payout from technology development and unwilling to tolerate the risk

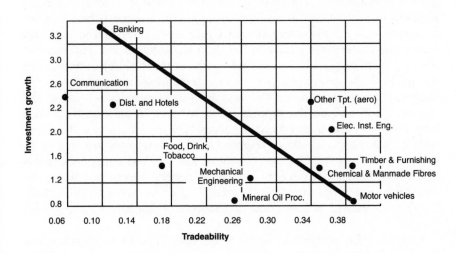

FIGURE 11.3   Tradeability and Investment Growth in UK Business 1979–87

Source: Muellbauer and Murphy (Ref. 11.5)

associated with such development and its commercialisation. This is in marked contrast to investors in countries such as Germany and Japan where free market economics are dampened by political policy and which tend to have more complex long term cross-shareholding structures. In these economies, investors have in the past been both more willing to look to the longer term, and more prepared to support investment in technology, although this may change as the investment market becomes more global.

For management, the extensive debate on short termism over the past decade has been futile. If you manage a publicly quoted company and your investors take a short term view, you have to live with the situation. All is not lost, however, as even the most hardened short term investor can be persuaded to take a longer term view if the arguments are strong enough.

This last section of the book discusses how to sell the value of technology to the external community and particularly to institutional shareholders. In the early 1990s, the UK Innovation Advisory Board took up the subject in a major project looking at short termism and the City (Ref. 11.6). As part of this project, Arthur D. Little helped produce *The Innovation Plans Handbook* (Ref. 11.7). Some of the ideas in this section, and many of the figures, draw upon that work.

To start with the basics, the value of a business to its shareholders is the value of the current business plus the net present value (NPV) of future growth opportunities. The value of the current business can be assessed in assets and profits, or in trading levels, but in essence is based on an informed view of the strength underlying assets and of the size and robustness of the profit stream in the short to medium term. The value of future growth opportunities depends both on the scale of opportunities for growth via geographic expansion, technology investment, brand exploitation and so on, on the ability of management to realise the opportunities, and on the probability of success. In an industry with a long and consistent track record of successful exploitation of technology, such as UK pharmaceuticals (Figure 11.4), the investors are willing to continue to support heavy investment in R&D. Alfred Rappaport, in his studies on shareholder value, found that, in general, investors will take the long term view if presented with a credible case for doing so (Ref. 11.8). If the track record is less good, investors will discount future growth heavily.

Takeovers in which the acquirer is better placed to develop the business than its current management show just how the potential value of growth opportunities can be. When Nestlé acquired Rowntree Mac-Kintosh, for example, Rowntree's market capitalisation rose dramatically to a level equal to four times asset value, reflecting the potential value that

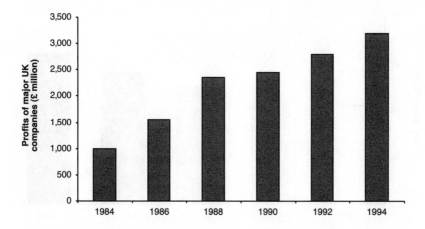

FIGURE 11.4   Profit Growth in the UK Pharmaceutical Industry
Source: Arthur D. Little analysis of accounts of major
companies

could be added to the Rowntree brands by placing them within the Nestlé
business structure. The subsequent growth in sales of KitKat and other
countlines as they were pushed through Nestlé's international distribution
network showed that this value could be realised. Sales of KitKat
increased from £240 million to over £430 million within five years. The
conclusion is clear: investors do place a real value on future growth
opportunities if they are convinced that those opportunities can be
realised. The same argument applies to technology development. If the
growth delivered by technology can be demonstrated adequately, investing in technology will be seen as a good thing.

Does technology investment help increase margins and deliver more
profitable business? Many academics have looked for strong causal links
between R&D investment and company performance. But, although
successful companies typically spend more on R&D than unsuccessful
companies, it is not clear whether R&D has led to success, or success has
encouraged management to spend on R&D.

Historical data do show a slight causal link between past R&D and
current performance. A rise in R&D investment is often reflected in a rise
in business sales and profitability some six- or seven-years later, a time lag
that is consistent with the speed of take-up of radical innovations in most
industry sectors. Furthermore, margins and R&D seem to be linked
(Figure 11.5). R&D investment doesn't just help grow the business, it helps
increase profitability.

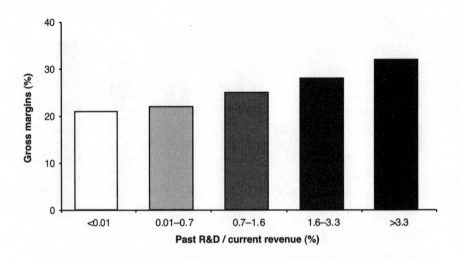

FIGURE 11.5   The Link Between Margins and R&D Investment
Source: Collier (Ref. 11.9)

So far so good. However, one of the reasons that accurate data are hard to come by is that variations in the ability of companies to manage R&D effectively tend to overwhelm variations in expenditure. Consequently, shareholders and investors are rightly cautious about accepting bland statements on the need for more R&D. They need to be convinced about the specifics: should the business be investing in technology and, if so, where's the evidence that the money will be well spent and the returns will justify the effort?

How can a business win support from the investment community for its growth plans? The following guidelines, using the image, value, satisfaction consumer buying model, should help in articulating the message and presenting it to maximum effect.

O   Agree internally on the ground rules on disclosure and communication channels
O   Develop the 'image' message to position the company's use of technology
O   Develop the 'value/satisfaction' message, conveying specific intentions and evidence of past performance
O   Play devil's advocate and adopt an investor's viewpoint: 'Would I invest in my company and, if not, what should I be doing differently?'

SET DISCLOSURE AND COMMUNICATION RULES

Many business leaders are nervous about disclosing anything to do with future products and processes. Because of insider trading legislation, information made available to shareholders must also be made publicly available. If you are worried about your competitors finding out your plans, the simplest course of action is not to tell anyone anything. But competitors can learn a great deal about you anyway, from published information, customers, suppliers and ex-employees. Provided project details are kept confidential, you can gain more from outlining your plans than you lose.

Communication not only gets your message across, but also demonstrates the level of your commitment. Limit your explanations about technology development to two lines on page 19 of the annual report, and no one will believe that you are serious about technology, whatever those two lines say. On the other hand, if you promote technology to the front page of the annual report, feature technology frequently in press releases, company newsletters and so on, and talk extensively and consistently to analysts about technology, they will start to take you seriously.

As a check, ask yourself:

○ Can the chief executive talk knowledgeably about the products and processes and about technology development? If not, what does he or she need to know (and believe in) to be credible? It may be worth revisiting the previous section and thinking again about internal selling.

○ Is the senior technical director always present at meetings with shareholders, analysts and the press? If not, why not?

○ Is the outside world ever exposed to the internal workings of our business? Have analysts and the press seen (and hopefully been impressed by) the manufacturing and assembly facilities, the research laboratories and the product test facilities?

If the answer to these questions is yes, fine. If it's no, decide how to put things right *before* you launch into promoting technology. As a sophisticated audience, investors and their advisors will not take kindly to a message that is either not consistent with its medium or lacks wholehearted commitment from the top of the business down.

DEVELOP THE 'IMAGE' MESSAGE

Define what image you want to get across, basing it on the strategy formulated along the lines outlined in earlier chapters. Are you a technology leader or follower? Are your products revolutionary or incremental?

How important is technology as a competitive weapon? Be very clear on these issues before you start outlining your views to the rest of the world.

Once you know what image you want to portray, you can decide how to articulate the message. The key points to get across at every opportunity are:

O   We have thought clearly about where to invest and have made our decisions on the basis of sustainable strengths.

O   We have allocated our technology resources to give a balanced portfolio that will lead to business growth.

O   We know how to manage development to get the desired results.

O   The balance of risks, returns, and timing is attractive, and the expected returns will be worth waiting for.

These assertions are not enough on their own. Unless you supply the evidence to support them, they will sound like window-dressing. As one financial commentator has observed, a vague reference to the need to increase R&D investment is often an attempt to disguise a temporary downturn in performance.

At the same time, avoid overkill. Describing each project in detail, with costs and revenue streams, is tedious, time-consuming and of no real benefit to the investor. Focus instead on the expected overall results, with more detail only for projects that will have a big impact on the business or need especially heavy investment.

Most of the information required to support these key messages can be fitted into the outline Innovation Manifesto shown in Figure 11.6. Substantiate each of the dash-points, and the investor will be satisfied.

The manifesto is not for distribution to the outside world. Use it as an internal reminder, providing you with the information you need to discuss the role of technology in the business with your shareholders and other key stakeholders.

The way you portray the message conveys a lot about how serious you are. The following statements all appeared in recent annual reports:

O   'Our intention is to achieve international ascendancy in the excellence of the overall performance of all our products, by innovation through continuous research and development in product and process technology.'

O   'Innovation and research is at the heart of our business to ensure that it has the technology, the products and the manufacturing processes to achieve higher profits in future years.'

- In the light of its business strategy, the company has decided where to invest and is building on sustainable strengths:
  - The planned investment is a logical, market-led consequence of business strategy.
  - The focus of the investment also supports the business strategy.
  - Investment in innovation is balanced with investments in other aspects of the business.
- Management is capable of managing the development effort to get the desired results:
  - It has a good track record with quantifiable results; organic growth has been a direct result of past innovation effort.
  - A structured development management process is in place; to ensure results, to decide when to continue investing, and when to stop.
- Resources have been allocated to give a balanced portfolio that will lead to business growth:
  - Some projects will lead to incremental improvements in the existing businesses.
  - Other major projects will result in new businesses or significantly different new products or services.
  - Some investment will pay for research to underpin the core business.
- The balance of risks, returns and timing is satisfactory:
  - Returns and their timing can be quantified.
  - Risks have been identified and are manageable.
  - The returns will ensure that the company can both maintain dividend growth and strengthen its long-term competitive position.
  - Inevitably, only some of the innovation effort will succeed, but overall, the company will be well placed for further growth.

FIGURE 11.6   Innovation Manifesto
Source: *The Innovation Plans Handbook*
This and other figures from *The Innovation Plans Handbook* elsewhere in this book are Crown Copyright, reproduced with the permission of Her Majesty's Stationery Office. (Ref. 11.7)

O   'We have dedicated £393 million to the research and development of new products and services. By 1994, we plan for at least 15 per cent of our sales to be from products launched within the previous five years.'

Each statement, no doubt, was intended to convey an image of technology excellence and commitment to innovation. However, the flowery words of the first and second quotations carry no conviction. In contrast, the third is much more positive – although 15 per cent seems a low proportion of sales attributable to new products.

DEVELOP THE 'VALUE/SATISFACTION' MESSAGE

Assume you have persuaded the investor that your organisation is serious about technology, that you have a sensible strategy and that top management is committed to the value of technology development. Will the share price rise? No. If anything, it may fall for a while, as investors become increasingly nervous. Up to now, they've been assuming that your company is like everyone else's. Now they know that you are more committed to technology and, by implication, to uncertainty.

All investments are risky, but some are more risky than others. Investing in a new piece of machinery may not improve your products, but it probably will. The risk that the machine will not work as planned, or that market conditions will change dramatically, is real, but usually small. In contrast the risk that a development project will fail is high, because all innovation is fraught with difficulty. Therefore, to keep investors happy, you need to convince them both that the investment can deliver value and that you are capable of ensuring that the value is delivered. You need a more detailed explanation than in the manifesto. Specifically, you need to explain:

O   How investment is split between incremental and radical development
O   How the business believes it can exploit technology
O   What the primary focus, if any, will be
O   What impact technology will have on the business.

At corporate level, it is hard to convey such messages without sinking into motherhood statements. One way is to use enough data to imply that you are systematic and rigorous in assessing specific projects without delving into too much detail. Pie charts on the nature and destination of technology investments, coupled with metrics showing the growth of new products and the value added by technology, will reassure investors about your ability to manage technology.

'Satisfaction' measures are particularly powerful: for example, comparing old and new versions of the same product to show both the rise in sales and margin, and the decline in production costs, can persuade investors that you can manage technology development efficiently to yield real benefits to the business.

You can also use predictive satisfaction measures. For example, a global industrial machinery company in a fiercely competitive market was looking to upgrade its product range dramatically, both improving product performance and cutting manufacturing costs. With an additional investment of £10 million in technology and product development over and above the annual R&D budget, management planned to increase sales by some 20 per cent and add an extra £60 million a year in profits, double the current level. Inevitably, at the start of such a project, sales and profit forecast are uncertain, while costs are much easier to assess. The dilemma for management is this. If it goes public on its expectations, it will create a hostage to fortune and alert competitors to its plans. If it keeps quiet, it will have a £10 million dip in profits over the next couple of years to explain away.

In such a case, the company needs to explain that it is upgrading the product range, expecting sales and profits to rise as a consequence. There is no need to be too specific about which products, or about expected levels of returns. However, the company should place a marker, stating, for example, that within three years it expects profits to rise by some 50 per cent.

Shareholders will often accept restructuring provisions presented in this way, provided adequate explanations are given. Technology investments could be equally acceptable, if adequately justified.

'WOULD I INVEST IN MY OWN COMPANY?'

If you can't convince the board and the investment community that your plans make sense, they probably don't. To test your logic, ask yourself the questions any investor would ask. At corporate level, this is a valuable exercise in checking that your strategy is right, and that you know *why*. For the business units, it is a validity check. There are four key questions to ask:

O   What is the company's business strategy, and is the company using technology in the best way to support it?
O   Are the company's technology development plans workable?
O   Has the company been realistic in assessing the risks?
O   What will the net financial impact be?

Probing these points confirms that management knows what it is doing and is giving itself the best possible chance of benefiting commercially from technology development.

The amount of probing that real investors would need to do and the weight they attach to each question would depend on their relationship with company management, on the company's track record, and on how important technology is to the company. If the relationship is good, and management has a record of success, investors will want primarily to understand trends, competitive intensity, the sums involved and the risks. However, where investment has significantly increased or decreased, where communication is poor, or where there is no track record, investors will want detailed answers to the four questions above. For corporate

- Is the company using innovation to support its business strategy?
  - What is the role of innovation in the strategy?
  - Are the plans for innovation consistent with the company's overall strategy, product and market strategies, and other investment plans?
- Are the company's plans for innovation workable?
  - Is the management team up to it?
  - Does the company have the necessary human resources and skills?
  - How strong is the company's track record?
  - Have the plans for major projects been thought through?
  - Is the innovation effort balanced?
  - Is the company planning to invest a realistic amount?
- Have risks been realistically assessed?
- What will the net financial impact be and is it properly accounted for?
- Do the risks and returns translate into long-term shareholder value?
  - Has the company estimated the impact on earnings?
  - How valuable are the growth opportunities offered?
  - How much should returns be discounted because of risk?

FIGURE 11.7   The Investor's Checklist
Source: *The Innovations Plans Handbook*
This and other figures from *The Innovation Plans Handbook* elsewhere in this book are Crown Copyright, reproduced with the permission of Her Majesty's Stationery Office. (Ref. 11.7)

management, the sub-points under the questions in the Investor's Checklist (Figure 11.7) provide a useful starting point.

Is the company using technology to support its business strategy?

Do you have a clear business strategy? If you do not, and many companies don't, this problem is bigger than a simple failure to communicate, and should be tackled first. If you do have a clear strategy, you need to communicate the role of technology within that strategy. The earlier chapters give guidelines on this.

The searching questions you would need to ask if you had not taken part in the development of the technology strategy include:

O   Are your technology plans consistent with your overall business strategy?

O   Will the planned development support your product and market strategies?

- Will the planned developments enable you to keep up with or outpace the competition?
- Will they result in competitive new products and processes?

O   Are the planned investments in technology consistent with your other investment plans? In other words, is the business giving technology the priority it deserves in relation to, say, dividends or investment in additional capacity?

O   Are you investing enough in developing human resources and skills in technology?

Are the technology development plans workable?

The key question here is whether you can implement the strategy. In short, is your management team up to the job? To find out, check whether your managers have the skills, qualifications and experience to deliver the goods. Their experience is important too. How good is their record of delivering what they promised and is there any evidence that they are committed to innovation?

Equally important, particularly if you are investing heavily in technology, examine the structure of your board to make sure that checks and balances are in place. In particular, do your non-executive directors understand technology, and do they have the wherewithal to monitor the development effort and check whether management is running into trouble?

If you are confident that the management team is up to the job, you will probably be content to let them get on with it. If you have doubts, or if the investment is unusually high, you may need reassurance that the plans for major projects have been thought through. In particular, ask yourself the questions listed in Figure 11.8 (see page 246).

Finally, the viability of the plans depends on the resources required for implementation. Check that the amount you are planning to invest covers what you are trying to do. Then stand back and look at the investment from a corporate standpoint.

O   How do your investment plans compare with that of other companies in the sector?

O   How they compare internationally?

O   Can you afford the investment, or will it place an undue strain on resources?

O   Do the plans match your competitive position and ambitions?

Overall, whether a technology development plan is workable is a matter of judgement. You cannot expect smaller, less well-resourced businesses to achieve the same objectives as their larger, more international competitors. To assume that your development team will be better than those

- Are the plans internally consistent?
- Is the financial analysis adequate?
- Is the timing realistic?
- Are the technical skills available?
- Are adequate management systems in place?
- Is the development effort balanced?

FIGURE 11.8   Assessment of Development Plans
Source:Adapted from *The Innovations Plans Handbook*
This and other figures from *The Innovation Plans
Handbook* elsewhere in this book are Crown Copyright,
reproduced with the permission of Her Majesty's
Stationery Office. (Ref. 11.7)

of your competitors is a mistake. You may strike lucky, but assuming that high quality of development will compensate for lack of resources relative to competitors is not a sound basis for investment.

You and your investors also need to be sure that the business has the resources to follow through on successful projects. You may be able to come up with 200 new product ideas and set up collaborative R&D ventures, but downstream shortages of marketing staff, lack of flexibility in the factory, or overloaded distribution channels could still prevent you from realising the full value of your investment.

Have risks been realistically assessed?

You should check that you have identified all pertinent risks (Figure 11.9) and made a realistic assessment of returns, carrying out a sensitivity analysis on the impact of variation in risk on the outcome.

Risks include:

O   *Competitors' actions* (both national and international). What are they doing? Are they likely to launch a competitive offering?

O   *Technology problems.* Does the innovation depend on a technology breakthrough? Is that likely? What could go wrong? What back-up options do you have?

O   *External influences.* When is innovation going to yield commercial results, and what will be the state of the business environment at that time? Does the innovation depend on others; for example,

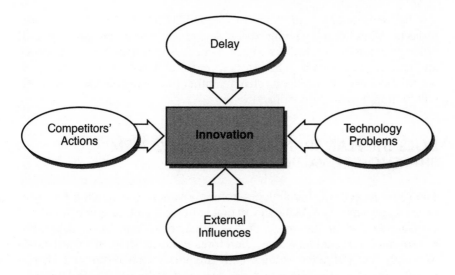

FIGURE 11.9   Innovation Risks
Source: *The Innovations Plans Handbook*
This and other figures from *The Innovation Plans Handbook* elsewhere in this book are Crown Copyright, reproduced with the permission of Her Majesty's Stationery Office. (Ref. 11.7)

is your new notebook computer project totally dependent on the availability of the next generation of memory ICs from Japan?

○   *Delay.* What will happen if key projects are late? Will a one-year delay mean that you miss a crucial time window, or force major customers to switch to a competitor?

Risks can be assessed both quantitatively or qualitatively. Whether you construct quantitative probability trees, or simply list the risks and make a judgement on their cumulative effect is not important. As long as the existence and potential consequences of a set of risks have been recognised, you can treat the predictions of revenue streams seriously.

What will the net financial impact be?

This is the most important question of all, and the hardest to answer. Assessing the full costs of an investment in innovation and determining the financial returns are difficult tasks.

For big innovation projects, you and the board should look for detailed financial calculations, drawing on the evaluation techniques outlined in Chapter 4 of this book. If necessary, develop risk/return financial models, test for sensitivities, and demonstrate validity by testing against past projects. Allow for a declining base-case, capital investment, taxation and other parameters, and build a robust picture. Robustness is more important than detailed accuracy. Investors want to know whether something is worthwhile, even if conditions change, rather than what the exact benefits will be under ideal conditions.

DOES THE PLAN TRANSLATE INTO LONG TERM SHAREHOLDER VALUE?

The value growth to shareholders from innovation is as much a function of the company's capabilities in manufacturing, marketing and financial management as of the merit of the initial idea. Translating risks and returns into shareholder value, therefore, is not a straightforward task. Although few definitive studies correlate innovation effort and shareholder value, the correlation between long term sales growth and innovation effort is indisputable.

To form a view on the impact of innovation on shareholder value, you should ask:

O   Has the company estimated the impact of innovation on earnings? Has management mapped out the cash requirements and revenue streams, taking account of the inevitable decline in sales of current products or services?

O   How valuable are the growth opportunities offered? Can the company realise the promised opportunities, or is it vulnerable to competitors' actions, to changes in customer preferences, or to supplier problems?

O   How much should the predicted cashflows be discounted to take account of risks? Although the calculation of NPV based on risk adjusted discount rates is now widely accepted, many organisations still use simpler, less accurate measures such as payback periods.

You should also consider the value of the proposed investment in innovation in the context of other influences on shareholder value. Technology and innovation are important to shareholder value, but so are other strategic actions. Big acquisitions, entry to new geographic markets, rationalisation of manufacturing facilities and changes to senior management can all have a big impact. Sometimes, in the short term, they can be more valuable than technology in helping you realise your strategic objectives, and may be a necessary prerequisite to investment in technology and innovation.

Therefore, the chief executive and other senior management, together with the investment community, need to be clear about the place of technology in your business. Technology is rarely the only driving force in a business, and the potential benefits arising from a technology advance are often lost in poor execution of the concept in marketing, production, procurement, and other functions. That is no reason to give up the strategic battle though. You may not succeed if you have technology, but at least you have a chance; without technology, you have no chance.

Finally, keep in mind that technology is the *only* functional area which routinely takes a longer term multi-functional perspective. In this regard, those who manage technology at a senior level are the de facto guardians of the long term strategies of the business. At corporate level, this is a key role in bringing a wide-ranging, outward looking, growth-oriented longer term perspective to bear on a corporation overloaded by the need to resolve immediate problems under unremitting pressure for short term results.

REFERENCES

1.1 SW Sanderson and V Uzumeri, *Strategies for New Product Development and Renewal*, Working paper, Center for Science and Technology Policy, Rensselaer Polytechnic Institute, Troy NY, May 1990.

1.2 Eric Larson *et al.* 'Beyond the Era of Materials', *Scientific American*, Vol. 254, No. 6, June 1986, also reprinted in *The Materials Revolution*, ed. Tom Forester, pub. Basil Blackwell, 1988.

1.3 Roger Porter, 'Looking into the Future', *Hoescht High Chem Magazine*, Vol. 15, 1994.

1.4 Joel Clark and Merton Flemings, Advanced Materials and the Economy, *Scientific American*, Vol. 255, No. 4, October 1986, also reprinted in *The Materials Revolution*, ed. Tom Forester, pub. Basil Blackwell, 1988.

1.5 Gary Hamel and CK Prahalad, 'The Core Competence of the Corporation', *Harvard Business Review*, May–June 1990, and 'Strategic Intent', *Harvard Business Review*, May–June 1989.

1.6 Andrew Campbell, Marion Devine and David Young, *A Sense of Mission*, pub. The Economist Books, 1990.

1.7 Tamara Erickson and David Shanks, 'Rethinking Growth and Renewal in the '90s', in *The Best of Prism*, Vol. II, pub. Arthur D. Little, 1996.

2.1 Michael Goold, Andrew Campbell, Marcus Alexander, *Corporate Level Strategy – Creating value in the multi-business company*, pub. Wiley, 1994.

251

2.2   Michael Goold and Andrew Campbell, *Strategies and Styles – The role of the centre in managing diversified corporations*, pub. Basil Blackwell, 1987.

2.3   Gerard Tellis and Peter Golder, 'First to Market, First to Fail?', *Sloan Management Review*, Vol. 37, No. 2, Winter 1996.

2.4   David Teece, 'Profiting from Technological Innovation', *Research Policy*, Vol. 15, No. 6, 1986.

2.5   The Innovation Advisory Board, *The Innovation Plans Handbook: Getting the Message Across – Improving communication on innovation between companies and investors*, pub. UK Department of Trade and Industry, 1991.

3.1   UK Department of Trade and Industry, *The 1997 UK R&D Scoreboard*, pub. Company Reporting Ltd., June 1997.

3.2   Accounting Standards Committee, *SSAP 13 (Revised) – Accounting for Research and Development*, pub. ICAEW London, January 1989.

3.3   Institutional Shareholders' Committee Pamphlet, *Suggested Disclosure of Research & Development Expenditure*, April 1992.

3.4   Bill Nixon, 'R&D Disclosure: SSAP 13 and After', *Accountancy*, February 1991.

3.5   Philip Roussel, Kamal Saad and Tamara Erikson, *Third Generation R&D – Managing the link to corporate strategy*, pub. Harvard Business School Press, 1991.

4.1   Gary Hamel and CK Prahalad, 'The Core Competence of the Corporation', *Harvard Business Review*, May–June 1990.

4.2   The Innovation Advisory Board, *The Innovation Plans Handbook: Getting the Message Across – Improving communication on innovation between companies and investors*, pub. UK Department of Trade and Industry, 1991.

5.1   Boston Consulting Group, *Perspectives on Experience*, pub. Boston Consulting Group, 1972.

5.2   Making Waves, part of the World Economy Survey, *The Economist*, 28th September 1996.

5.3   GK Webb, 'Product Development and Price Trends for Fibre Optic Components', *Technovation*, Vol. 16, No. 3, March 1996.

5.4   George Day and David Montgomery, 'Diagnosing the Experience Curve', *Journal of Marketing*, Vol. 47, Spring 1983.

5.5   Stephen Schnaars, *Megamistakes – Forecasting and the myth of rapid technological change*, pub. Free Press, 1989.

5.6   Ed. Leo Howe and Alan Wain, *Predicting the Future – the 1991 Cambridge Darwin Lectures*, pub. Cambridge University Press, 1993.

5.7   John Gillot and Manjit Kumar, *Science and the Retreat from Reason*, pub. Merlin Press, 1995.

5.8   Lucy Rowbotham and Nils Bohlin, 'Structured Idea Management as a Value-Adding Process', *Prism*, Second Quarter 1996, pub. Arthur D. Little.

5.9   Toru Nishikawa, 'New Product Planning at Hitachi', *Long Range Planning*, Vol. 22, No. 4, 1989.

5.10   Ellinor Ehrnberg, *Technological Discontinuities and Industrial Dynamics*, Chalmers University of Technology, 1996.

5.11   Richard Foster, *Innovation – The Attackers' Advantage*, pub. Summit Books, 1986.

5.12   CEH Morris, *Steel – A metal and a material*, Proc. Instn. Mech. Engrs., 1989.

6.1   MJ Neale, *Wealth from Technology*, Proc. Instn. Mech. Engrs., Pre-print 5, 1990.

6.2   David McDonald and Harry Leahey, 'Licensing has a Role in Technology Strategic Planning', *Research Management*, January–February 1985.

6.3   James Welch *et al.* 'The Bridge to Competitiveness – Building supplier–customer linkages', *Target*, Vol. 8, No. 6, November–December 1992.

6.4   Andreas Zitzewitz *et al.* Global Alliances – 256M. DRAM, Motivations, Challenges and Success Factors, Outsourcing R&D Conference, London, June 1995.

6.5   'Making Alliances Work – Lessons from companies' successes and mistakes', *Business International*, March 1990.

6.6   Elizabeth Garnsey and Malcolm Wilkinson, 'Global Alliance in High Technology – A trap for the unwary', *Long Range Planning*, December 1994.

6.7   David Gibson and Everett Rogers, *R&D Collaboration on Trial – The story of MCC*, pub. Harvard Business School Press, 1994.

7.1   Ranganath Nayak and John Ketteringham, *Breakthroughs*, pub. Mercury books, 1987.

7.2   Richard Gourlay, 'How Big Brother can Offer a Strong Defence', *Financial Times*, 20th November 1990.

8.1   Philip Roussel, Kamal Saad and Tamara Erikson, *Third Generation R&D – Managing the link to corporate strategy*, pub. Harvard Business School Press, 1991.

8.2   Paul Adler and Kasra Ferdows, 'The Chief Technology Officer', *California Management Review*, Spring 1990.

8.3   Jean-Philippe Deschamps and Ranganath Nayak, *Product Juggernauts*, pub. Harvard Business School Press, 1995.

8.4   Herman Vantrappen and John Collins, 'Controlling the Product Creation Process', *Prism*, Second Quarter 1993, pub. Arthur D. Little.

8.5   Arthur D. Little, *Total Product Management – A management overview*, pub. UK Department of Trade and Industry, 1991.

8.6   Ross Horwich, *A Review of Corporate Research & Development Funding*, Sloan Fellowship Masters Programme Project, pub. London Business School, August 1992.

9.1   V. Nolan, *The Innovator's Handbook*, pub. Sphere Books, 1989.

9.2   Tom Peters, *Liberation Management*, pub. Alfred Knopf, 1992.

9.3   Thomas Allen and Alan Fusfeld, 'Design for Communication in the Research & Development Lab.', *Technology Review*, May 1976.

9.4   Clive Maier, 'All Together Now', *Design*, April 1994.

9.5   Richard Freeman, 'Innovation and Growth – Does UK industry and the city recognise that innovation is essential for profitable and sustainable growth?', *Innovation and Short-Termism*, Financial Times conference, London, June 1990.

9.6   RM Belbin, *Management Teams – Why they succeed or fail*, pub. Heinemann, 1981.

9.7   Horace Freeland Judson, *The Eighth Day of Creation*, pub. Penguin Books, 1995.

9.8 Peter Scott-Morgan, *The Unwritten Rules of the Game*, pub. McGraw-Hill, 1994.

9.9 Philip Roussel, Kamal Saad and Tamara Erikson, *Third Generation R&D – Managing the link to corporate strategy*, pub. Harvard Business School Press, 1991.

10.1 A Griffin and A Page, 'An Interim Report on Measuring Product Development Success and Failure', *Journal of Product Innovation Management*, Vol. 10, pp.291–308, 1993.

10.2 Charles House and Raymond Price, 'The Return Map – Tracking product teams', *Harvard Business Review*, January–February 1991.

10.3 Christoph Loch, Lothar Stein and Christian Terwiesch, 'Measuring Development Performance in the Electronics Industry', *Journal of Product Innovation Management*, Vol. 13, pp.3–20, 1996.

11.1 *Results of the Arthur D. Little International Survey on the Marketing/R&D Interface*, pub. Arthur D. Little International Inc., 1993.

11.2 Ross Horwich, *A Review of Corporate Research & Development Funding*, Sloan Fellowship Masters Programme Project, pub. London Business School, August 1992.

11.3 Lowell Steele, 'Selling Technology to your Chief Executive', *Research Management*, January–February 1987.

11.4 Jean-Philippe Deschamps and Ranganath Nayak, *Product Juggernauts*, pub. Harvard Business School Press, 1995.

11.5 Data produced by John Muellbauer and Anthony Murphy, published in *Economic Policy*, October 1990, and quoted in Will Hutton, 'Why Britain Can't Afford the City', in *Management Today*, September 1991.

11.6 'The Innovation and Short-termism', Financial Times conference, London, June 1990.

11.7 The Innovation Advisory Board, *The Innovation Plans Handbook: Getting the Message Across – improving communication on innovation between companies and investors*, UK Department of Trade and Industry, 1991.

11.8 Alfred Rappaport, 'CFOs and Strategists: Forging a common framework', *Harvard Business Review*, May–June 1992.

11.9 Donald Collier *et al.* 'How Effective is Technological Innovation?', *Research Management*, September–October 1984.

INDEX

257

Safer by Design

A Guide to the Management and Law of Designing for Product Safety
Second Edition

Howard Abbott and Mark Tyler

A Design Council Title

Product safety begins with design or formulation whether it is for a complex engineering product or a simple household article. Those who suffer damage from a design defect can win compensation without having to prove negligence. Manufacturers, suppliers and importers can all be responsible for ensuring that their products are safe. To help protect them against prosecution, customer dissatisfaction and commercial loss requires a programme of risk reduction, which begins with the management of design. Design and product development require a balanced approach to the new realities of the legal situation, both for companies and individual designers.

Part 1 reviews the strategy needed to manage design in the fresh legal climate and includes guidance on techniques that can be used. Part 2 is a jargon-free guide through the difficult area of international product liability law. It has been entirely rewritten to reflect the many recent changes to influence European law and a designer's personal liability. Part 3 brings home vividly the physical, legal and commercial risks of product defects and demonstrates ways in which they could be prevented. There are over 20 real life, fascinating and instructive case histories, many of them new, ranging from exploding office chairs to ro-ro ferries and from washing powder to aircraft.

Safer by Design is exceptional in providing management and risk assessment advice, coupled with legal guidance and actual practical lessons.

Gower

Japanese Design and Development

Nobuoki Ohtani, Suzanne Duke
and Shigenobu Ohtani

A Design Council Title

Japanese manufacturing companies continue to dominate the world markets. But are their management and production systems best suited to satisfying changing customer demands? What does it mean today to talk of 'Japanese' methods and what more can western managers learn from them?

This timely book explores the influences and pressures which characterize Japanese companies and examines the ways in which some of the best known are refocusing their development processes to improve input into, and management of, the early stages so that the products succeed across the whole range of available markets. Detailed case studies of Toyota, Rover/Honda, Canon, NEC, Sharp and Okamoto are used to illustrate the benefits of leading Japanese companies' approach to design and development at both strategic and operational levels. The authors also take a penetrating look at Japanese management culture and its effects on product development. They conclude that Western companies still have much to gain from adopting certain traditional Japanese techniques.

Designers and managers seeking to understand how better use of design resources, together with better design management and strategy, can improve customer satisfaction will find much here to help them.

Gower

The New Guide to Identity

How to Create and Sustain Change Through Managing Identity

Wally Olins

A Design Council Title

It is, of course, commonplace for corporations to operate sophisticated identity programmes. But identity has now moved way beyond the commercial area. We live in a world in which cities, charities, universities, clubs - in fact any activity that involves more than two or three people - all seem to have identities too. However, very few of these organisations have released the full potential that effective management of identity can achieve.

In this book, the world's leading authority on corporate identity shows how managing identity can create and sustain behavioural change in an organisation as well as achieving the more traditional outcome of influencing its external audiences.

The New Guide to Identity provides a simple clear guide to identity, including what it is and how it can be used to full effect. If a change of identity is required, the whole process is described from start-up (including investigation and analysis of the current identity), through developing the new identity structure, to implementation and launch. For anyone responsible for the identity of an organisation, or for designing it for someone else, or attempting to achieve change in their organisation, or studying the subject, this straightforward guide is essential reading.

Gower

Product Development and the Environment

Paul Burall

A Design Council Title

Environmental concerns are creating new threats and opportunities for business. Legislation aimed at cutting pollution and encouraging recycling, retailers demanding environmental responsibility from suppliers, consumers seeking green products - these are just three of the factors making the development of environmentally-responsible products essential for success.

Burall has written a practical guide for managers and designers seeking to exploit the expanding markets for the efficient and clean products demanded by a world seeking a sustainable future. He explains how the objectives of environmentally-responsible product design parallel management objectives: both seek the most efficient use of resources. Critical of the current emphasis on recycling, he outlines how designers can minimise the lifetime environmental impact of products.

The book describes the role of various design tools and explores management and marketing issues. It ends with a speculative look at some of the technologies that are likely to play a role in achieving greener products.

Paul Burall covers the legal, management and public relations features of the subject as well as the marketing, technical and design aspects. Anyone concerned with design will find this book provides a comprehensive and practical approach to the environmental issues as well as an indication of future trends.

Gower